History in Higher Education: New Directions in Teaching and Learning

History in Higher Education:
New Directions in Teaching and Learning

Edited
by

Alan Booth

and

Paul Hyland

BLACKWELL
Publishers

Copyright © Blackwell Publishers Ltd 1996

First published 1996

2 4 6 8 10 9 7 5 3 1

Blackwell Publishers Ltd
108 Cowley Road
Oxford OX4 1JF
UK

Blackwell Publishers Inc.
238 Main Street
Cambridge, Massachusetts 02142
USA

British Library Cataloguing in Publication Data

A CIP catalogue record for this book is available from the British Library.

Library of Congress Cataloging-in-Publication Data

History in higher education: new directions in teaching and learning/edited by Alan
Booth and Paul Hyland.
    p.   cm.
    Includes bibliographical references and index.
    ISBN 0-631-19135-6 (acid-free paper). – ISBN 0-631-19136-4 (pbk.)
    1. History – Study and teaching (Higher).   I. Booth, Alan.   II. Hyland, Paul.
D16.2.T38   1996
907.1'1 – dc20   95-17968
                                                    CIP

Typeset in 11 on13pt Ehrhardt by Best-set Typesetter Ltd., Hong Kong
Printed in Great Britain by Hartnolls Limited.

This book is printed on acid-free paper

Contents

Acknowledgements   vii

List of Contributors   ix

1   Introduction   1
    Alan Booth and Paul Hyland

Part I   Curriculum Issues

2   Planning a History Curriculum   21
    Alex Cowan

3   Race in a World of Overlapping Diasporas:
    The History Curriculum   39
    Earl Lewis and Jeanne Theoharis

4   Gender in the Curriculum   55
    Cathy Lubelska

5   Teaching History Theory: a Radical Introduction   75
    Keith Jenkins

Part II   Reviewing Traditional Methods

6   Teaching and Learning in Lectures   97
    Peter N. Stearns

CONTENTS

7 Seminars for Active Learning   111
   George Preston

8 Measuring and Improving the Quality of Teaching   128
   Paul Hyland

Part III   Teaching with Multi-media

9 Computer-assisted Teaching and Learning   155
   Donald A. Spaeth

10 Structured Distance Teaching   178
    Arthur Marwick

11 Teaching and Learning through the Visual Media   191
    John Ramsden

Part IV   Linking History with Society

12 History and the Community   207
    Michael Winstanley

13 Learning from Experience: Field Trips and Work
    Placements   224
    Christine Hallas

14 History, the Curriculum and Graduate Employment   242
    Peter J. Beck

Part V   Assessment and Quality

15 Changing Assessment to Improve Learning   261
    Alan Booth

16 Assessing Group Work   276
    Alan Booth

17 Assessing the Quality of Education in History Departments   298
    George Brown

Index   321

Acknowledgements

Working on this book we have become very conscious of the many debts we owe to many people who, often unconsciously, have helped to develop our thinking as teachers of history. We would particularly like to thank colleagues and students in the history departments at Nottingham and Bath who have kindly offered their own experiences and ideas, and responded patiently to our attempts to convince them of the merits of some new teaching method or other. So too have the contributors to this collection responded with good humour and enthusiasm, and added greatly to our knowledge on many topics.

More individual debts of gratitude are also due. We would like to thank George Brown for his advice, encouragement and vast expertise in the field of teaching and learning – which we have plundered on countless occasions. Margaret Tremeer has corrected more errors in our papers than we dare to mention, and Tessa Harvey at Blackwell has been a constant source of energy and assistance. More personally, Jeanne Booth and Pauleen Hyland have kept us going, not only through many discussions about higher education and how to improve their husbands' teaching, but in sharing all the joys and pains of bringing this project to fruition.

The editor and publisher would like to thank the Open University for permission to quote material in Chapter 10 © Copyright The Open University.

Contributors

Peter J. Beck is Professor of International History at Kingston University. His publications include *The International Politics of Antarctica* (1986), *The Falkland Islands as an International Problem* (1988), *British Documents on Foreign Affairs* (1992), and with David Stevenson, *Careers for History Graduates* (1994). He edited the *PUSH Newsletter* (1989–92), and his experience of introducing innovatory teaching methods in group work is recorded on the *Royal Society of Arts/CNAA National Capability Database*. He was a member of the CNAA History Board (1982–7), and is currently on the History panel of the Humanities Research Board.

Alan Booth is Lecturer in History at the University of Nottingham. He has written widely on the 1790s in books and journals, including *Past and Present, Social History* and *International Review of Social History*. He has also published articles on the teaching and learning of history in *The Historian* and *Studies in Higher Education*, and contributed to a number of edited collections on teaching and assessment. He has been involved in many projects introducing innovative methods into the teaching of history and the humanities, and is currently engaged in producing a teaching and learning package for humanities and social science tutors throughout higher education in Romania.

George Brown was Reader in University Teaching Methods at the University of Nottingham, where he worked closely with many members of the Faculty of Arts on developments in teaching. He has published over two hundred articles and texts on teaching and assessment in higher education. He was the National Co-ordinator of Academic Staff Training and Development for the Committee of Vice Chancellors and Principals from 1984 to 1989. Since his retirement he has been involved in providing workshops and courses on teaching, learning and assessment, has contributed to the training of auditors and subject quality assessors, and has served as a Higher Education Adviser to the Department of Employment, UNESCO and the World Bank. He is currently co-directing a project on the assessment of student learning at the CVCP Universities and Colleges Staff Development Agency at the University of Sheffield.

Alex Cowan is Senior Lecturer in History at the University of Northumbria, and an Executive Officer of History in the Universities Defence Group (HUDG). He teaches courses in early modern social history and information technology for historians. He has published essays on urban elites in Venice and Lübeck and is completing an urban history of early modern Europe. He has also published articles on history teaching in the 'new' universities, in *The Historian* and *The History Teacher*.

Christine Hallas is Head of the School of Humanities and Cultural Studies at Trinity and All Saints, University of Leeds. Her teaching and research is in modern British social, economic and rural history. She is interested in pedagogy and, in particular, the 'hands on' approach to the teaching and learning of history as exemplified by history and workplace and fieldwork activities. She has published articles on history and placement schemes in *PUSH Newsletter*.

Paul Hyland is Reader in Literary History and Head of the School of History and European Thought and Culture at Bath College of Higher Education. He has conducted and supervised several research projects on history teaching and learning problems. He is editor or co-editor of *Irish Writing: Exile and Subversion* (1991), *Writing and Censorship in Britain* (1992), *The London Spy* (1993), *Writing and Africa* (1995), and the quarterly journal *Irish Studies Review*.

Keith Jenkins is Senior Lecturer in History at the Chichester Institute of Higher Education. He has written many articles on the teaching of history and historical theory, including several for the journal *Teaching History*. His book *Re-Thinking History* was published in 1991, and a further book *'What Is History?': From Carr and Elton to Rorty and White* was published by Routledge in 1995.

Earl Lewis is Associate Professor of History and Afro-American and African Studies at the University of Michigan. He has published articles on African American migration and urbanization, the black family, race, and identity. He is the author of *In Their Own Interests: Race, Class and Power in Twentieth-Century Norfolk, Virginia* (1991), and, with Robin D.G. Kelley, general editor of a forthcoming eleven-volume history of African Americans for young adults.

Cathy Lubelska is Principal Lecturer in Social History and Women's Studies, and Course Leader for Women's Studies at the University of Central Lancashire. Her current research interests include the exploration of experiential approaches within feminist women's history, gender and professionalization, and the history of women's health and health care. She has published work on curricula issues in *North West Journal of Historical Studies, Out of the Margins: Women's Studies in the 1990s*, ed. J. Aaron and S. Walby (1991), and is co-editor of *Making Connections: Women's Studies, Women's Movements, Women's Lives* (1993) and *Changing the Subject: Women in Higher Education* (1994).

Arthur Marwick is Professor of History at the Open University, and has held Visiting Professorships at Stanford University, L'École des Hautes Études en Sciences Sociales in Paris, Rhodes College, and the University of Perugin. His main research interests have been in total war and social change, class, personal appearance in history, and the nature and purposes of historical study. He has published seventeen books and is currently working on cultural and social change in the 1960s in Western Europe and the United States.

George Preston is Senior Lecturer in the Faculty of Education and Human Sciences at Bath College of Higher Education. He has undertaken many research projects on the development of teaching and learning in higher education, several of which have involved collaboration with historians at Bath and other institutions. These have been reported in various journals and conferences. His current teaching and research is centred upon health education and the training of teachers.

John Ramsden is Reader in Modern History at Queen Mary and Westfield College, University of London, Literary Director of the Royal Historical Society, a former member of the Executive of the British Film and Video Council, and Chairman of the Inter-University History Film Consortium. He has produced three books and various articles on the British Conservative Party, a film *Stanley Baldwin* for IUHFC, and a textbook with Glyn Williams, *Ruling Britannia: A political history of Britain since 1688* (1990).

Donald A. Spaeth is Deputy Director of the 'Computers in Teaching Initiative' Centre for History, Archaeology and Art History, at the University of Glasgow, which helps UK academics to incorporate computers into their teaching. His publications include *A Guide to Software for Historians* (1991), and with V. Davis, P. Denley and R. Trainor, *Towards an International Curriculum for History and Computing* (1992). His research interests are in the social history of religion in early modern England.

Peter N. Stearns is Heinz Professor of History and Dean of the College of Humanities and Social Sciences at Carnegie Mellon University. He teaches a first-year World History course, and has been active in various curricula and teaching programmes. His book, *Meaning over Memory: Recasting the Teaching of History and Culture* (1993), deals with curricula issues in the field. He is also editor of the *Journal of Social History*, and incoming Vice-President of the American Historical Association and Head of its Teaching Division.

Jeanne Theoharis is a Ph.D. candidate in American Culture at the University of Michigan. Her dissertation 'Urban Teenagers, City Schools, Ethnography, and the Politics of Representation' uses the writings of a group of black students in Boston to examine contemporary African American urban life and public education. She has been an instructor for the American Culture Program and before coming to Michigan, was a highschool teacher.

Michael Winstanley is Senior Lecturer in History at the University of Lancaster. He specializes in nineteenth- and early twentieth-century social history and has a particular interest in the regional history of north-west England. His publications include work on retail development, rural society, crime and policing, press reporting, the cotton industry, county historians and popular radicalism. He is secretary of the local branch of the Historical Association and co-edits a series of illustrated pamphlets produced by Lancashire County Books which is designed to make the results of academic research more widely available in the region.

1

Introduction

Alan Booth and Paul Hyland

This book appears at a challenging time for history teachers in higher education. The recent expansion of student numbers and concurrent reductions in public expenditure have inevitably led to resources being spread more thinly, and to mounting pressure for universities and colleges to demonstrate efficiency gains and new kinds of accountability in almost every aspect of their activity. In Britain, the advent of a mass system of higher education poses questions about the whole meaning of a university education, and a similarly fundamental reappraisal of the nature and purpose of higher education is occurring across the developed world. This is, of course, of more than passing professional interest to a discipline founded upon the analysis of change and continuity. It is easy to envisage future generations of history students discussing this shift from 'elite' to 'mass' systems of higher education; debating whether in the late twentieth century institutions experienced a seismic leap from 'pre-modern' to the 'modern', and assessing the consequences of such rapid change for the idea of 'the university' and the relationship between higher education and society.[1]

The challenges accompanying present changes, however, have a more immediate resonance for teachers of history. In Australia, Canada and the United States, as well as in Britain, 'doing more with less' has become a necessity: teaching more students than ever before, under what are often much-less-favourable conditions. Ill-equipped and inappropriate teaching rooms and inadequate library and IT facilities are just a few of the recurrent causes of frustration and complaint. Growing numbers of students with increasingly diverse backgrounds, abilities and interests pose new challenges for the teaching of history in almost every institution. So in the 1990s, most history tutors can no longer expect to greet each year a constant body of young students with broadly similar levels of knowledge, skills, qualifications and expectations. And as hitherto under-represented groups take more of their rightful place as staff and students in higher education, so many of the old assumptions about the content and purposes of the history curriculum require radical revision. Economic realities pose further problems. For many students, books are expensive commodities, and as many have to work part-time to pay their fees and maintain a living so new limits are imposed upon their opportunities for studying. Thus, the world of teaching and learning in higher education is changing rapidly, and the challenges facing both teachers and students have become correspondingly greater.

What are the key elements of a historical education? How can these best be realized within modular and free-standing programmes? How can they be matched with more student-centred learning and the changing patterns of graduate employment? How can we improve our teaching and the nature of student learning? The need for systematic reflection on such issues has never been more pressing. Yet these kinds of questions require our attention at a time when institutional pressures are mounting. The administrative duties associated with rapid change are rising annually, and the financial requirements for most institutions and tutors to meet new targets on research and publication cannot be ignored. Staff appraisal and Quality Audits have, in a short time, become commonplace. So, preoccupations with performance indicators, the next Research Assessment Exercise, and the requirements of burgeoning educational administrations dedicated to demonstrating 'Quality', are symptomatic of the new conditions within which historians and other tutors often appear merely to be scrambling to respond to ever more stringent and complex demands that are made upon them.

The 'pursuit of excellence' in all aspects of professional activity has become the catchphrase of every institution, deeply conscious of the need to secure or raise its position in fiercely competitive higher education systems. For tutors, the result has been that:

> the average university or polytechnic teacher is now expected to be an excellent teacher: a man or woman who can expertly redesign courses and methods of teaching to suit different groups of students, deal with large mixed-ability classes, and juggle new administrative demands, while at

the same time carrying a heavy research responsibility and showing accountability to a variety of masters as both a teacher and a scholar.[2]

Too often these and other requirements, such as income generation, are
in competition, and in the context of multiple demands, long-term priority will naturally be given to those which offer tangible rewards. So, in
higher education systems where research performance carries the only
prospect of increased funding for departments and promotion opportunities for individuals, most effort will be made in that direction. As
Peter Stearns puts it in attempting to explain a history of 'distressingly
few commitments to curricular discussions by major researchers' in the
humanities in the United States, a significant part of that reluctance
'stems from the undeniable penchant of major universities to value research over teaching in doling out salaries and granting tenure'.[3] In
Britain too, the Higher Education Funding Councils' Research Assessment Exercise has reminded even the most dedicated teachers that academic careers are made primarily upon research, and almost never in the
field of teaching. Moreover, the nature and importance of the links
between these critical activities has hardly been explored at all.[4]

In these circumstances, simply maintaining current levels of creative
and strategic thinking is not easy, and sticking to the 'tried and tested' is
a great temptation. In history the temptation to tradition is particularly
strong; for, although there have always been committed innovators in the
teaching of the subject, the profession as a whole has not encouraged this
aspect of activity. In general, experiments at the forefront of teaching
have had little influence on the ways most university history tutors teach,
or think about the curriculum. Put starkly, it seems difficult to disagree
that 'a subject concerned with the past seems all too often to perpetuate
the unimaginative teaching methods of the past'.[5] This traditionalism is
rooted both in the culture of many disciplines in higher education, and
in contexts and traditions that are more particular to historians.[6] So,
in addition to the high priority that is usually given to research and
publication in the making of staff appointments and promotions, the
often desultory nature of pedagogic training for new tutors, and the
widespread, and sometimes understandable, distrust of teaching and
learning theory, the development of history teaching suffers from the
self-confidence that springs from being a long-established discipline
in higher education. In Britain the dominance of Oxford and Cambridge models of tuition in the experiences and ideals of most senior and
many junior members of departments has not assisted the profession in

coming to terms with change; just as in the United States, for many
tutors, bitter recent debate surrounding the content of the humanities
curricular 'canon' has made caution rather than change seem the safer
option.[7]

In such contexts, an appeal to the profession to commit the same
energy, enthusiasm and imagination to teaching issues as to research is
not likely to be embraced by all; although we know from experience that
many history tutors already work extremely hard at their teaching. We
would argue, however, that the need to promote and enhance the value
of history teaching is greater than it has ever been. If the quality of
teaching is to be maintained and improved, more reflection, discussion
and evaluation are required – not less. Effective teaching and learning are
vital to the well-being of history staff and students in higher education,
and thus to the future of the discipline itself. Even those working in
institutions whose principal intention is to raise their income and status
from research have a vital interest in this respect – for very little of the
current quality and volume of history writing could be sustained without
a large, diverse and attractive body of undergraduate programmes. In
this sense, research and publication are the servants of all staff and
students, for it is largely through their changing needs and interests
as teachers and as learners that the demand for new knowledge and
scholarship is stimulated, as well as being more generally disseminated.
Unlike disciplines which can draw substantial income from their scientific or commercial applications, the growth and development of history
thus depends very largely upon its continuing appeal and relevance to
students, whose enrolments support and generate the great majority of
appointments. These in turn, through their research, ensure that the
curriculum is developed to meet the needs and interests of new students.
But the revitalization of the curriculum through staff research needs to
be matched by an equal emphasis upon how we teach, informed by
awareness of how students learn, and how the answers to these questions
also critically affect the nature and value of every history student's
education.

New thinking is just as important to the health and improvement of
teaching and learning as it is to historical research. Not that new ideas
should simply be adopted in preference to old, but they must be generated and given a fair hearing as part of a continuous professional debate
about the goals and effectiveness of current practice. Systematic, self-
critical reflection is, and always has been, an essential feature of good
teaching, and its absence makes the teaching of history not only less

rewarding but also much more difficult in a period of relatively diminish-
ing resources and considerable change. For contrary to some long-held
notions, good teaching is neither easy nor largely a function of the
historian's knowledge and scholarship in any given field. Such misconceptions give rise to many of the common complaints about students'
lack of learning or the shallowness of their understanding: 'Students
don't remember what I've told them in the lectures'; 'It is difficult to get
students to contribute to seminar discussions'; 'Most of these essays are
very uninspiring'. But by recognizing that good teaching is intellectually
and personally every bit as demanding as good historical research, we can
take the first step towards improving student learning and to protecting
and enhancing the discipline of history itself.

Fortunately, there are indications that the teaching of history is beginning to receive the higher profile that it deserves. Chet Meyers and
Thomas Jones, Professors of Humanities and History respectively at
Metropolitan State University, write of an emerging national dialogue on
teaching issues in the United States:

> Teachers are beginning to talk with each other about teaching and, as a
> result, to change the ways they teach. Though hardly a revolution, this
> conversation about teaching breaks a long tradition reflecting an almost
> feudal mentality in which teachers surrounded their classrooms with
> psychological moats and fortifications. And, when the teaching nobility
> did meet, their conversations revolved around research and disci-
> pline-related issues – not teaching. Happily, signs indicate a changing
> perspective.[8]

They attribute this change to a growing awareness among tutors that
their traditional methods are not working as well as previously, and that
the experience of an increasingly diverse student body is emphasizing the
need to re-think conventional wisdoms about teaching. Others note that
the increasing threat to research income in many institutions is placing
greater emphasis upon tuition funding, and thus teaching issues.[9] If this
process is only in its infancy, it is significant that much stronger Faculty
development programmes are springing up; that historians are increasingly keen to contribute to conferences, journals and books on developing teaching. Reflecting on this, the editor of the 'teaching innovations'
column of *Perspectives*, the newsletter of the American Historical Association, has recently recalled how rapidly attitudes are changing. In
1988, as the new editor, he frequently had to hustle for contributions,
often without success; he now receives a significant number of unsolic-

ited submissions, including many from 'prominent scholars at major research institutions'. 'As we enter the 1990s and head towards the turn of the new century', he writes, 'the need to recognise and encourage effective teaching is increasingly pronounced.'[10]

In Britain there are similarly encouraging signs that teaching matters are rising in the agendas of academic historians. Here too, resource pressures and large-class problems are important in generating unease about the efficacy of traditional teaching methods. The need for institutions and departments to meet increasingly exacting Quality Assurance thresholds has also become a feature of higher education in the 1990s, and has encouraged the development of more-systematic course review procedures and staff development initiatives in teaching matters for both new and established tutors. So too, for all its widely recognized failings, has the Higher Education Funding Councils' Quality Assessment Exercise lent support to the importance of greater variety in methods of teaching and assessment as part of a wider appreciation of the benefits of more 'active' methods of teaching and learning, and engaged historians in serious debate about the meaning of effective teaching in History.[11] Moreover, although there is still no public funding currently earmarked for research into history teaching, money has become available for practical teaching development. For several years in the early-1990s, the Partnership Awards, sponsored by industry, offered an annual prize for innovation in the teaching of history. In addition, important government-funded initiatives encouraging innovation have appeared since the late-1980s. Most notable has been the Enterprise in Higher Education initiative which, from an early and unhelpful emphasis upon 'leadership' and 'entrepreneurial' skills, has encouraged some valuable experiments in the field of active learning in history. Here, work by historians in a number of participating institutions, in areas such as small-group teaching, group project work, work-based learning, learning contracts and computer-assisted teaching and learning, has encouraged fresh thinking about the teaching of the subject from a skills perspective.[12] This has been complemented by the continuing success of the Higher Education Funding Councils' 'Computers in Teaching Initiative', whose Centre for History at the University of Glasgow has been a key influence in disseminating advice and good practice in computer-assisted learning, and co-ordinating developments in that field.

Evidence of a growing awareness of the value of sharing ideas and new initiatives in teaching is also apparent in the variety of articles published by *PUSH Newsletter* (1989–92), and in the pages of *Teaching History* which, whilst concentrating on school teaching, invites contributions from tutors in higher education. Other journals, such as the long-established *History Today* or the newly founded *History Review*, *Modern History Review* and *History Ireland*, are further testimony to the care with which many historians are trying to address the needs of students and public audiences, by reviewing recent scholarship and debates in a clear and attractive manner. As yet, few contributors are as much concerned with how we teach and how students learn as they are with the historical subject-matter, but this too may change as more historians appreciate the importance of understanding the processes of student learning. The success of the Open University, especially through the widespread adoption of its innovative materials, whether television and radio broadcasts or course handbooks and posters, has also assisted the spread of good practice in planning and thinking about the teaching of history. So too has the notable improvement in the quality and variety of student textbooks in recent years.

This book is therefore both a confirmation of the notable upsurge of interest in history teaching in higher education, and a contribution to what we hope will be a growing dialogue about the teaching and learning of the discipline. Our objectives are essentially twofold. First, to provide an account, from various perspectives, of some recent developments in the teaching of history, in order to stimulate discussion about the needs of staff and students in the future. Secondly, to offer some practical advice and ideas for tutors who are interested in improving their own teaching; whether by refreshing traditional methods or introducing new ones, or simply thinking through what they do as course designers, teachers and assessors in more systematic ways. We have therefore deliberately accommodated the traditional as well as the innovative; including chapters on the staples of history teaching, notably lectures and seminars, in the conviction that fine-tuning can be just as effective as innovation. We have also attempted to be as pragmatic as possible in offering advice, and to avoid being overly prescriptive in putting forward ideas for change. Wherever possible the sort of high-flown educational theory that might be expected to irritate some history tutors has been avoided, though our own conviction is that an awareness of recent developments, particularly in the field of student learning, can frequently be a helpful means of improving teaching, and this is explored briefly in the following section.

Encouraging Active Learning

Underlying this book is the belief that effective teaching is about facilitating student learning. Moreover, as Paul Ramsden puts it: 'to teach is
to make an assumption about what and how the student learns; to teach
well implies learning about students' learning'.[13] This does not mean that
history tutors have to become experts in educational research and theory,
but that questions about how our students learn best need to be carefully
considered when designing and revising curricula, teaching methods and
assessment procedures. Although the specific ways in which students
learn history, and what their various experiences of the subject are,
remain relatively unexplored, recent educational literature about the
ways in which students learn can provide much information that is of
great practical value.

In terms of course design, teaching methods and assessment, much
research and thinking has recently revolved around the concept of
'active learning', which emphasizes that learning is fundamentally an
active process and that it is best promoted when learners are directly
engaged through their own interests, enthusiasms and talents rather than
expected merely to receive information.[14] In many respects this has long
been understood by historians, if not always acted upon. Though much
of Geoffrey Elton's analysis of history teaching, published in 1967, looks
awkwardly elitist in the context of today's mass-participation systems of
higher education, few history tutors would disagree with him that whilst
the transmission of knowledge has a place,

> it is perfectly obvious that instruction which confines itself to expounding
> some knowledge and demanding its absorption by the student does not
> deserve the name of teaching because nothing of value is done to the
> student mind. . . . All teaching requires the active participation of both
> the teacher and the taught.[15]

Nor would many dispute his insistence on the importance of the development of critical thinking and the deepening of the historical imagination.[16] The studies of active learning emphasize that these and other
qualities and skills are best developed by enabling and encouraging
students, both individually and collectively, to participate more fully in
the processes of learning. Briefly stated, the characteristics of active
learning are the following:

Responsibility for one's own learning. This stems especially from research into the effects of personality on learning, which has shown that

how students perceive themselves and why they succeed or fail have a strong influence upon motivation and the depth of understanding achieved.[17] Students are most likely to initiate, become personally involved in, and sustain learning when they believe that success or failure is dependent upon their own efforts rather than upon factors perceived as being largely outside their control. Thus increasing students' sense of control over what they do, providing them with opportunities to exercise independence and developing the necessary skills with which to do this, can make them more effective learners. This might involve a wide spectrum of approaches, from allowing students greater choice over essay titles to more truly student-centred activities such as student-run seminars or self-assessment and peer assessment. This type of teaching inevitably also affects the relationship between tutor and student; the former guiding, advising and encouraging students as much as transmitting a predetermined body of information. It does not reduce the importance of the tutor, rather the reverse; but it does put students at the centre of teaching and learning, shifting the focus of attention away from the tutor as the source of all authority and inspiration. The tutor is still critical as educator, but in a more subtle and complex way than is the case with didactic teaching.

A personal search for meaning is a critical feature of active learning; that is, constructing meaning for oneself on the basis of critical reflective practice rather than merely receiving and reproducing knowledge. This feature has close links to studies of student learning styles which, while revealing that people learn in different ways, have identified two dominant general learning orientations: knowledge-seeking and understanding-seeking.[18] Knowledge seekers search for facts, use memorization skills and tend to work methodically through a problem in logical order. They are not interested in speculating or finding deeper meanings, or even perhaps in the value and utility of the knowledge they are acquiring. Understanding-seekers try to relate material to their own and others' experiences, looking for underlying themes and structures, exploring links between topics and preferring to work from the whole picture inwards and to use evidence more intuitively. Most students have a predominant style, and both knowledge-seeking and understanding-seeking are necessary to historians, for it is clearly necessary, say, to have a grasp of the terms of a peace treaty before assessing its impact and significance. In general, however, history tutors would wish particularly to foster the higher levels of thinking associated with personal and critical understanding.

Understanding seeking can be seen as part of a 'deep' approach to learning. Much research has shown that in coming to a specific study task students will generally adopt either a 'surface' or a 'deep' approach.[19] The former is characterized by an intention to reproduce material, and involves memorization and failure to distinguish guiding principles. It frequently involves a lack of attention to purpose or strategy, a concentration on facts and a passive acceptance of ideas. It is often particularly encouraged by assessment procedures which seem to the student to reward derivative learning and recitation rather than reflection. A deep approach involves the intention to understand and transform material by critical engagement with the content; relating ideas to previous knowledge and experience; distinguishing guiding principles; relating evidence to conclusions and actively examining the reasoning of an argument. Deep learning is a more sophisticated form of learning which requires a clear and well-structured course content; flexible and imaginative teaching which seeks and values student insights and opinions, and assessment methods that stimulate individual interest, involvement and self-expression.

Whilst these dispositions are relatively stable, it has been argued that by developing more active teaching and assessment methods, as well as giving attention to the wider contexts of education, we can encourage more students to adopt a deep approach to learning. Opportunities for students to discuss their work together, as in seminars and project work, have been particularly cited as important teaching methods in this respect, as have assessment tasks which promote originality and critical reflection.[20]

Reflection on the process of learning. In promoting active learning, students need to be encouraged to adopt a reflective approach, both to their subject and the ways in which they learn it. This connects with work on experiential learning, particularly that of Kolb whose research established the widely influential idea of the 'learning cycle'.[21] Kolb argued that when adults come to learn anything there is a natural cycle which follows four stages. The starting point is personal experience, followed by observation and reflection on that experience, leading to the development of abstract concepts and generalizations in order to make sense of the reflections. These concepts or principles are then tested, refined or altered in a phase of experimentation, and the cycle is completed by linking the findings back to the original experiences. The implication is that experience is critical to learning for understanding. However, it is not sufficient merely to have an experience; without critical reflection it will quickly be forgotten. In teaching terms this has been a powerful argument for teaching methods which emphasise the value of 'real world' experience, such as field trips and work placement, and assessment methods which emphasise participation, as in self-evaluation and peer evaluation.

Transferability of knowledge, skills and understanding. Students learn best by applying their knowledge, skills and understanding, and by connecting their experiences and ideas with what they already know. Research on experiential learning emphasizes that when teaching directly encourages students to 'learn by doing' and taps into student experience, it is more likely to produce effective learning. This might explain the popularity of computer-assisted teaching and video among history students as devices for making the subject interesting, given the centrality of media technology in today's society and the flexibility that it allows in terms of adjusting the pace and pattern of learning to individual needs. Transferability involves skills transfer between academic disciplines, from history to English for example, as well as into the wider work environment, and means explicitly emphasizing and developing the sorts of communication, analytical and reflective skills at the core of history teaching. This does not mean that historical content has to be abandoned in favour of general skills development, but rather an acceptance that understanding in history involves developing both subject-specific and general skills, that even the latter are best learned in subject-specific ways, and that students should be encouraged to perceive their historical understanding and skills in a broader context.

Collaborative activity. Whilst higher education and, indeed, school systems have traditionally fostered individualism and competition, the literature on active learning emphasizes the social nature of learning. It suggests that collaborative work provides a wider range of possibilities for active learning than perhaps any other teaching medium. This springs from work in humanistic psychology, where Rogers in particular has pointed to the importance of social influences upon student learning.[22] Working together in groups can thus provide the sort of encouragement and mutual support conducive to effective learning. Of course, group-work has a long tradition in history, where seminars are a staple strategy, though students co-operating in preparing for individual assignments or even within lectures can be equally beneficial. If the reality of 'working together' is frequently very different, and this is dealt with in a later chapter, group work can none the less be a powerful force for active history learning. It emphasizes that although students are often most used to working as individuals, many advantages arise from collective activities in terms of motivation, negotiation, problem-solving and communication skills. As one researcher comments: 'Breaking down the isolation of learning in higher education seems an important trend in many of the attempts to improve the quality of student learning.'[23]

Whilst teaching activities and assessment procedures are important determinants of whether students adopt deep or surface approaches to learning, Noel Entwistle in particular has emphasized the importance of the total 'learning environment' to effective learning. This includes not only the academic strategies employed at course and undergraduate programme level, but also the broader physical, social and psychological contexts of institutions which affect each student's educational opportunities and experiences.[24] Many of these might be felt to be beyond the control of the individual tutor, but certainly departments might be expected to review what their course programmes are intended to achieve; the concept of progression; the appropriate degree of diversity and prescription; what content is to be privileged; what skills are to developed; how historical understanding is best developed; appropriate level of workload and so on. The culture of each department is therefore an important issue: What priority is given to teaching? What is the relationship of staff to students? Does the head of department encourage effective and innovative teaching? Promoting active learning is a challenge for every level of the institution.

Structure and Content

The seventeen chapters of this book address a broad spectrum of issues of central concern to the teaching of history in higher education. We have not attempted to put together a comprehensive guide to history teaching, or an agreed response to all the questions that can be asked about its future direction; indeed, to have done so would have been presumptuous given that the study of history teaching and learning is still in its infancy. Moreover, for wholly practical reasons we have confined our attentions to the teaching of undergraduates, though most of the essays also contain much that is of value to the teaching of postgraduates on the rapidly growing number of Masters courses.

In the opening section 'Curriculum Issues' we confront the problem that while all teaching and learning must have 'content', what that content should now consist of is by no means clear or agreed upon. Alex

Cowan shows us that in order to answer questions about the kinds of courses, depth and breadth, periods and places, skills and knowledge, and degrees of prescription or freedom that might be offered on a history programme, we have to re-think its central purposes, not least in the light of the growing diversity of students. The needs and experiences of students are also central to the chapters by Earl Lewis and Jeanne Theoharis, and Cathy Lubelska. These chapters explore how race and gender have played a major part in shaping and defining the discipline, and offer practical ways forward for re-thinking the curriculum in these terms. In the final chapter, Keith Jenkins argues for the place of a far more explicit theorizing in the undergraduate curriculum, and suggests how students might be introduced to this complex contemporary issue.

How to improve traditional methods of teaching and learning is the focus of the three chapters in the second section. Peter Stearns argues that far from being outmoded and ineffective, the lecture has much to offer as a teaching medium with many opportunities for group learning. George Preston concentrates upon the practicalities of group work, emphasizing the importance of engaging students more fully in the processes of teaching and learning and advising on how this might be achieved. Finally, Paul Hyland asks how, as individuals and departments, we might measure and improve the quality of history teaching through more diagnostic methods of evaluation and our own action-research.

The challenges and opportunities afforded by the growing range of educational media are the concern of Part III. The use of new technologies is now well established, if unevenly developed, on undergraduate history programmes at many universities. Donald Spaeth explores the uses of the computer to history tutors and how computer-assisted methods can be introduced effectively. Arthur Marwick draws upon the unique experience of the Open University to explain what is required to produce effective distance learning packages in history; while John Ramsden explains the value of the visual in history, and how tutors can use the visual media to enhance the learning experience of their students.

The linkages between the study of history at university and the needs and interests of society, locally and nationally, have become more prominent in recent years, and these form the focus of Part IV. Michael Winstanley demonstrates one way of addressing the issue through 'community history', and shows how this can both enrich the educational experience of students and promote the understanding of history among many people who might otherwise be reckoned well beyond the reach and concerns of the academy. Christine Hallas examines the practicalities of planning field trips and work placements, and their value as a bridge to the outside world, while Peter Beck's chapter explains the continuing relevance of the skills and qualities of history graduates to the world of work and the welfare of society as a whole.

In the final section, Alan Booth discusses the importance of assessment in terms of its influence on student learning and motivation, and suggests some practical ways of changing assessment procedures to encourage students to develop a wide range of skills and adopt deep approaches to their studies. The following chapter 'Assessing Group Work' provides an example of how group assessment can be used by tutors to promote many kinds of active and co-operative learning hitherto neglected by historians. In the closing chapter George Brown explores the issues underlying current approaches to the assessment of university teaching, particularly in Britain, and considers how the various values and attitudes embedded in these methods will continue to influence not only the future of history teaching but also the whole of higher education.

This book, then, brings together the research and experience of historians and educationalists working in a great variety of educational contexts in Britain and the United States. The contributors would not claim to be 'experts' in teaching, for all teaching is ongoing and no self-respecting teacher thinks that there is nothing more to be said or learnt. We do hope, however, that it encourages others to attempt the further work required to establish a rich and diverse body of research and analysis for teaching and learning in history. For, individually and collectively, the chapters in this book point to a new awareness of the need to advance this kind of scholarship, and address questions and issues which are of fundamental importance to everyone who is interested in the future of the discipline.

Notes

1   For a discussion of the changing nature of higher education in Britain, see R. Barnett, *The Limits of Competence: Knowledge, Higher Education and Society* (Open University Press, Buckingham, 1994); G. Williams and H. Fry, *Longer Term Prospects for British Higher Education* (Institute of Education, London, 1994). On the shifting nature of American higher education, see A. Levine et al., *Shaping Higher Education's Future: Demographic Re-*

alities and Opportunities 1990–2000 (Jossey-Bass, San Francisco, 1989);
L. B. Mayhew et al., *The Quest for Quality: The Challenge for Undergraduate Education in the 1990s* (Jossey-Bass, San Francisco, 1990).

2 P. Ramsden, *Learning to Teach in Higher Education* (Routledge, London, 1992), p. 2.

3 P. N. Stearns, *Meaning over Memory: Recasting the Teaching of Culture and History* (University of North Carolina Press, Chapel Hill, 1993), p. 111.

4 For an interesting argument suggesting 'scholarship' as a key link which could be used in the assessment of teaching quality, see L. Elton, 'Research, Teaching and Scholarship in an Expanding Higher Education System', *Higher Education Quarterly*, 46 (1992), pp. 252–68. How to reward teaching excellence is explored in L. Elton and P. Partington, 'Teaching Standards and Excellence in Higher Education', *Occasional Green Paper No. 1* (CVCP, Sheffield, 1991).

5 R. Pearce, 'Quality in the Teaching of History', in *The Audit and Assessment of Teaching Quality*, ed. P. T. Knight (Standing Conference on Educational Development, Birmingham, 1993), p. 27.

6 For a fascinating investigation of academic disciplinary cultures, including their seemingly inborn resistance to innovative ideas, see T. Becher, *Academic Tribes and Territories: Intellectual Enquiry and the Cultures of Disciplines* (Open University Press, Milton Keynes, 1989).

7 Ibid., especially ch. 3.

8 C. Meyers and T. B. Jones, *Promoting Active Learning: Strategies for the College Classroom* (Jossey-Bass, San Francisco, 1993), p. 3.

9 Stearns, *Meaning over Memory*, especially ch. 5.

10 *History Anew: Innovations in the Teaching of History Today*, ed. R. Blackey (California State University Press, Long Beach, 1993).

11 See the critical comments by History in the Universities Defence Group, *Report of a Working Party to Review the Teaching Quality Assessment of History by the Education Funding Councils for England and Wales, 1993–1994* (HUDG, London, 1994).

12 For a short critical review, see Barnett, *The Limits of Competence*, pp. 89–92.

13 Ramsden, *Learning to Teach*, p. 6.

14 In Britain this has been particularly promoted through the practical materials contained in the CVCP-funded series of modular volumes *Effective Teaching and Learning in Higher Education* (CVCP, Sheffield, 1992). For a synopsis of these, see *Effective Teaching and Learning in Higher Education: A Compendium of Resources for the Professional Development of Academic Staff*, ed. P. Cryer (CVCP, Sheffield, 1993). For a useful text outlining this approach in the United States, see Meyers and Jones, *Promoting Active Learning*.

15 G. Elton, *The Practice of History* (Methuen, London, 1967), p. 144.

16   This is not the place to explore what historians mean by critical thinking and understanding, but see Stearns, *Meaning over Memory*, pp. 153–60 for an attempt to address the analytical objectives of a humanities degree along these lines. For a strenuous and fascinating defence of the relevance of these terms in a modern system of higher education, see Barnett, *The Limits of Competence*, chs 7, 8.

17   M. Wittrock, 'Students' Thought Processes', in *Handbook of Research on Teaching*, ed. M. Wittrock (Macmillan, New York, 1986), pp. 297–314.

18   See N. Entwistle, *Styles of Learning and Teaching* (David Fulton, London, 1989 edn).

19   Recent research has also identified a 'strategic' approach, where the intention is to achieve the highest possible results and is therefore characterized by a close regard to assessment requirements and well-organized study methods. This can involve both deep and surface approaches to a task. On these study pathologies, see N. Entwistle, *The Impact of Teaching on Learning Outcomes in Higher Education: A Literature Review* (CVCP, Sheffield, 1992); N. Entwistle and P. Ramsden, *Understanding Student Learning* (Croom Helm, London, 1983); F. Marton and R. Säljö, 'Approaches to Learning', in *The Experience of Learning*, ed. F. Marton, D. J. Hounsell and N. Entwistle (Scottish Academic Press, Edinburgh, 1984), pp. 36–55; J. B. Biggs *Student Approaches to Learning and Studying* (Australian Council for Educational Research, Melbourne, 1987); G. Gibbs, *Improving the Quality of Student Learning* (Technical and Educational Services, Bristol, 1992).

20   See N. Entwistle, S. Thompson and H. Tait, *Guidelines for Promoting Effective Learning in Higher Education* (University Centre for Research on Learning and Instruction, Edinburgh, 1992).

21   D. A. Kolb, *Experiential Learning: Experience as the Source of Learning* (Prentice-Hall, New York, 1983). On the importance of reflective practice for student learning, see R. Barnett, *Improving Higher Education: Total Quality Care* (Open University Press, Buckingham, 1992), ch. 11.

22   C. Rogers, *Freedom to Learn* (Merrill, Columbus, 1978).

23   Entwistle, Thompson and Tait, *Guidelines for Promoting Effective Learning*, p. 7.

24   Ibid., pp. 8–9, and especially Entwistle, *The Impact of Teaching on Learning Outcomes*, pp. 41–4.

Further Reading

The last ten years have seen a tremendous growth in the number of books on teaching and learning in higher education, but the following are particularly useful and provide references to other works.

For those beginning to teach and looking for a review of the research literature as well as practical advice, G. Brown and M. Atkins, *Effective Teaching in Higher Education* (Methuen, London, 1988) can be recommended. W. J.

McKeachie, *Teaching Tips: A Guidebook for the Beginning College Teacher* (D. C. Heath, Lexington, 1986) is also a good practical guide to a wide range of teaching and assessment tasks.

For experienced teachers of history, the following texts integrate theory and practice in a meaningful and creative way. P. Ramsden, *Learning to Teach in Higher Education* (Routledge, London, 1992) offers a challenging view of the meaning and practice of all the key aspects of teaching activity. N. Entwistle, S. Thompson and H. Tait, *Guidelines for Effective Teaching* (University Centre for Research on Learning and Instruction, Edinburgh, 1992) is a clear, pragmatic guide, with good examples, firmly founded upon the recent research into teaching and learning.

Those interested in exploring the ways in which students learn should turn in the first instance to N. Entwistle, *The Impact of Teaching and Learning Outcomes in Higher Education* (CVCP, Sheffield, 1992) which provides an overview of the research literature. His *Styles of Learning and Teaching* (David Fulton, London, 1989 edn) offers a more heavily theorized approach, as to a lesser extent does N. Entwistle and P. Ramsden, *Understanding Student Learning* (Croom Helm, London, 1983). J. B. Biggs, *Student Approaches to Learning and Studying* (Australian Council for Educational Research, Melbourne, 1987) is also full of insights.

For a practical approach to 'active' learning, the twelve volumes in the series *Effective Teaching and Learning in Higher Education* (CVCP, Sheffield, 1992) cover all aspects of teaching activity and are invaluable, if uneven in quality. All include exercises which can be used with students and staff. The volume by P. Denicolo, N. Entwistle and D. Hounsell, *What is Active learning?*, is a straightforward introduction to the topic. So too is C. Meyers and T. B. Jones, *Promoting Active Learning: Strategies for the College Classroom* (Jossey-Bass, San Francisco, 1993) which contains many examples relevant to history.

Innovations in the teaching of history are the subject of *History Anew: Innovations in the Teaching of History*, ed. R. Blackey (California State University Press, Long Beach, 1993) which contains reprints of articles from *Perspectives*, the newsletter of the American Historical Association. Innovations in teaching are also described in G. Gibbs, *Improving the Quality of Student Learning* (Technical & Educational Services, Bristol, 1992), several of which are relevant to history. *Course Design for Resource Based Learning: Humanities*, ed. J. Wisdom and G. Gibbs (Oxford Centre for Staff Development, Oxford, 1994) also contains several case-studies from history.

Finally, for those who wish to reflect on the changing idea of higher education, and especially its new vocabulary of skills and competencies as opposed to the more familiar language of understanding and critical analysis, R. Barnett, *The Limits of Competence: Knowledge, Higher Education and Society* (Open University Press, Buckingham, 1994) provides a stimulating analysis of great relevance to historians.

PART I

Curriculum Issues

2

Planning a History Curriculum

Alex Cowan

Only a generation ago, when the first experiments in changing the style and content of history degrees began to take place in British universities, those concerned shared some implicit assumptions about the prior knowledge and experience of their undergraduates, which permitted them to engage immediately in a debate about content. Even then, the notion of a 'canon' of material about the past to be covered in a history syllabus was being brought into question. Now, the diversity of history courses is such that it is unlikely that a student in one institution will ever follow the same pattern of study as a student in another. Yet the external pressures to consider and justify each history syllabus have become ever greater. Not only is there a National Curriculum for history in the schools, but a process of validation and evaluation which first began in those higher education institutions under the aegis of the Council for National Academic Awards; this latter has now been extended by the introduction of Teaching Quality Assessments by the recently established national Funding Councils.

This growing requirement to justify an academic programme in terms of its content, how it is taught and how student progress is assessed, has developed in parallel with a sense among many historians that received models of history syllabuses are in need of revision, and that many of the assumptions behind what presently exists require explicit discussion. There are many reasons for this, including the need to find ways to meet the intellectual aspirations and experience of a rapidly changing body, the emergence in senior positions of men and women whose own intellectual development began in the sixties, and the knock-on effect of changes to neighbouring disciplines such as sociology and literary criticism throughout the western world. Perhaps the most important of all, however, is the sense that history as an academic discipline is under threat. We live in a world in which the importance of the study of the past is no longer self-evident, and the provision of history courses has to be seen as an area of educational activity in competition with others whose coherence and justification are often more easily perceived.

In these circumstances, there can be little doubt of the importance of constructing an effective history curriculum. The way forward is not so clear. There is an urgent need for further debate among practitioners rather than theorists so that we can identify a framework within which new history curricula can be designed. It is equally important to identify the higher education context within which history teaching is taking place. This chapter will focus on three areas of discussion: the history curriculum as it was, and the external pressures for change; the potential aims and objectives in constructing a history syllabus; and major content issues. It ends with the examination of a single case-study, the undergraduate programme in historical studies at the University of Northumbria at Newcastle, which represents one attempt to confront many of these issues.

The History Curriculum

By comparison with the present day, those with a responsibility for the university history curriculum some forty years ago had a relatively easy task. The main purposes of historical study were to further scholarship, to train future historians, and to develop individuals with a rounded cultural confidence which would render them capable of taking up responsible posts in commerce, industry or the civil service with the greatest of ease. There were no debates about teaching method, and very little discussion of content, for the students who became undergraduates at Oxford, Cambridge or the great civic universities fulfilled their tutors' expectations in advance. Candidates for the limited number of places available on history courses were expected to have a general overview of British history, a solid grounding in English literature and a fair command of Latin. They were also already trained by their schoolteachers in the central academic exercises expected of them at university: reading, essay writing and answering questions on examination papers. Once they arrived at their chosen university these skills were put into practice in an environment of survey lecture courses and intensive personal tutorials, supplemented in some places by seminars in which students occasionally spoke to each other. The lecturing staff offered a curriculum which was a mixture of surveys in British history, complemented by research-led specialist courses. Undergraduate education became an extension of secondary education in which little was made explicit about the expectations of the teaching staff and the approach to education was embodied in a circular justification that students read history in order to gain more understanding, which enabled them to *read* history, which was expected to be an end in itself.

Very few of these conditions now remain. Instead of relying on the comforting assumptions that students came from similar backgrounds and shared similar interests to those of their teachers, anyone who begins to consider how to design a history curriculum is obliged to take several steps back from questions about content and even from modes of delivery to consider the contrasting experience of potential students of history and the need to take account of prevailing attitudes and forms of organization in present-day higher education.

The student body has become far more diverse. Some present-day undergraduates left school without formal qualifications and have returned to full-time education after several years at work or of bringing up a family. Others may come from households where they are the first member of their family to enter higher education and therefore lack some of the social conditioning which allowed most undergraduates in the past to adapt rapidly to university life. Even those more traditional students who move easily to university from their final year at secondary school at the age of eighteen or so, have little in common with their predecessors of the 1950s and 1960s. The expansion in student numbers in response to government policy to increase the proportion of eighteen-year-olds in higher education on the one hand, and the rising demand for degrees from mature students, particularly in the humanities and the social sciences, have altered the profile of the potential undergraduate. Many more students begin their degrees without the confidence engendered by knowing that they have scored particularly highly at school in their chosen subjects. To put it bluntly, designing a history curriculum needs to take groups of mixed ability into account.

The institutional context has also altered in a number of ways. Potential students and curricula planners alike are now faced with a unified system in which there are over a hundred universities and twenty-two colleges and institutes of higher education at which history is being taught.[1] History courses now have to take into account the needs of an army of part-time students who may only enter the institution once a week and are faced with the dilemma that the time at which their class ends corresponds with the closing time of their university library. As more and more universities and colleges become modular and organize their teaching into semester-length courses, the picture keeps on changing, requiring even more flexibility in our expectations of students of history. While the most recent published digest of UK history degrees offers a picture of comforting diversity in which single honours degrees largely characterized the 'old' universities and joint and multidisciplinary degrees were the *imprimatur* of the polytechnics and colleges of higher education,[2] the most recent developments have seen the emergence of history 'routes' in modular degrees in the 'new' universities and an increase in the range of subject combinations in the 'old'. In spite of changes in government policy which have put a severe brake on the earlier expansion in student numbers, the potential for change in higher education remains considerable. Already, many universities are franchising out first-level courses to further education colleges. The introduction of credit transfer schemes not only makes it possible for a student to begin a degree course in one UK institution and complete it at another, but to do so at universities in various countries of the European Union.

Changes have taken place in the school curriculum which have altered the nature of the intellectual baggage which school-leavers bring with them to university when studying history, or, for that matter, any other academic subject. Latin has gone from the curriculum of all but a minority of secondary schools. While English literature remains a popular choice at school alongside history, the way in which it is taught and the range of books studied rarely offer a satisfactory basis for the study of history. Until very recently, the content of history courses taught in secondary schools has been astonishing by its diversity and the inability of children to relate one aspect of the past which they have studied to any others. For an overview, they are obliged to cast their minds back to the age of thirteen or earlier. Historical novels, which so often acted as a major stimulus of interest in the past have fallen in popularity in competition with science fiction, crime and horror novels.

The study of history as an academic discipline is increasingly in competition with other degree programmes using methods which seem to be a world away from individual library study. Since the seventies and the expansion of higher education in the United Kingdom, potential students have been offered a bewildering range of degree courses, combining two or three different subjects, or offering the promise of well-paid jobs because they have been designed to prepare for a specific range of employment. Now, more than ever, traditional subjects such as history are at the mercy of market forces on the one hand, where students choose to study degrees for which they can see a purpose, and at the mercy of institutional constraints on the other. Universities no longer favour subjects which bring in relatively limited fees, and offer less money to support teaching. Historians, like their colleagues in literature, philosophy and theology, have to teach more students for less.

Even if they know how to 'read', current students are unlikely to find much to read. They are in competition for books and journals with many more students than before. Libraries are unable to keep up with the increase in demand for their services, either in terms of making books available in sufficient numbers, or by providing enough study spaces in an environment conducive to study. Demands on libraries have also increased as student incomes have fallen to a level at which book purchases now have a very low priority. It is clear that anyone planning a history curriculum afresh would be unwise to rely on most of the old assumptions about the skills and experience of potential students.

On the positive side, we can begin to make some new assumptions about this diverse group of people whom we recognize as history undergraduates. Major changes have been taking place in the ways in which history is taught in primary and secondary schools, enabling children to develop a greater range of historical skills in their approach to the past. Three areas of activity in particular are important. Much more emphasis is being placed on problem-solving rather than memorizing factual information. An approach which some would have reserved for final-year undergraduates or students engaging in research is now being used by eleven-year-olds. Far greater use is being made of primary sources of all kinds. Many students now begin their degrees with an understanding of the importance of primary sources in themselves and of the necessity to confront one source with another. The formal essay has been replaced in part by project work, enabling students to learn by experience how to organize their own time, work to deadlines, seek out information from a variety of sources and places and present it in an effective way. We might add that a general cultural change in primary and secondary education now places discussion and group work on the same level as individual activity.

It will take time for all these changes to work their way through the education system into higher education, not least because of the growing proportion of adults now joining school-leavers, but undergraduate history programmes are now in a position in which they must both take advantage of them and must respond to the expectations which they have generated. Many undergraduate history programmes have failed to adapt so far, leading to frustration among students.

If the disappearance of a classical, literary secondary education is to be lamented, there are other cultural developments which need to be taken into consideration, although with considerable care. Cultural conditioning about the past is now more visual than ever before, from cartoon histories of the American War of Independence, Hollywood epics full of swords, ruffles and crinolines, and *Bill and Ted's Amazing Adventure*, to the welter of television documentaries using newsreel, reconstructions, and computer graphics. However much the visual influences to which students have been exposed are both superficial and subjective, they offer stimuli which can be built on, deepened and corrected. Today's students, without being aware of it, have a much more sophisticated, critical and multidimensional approach to visual material than their predecessors. This offers new opportunities in curriculum design.

Curriculum Issues

These changes in the student body and their formative experiences leave us in little doubt that the history curriculum urgently requires revision. The problem is what should be done. There is no overall agreement about the shape of such a new curriculum. Nor should there be, for diversity of provision is one of the most enduring characteristics of higher education in the democratic world. On the other hand, there are a number of issues which should be taken into account when designing a history curriculum.

As a starting point, the changes in the student body which have been taking place during the last decade indicate that the focus of the curriculum either has shifted or needs to shift from the requirements of the tutor to those of the student. In other words, curriculum development in history, in common with other disciplines, must take into account the purposes of the undergraduate programme as well as its content, and each component of that programme requires designing with its educational as well as scholarly purposes in mind. This is far from suggesting

that content does not matter, only that there needs to be a close relationship between the content of an element of the history curriculum and its
function. Once this has been established, other issues become important.
Should there be any prescription over content at all, or should programmes be constructed by students from a wide range of available
courses? Do courses in national history still have a role in the curriculum
and, if so, what importance should be accorded to them? Are outline
courses out of date or is there a place for them in today's curriculum?
Should the curriculum reflect the chronological diversity of the past or is
it appropriate to limit content to the twentieth century? Is the acquisition
of transferable skills out of place in a non-vocational discipline? What is
the role of 'research-led' teaching?

Recent British government policy, with its emphasis on transferable
personal skills and 'enterprise' has had a marked effect on the direction
of curriculum planning in higher education. In some disciplines, the
acquisition of personal transferable skills has become the ultimate outcome. While this is most unlikely to attract support from historians
teaching in higher education, the link between undergraduate study and
the development of certain skills can now be made explicit. This is not
the same agenda as that put forward by governments, but one which
recognizes that the skills which can be developed are inherent in the
study of the discipline itself and contribute to an enhanced understanding of the past. Even here, the gap between the study of an academic
discipline for its own sake and the development of a programme of study
which enhances certain skills and approaches beneficial to future employment may not be as wide as we like to imagine. At the end of
the eighties, the Council for Industry and Higher Education turned its
attention to the humanities and concluded:

> As they respond to change and try to manage the present, companies
> are coming to see their competitive power in virtually continuous innova-
> tion in an uncertain world. Somewhat to its own surprise, *business is
> beginning to describe managerial virtues in the humanities' own vocabulary* of
> 'imagination', 'vision', 'sensitivity', and 'creativity'. Moreover in such a
> climate, the iconoclasm of a trained critical mind is a powerful business
> qualification [their emphasis].[3]

Peter Stearns offers a useful series of headings under which we can
gather the skills acquired by the successful student of history: the ability
to interpret and combine source materials, the ability to deal with diverse
interpretations of issues concerning society and culture, the ability to

mount arguments directed at analytical questions, the capacity to test models applied to social and cultural phenomena, the ability to assess causation and the impact of historical change, and the ability to compare societies and cultures in order to enhance understanding.[4] If history curricula in different institutions are to have at least one point in common, it is surely to ensure that by the time they graduate, students have developed these skills to a significant degree and are aware that they have done so.

There is an educational as well as an organizational imperative which requires all degrees to identify elements of progression and levels of achievement which have to be consistent with the quality of undergraduate provision elsewhere. Policies vary from one university or college to another, but as an increasing number of institutions are introducing modular systems, two major patterns of progression are developing. One, based on the traditional three-year English undergraduate degree, divides all courses into three academic levels and requires that successive levels should confront students with educational experiences of growing complexity, representing either the enhancement of skills which have already been developed to a certain extent, or the introduction of additional approaches appropriate to a higher level. The other, which is strongly influenced by long-standing practice in the 'old' universities, makes a distinction between an introductory first level, designed to prepare students from a variety of educational backgrounds for serious undergraduate work, and advanced courses which may be studied at any point before graduation. This approach takes account of both practical and intellectual factors. Opening up courses to a greater variety of students enables a wider choice of courses to be offered. Identifying advanced courses also leaves much greater flexibility over the question whether the kind of historical skills identified by Stearns and others can be measured mechanically in terms of short, semester-length units.

Any approach to curriculum design which places content at a lower level than the development of a range of competencies runs the risk of overkill.[5] There is a case for arguing that a history programme does not need a curriculum at all. It should consist entirely of diverse elements based on the research interests of teaching staff and selected by students to build up a programme of their own liking. Even if these interests, for one reason or another, are highly arbitrary, the overall experience could be said to comprise a history degree on condition that the individual courses have been designed to ensure academic progression. While such an argument fits well with an extreme form of modularity, in which no course is privileged above any other and students have a free choice to build up their personal study programmes, it ignores the long tradition in which content has played an important part in the history curriculum. Many of the content issues which are raised here are far from new, but are included because debates round them continue.

The universal presence in the curriculum of courses in the history of one's own country is both understandable and open to question. Their inclusion can be seen as the continuation of a process of cultural conditioning since early childhood by which students begin to identify with the country in which they live. In practical terms, too, there is likely to be a closer match between such courses and the research interests of most teaching staff.

National history courses in Britain and the United States provide students with greater access to primary and secondary sources in their own language. As Sir Geoffrey Elton wrote in 1967, 'In practice, I suppose, this [programme] is likely to mean that a student would have to work on the history of his own country, and despite a good deal of opposition to this principle, I cannot see what may be wrong with it.'[6] Even then, critics of such an approach argued that to privilege national history was to encourage a narrow Anglo-centric view of the past and to bring about the very ignorance and subjective understanding which a humanistic education is intended to offset.

Past experience has shown that definitions of national history change according to the status of the country concerned. There is an argument that in the modern world too much emphasis on national history is out of place unless it is studied in a broader context. The decline of the United Kingdom as a world power and its increasing association with mainland Europe have engendered a number of courses which place the history of Britain in a European context. Similarly, the world economic changes since the end of the Second World War suggest that the degree-level study of United States history could benefit from its consideration in the context of the history of the Pacific Basin. These are only two suggestions. The history of the UK could be equally well studied in the context of Empire and Commonwealth, while the history of the United States might benefit from a consideration of its place in the history of North and Central America as a whole.

The use of outline courses to review long periods of mainstream history is falling out of favour in British and American universities. Not only do these outlines require teams of staff who are unable to apply more than a small part of their specialist expertise, the range of material

and the speed with which it must be covered can leave students with a
superficial understanding of the past and reinforce their sense that the
acquisition of factual knowledge is what counts, rather than the development of their critical skills and understanding of the past.[7] What is more,
the place of outline courses as compulsory elements at the heart of
history programmes places a great strain on library resources which are
already unable to cope with existing numbers of students. On the other
hand, outline courses can provide a very useful framework in the earlier
stages of the undergraduate programme for more detailed study later on.
By acting as a compulsory core for a programme, they help to define that
programme and to offer a long-term perspective for students for whom
this was not present at secondary school. By integrating newer approaches such as gender history with mainstream concerns, these issues
can be seen in context. Of course, students should be protected from
being overwhelmed by the scope of an outline course, but it is possible
with careful planning to establish a good balance between the specific and
the general.

   All curriculum planning passes through a stage in which the case for
the inclusion of more and more material is put with such enthusiasm that
it becomes necessary to engage in serious pruning. At this point, rival
arguments tend to be put for restricting the chronological range of
subjects studied to the twentieth century or at least to the industrialized
world, or for the inclusion of topics from at least the thirteenth or
fourteenth centuries, if not earlier. Supporters of the 'contemporary
history' argument have a number of points in their favour. Most students
about to study history at university are already familiar with this period.
They respond to the issues under discussion more readily because they
can see their immediate relevance to present-day concerns. There is a
greater continuum with modern politics. By limiting courses to a shorter
period, it is possible to study the past in greater depth. Besides, it is
argued, there is little point in offering courses in earlier periods of history
when the pattern of student choice always favours modern history.

   There is an equally strong case for including the history of earlier
periods, not only in order to give students a much longer-term perspective on the past, but also to counter what are sometimes seen as weaknesses in the way in which students study modern history. Enthusiasm
for the historical roots of present-day issues can often be a poor disguise
for a highly subjective look at the past. By engaging with periods of time,
and forms of social and economic organization with which they are
unfamiliar, it is possible for students to develop a more complex under-

standing of the past. There is often far more methodological adventurousness in the study of periods for which there are limited sources which are more difficult to analyse. Such studies can form a useful bridge to neighbouring disciplines such as sociology and anthropology. The issue of putting a quart into a pint pot can be resolved by offering students a wide range of choice, but it is then the responsibility of those designing the curriculum to decide whether to leave students with an entirely free choice, in which case modern history will attract most of the students, or to build in the requirement that all students choose courses from a range of periods.

The debate about the best balance between objectives and content in the curriculum has been particularly lively in the case of information technology. Here is a skill which is both particularly useful to the graduate who is looking for employment, and increasingly relevant to the study of many aspects of the past. Should information technology be taught as a specific skill in a course which stands alone, or should students acquire IT skills by taking courses into which they have been fully integrated? IT courses, it is argued, are best taught by specialists in computing, leaving historians to teach what they know best. Should IT skills be needed for more advanced courses, it may be assumed that students have already acquired them. This argument is usually used in institutions where IT applications in the humanities are in an early stage of development, and it is deemed necessary to pay lip-service to institutional claims to teach all students transferable personal skills. Others would argue that even when history staff teach their students IT, too much emphasis is placed on the skill, and not enough on its applications to history. IT should be incorporated into history courses. This argument gains in strength as computers become more user-friendly, and opportunities grow for students to use computer-assisted learning packages in history such as those being developed by the History Courseware Consortium in the UK. There is also a third way, in which the main purpose of IT courses in history is to develop students' capacity to create and use databases in a framework of discussions about the past. The latter two approaches are distinguished in part by the emphasis given to the development of IT skills, and in part by the practicalities of incorporating IT into a wide range of history courses.

Much has been made so far of the student body and its diverse needs. What of the teaching staff? Along with the library, they represent the most precious resource available to an institution, and their experience and talents are the basis of all successful teaching. Two related questions ought to be taken into consideration when planning a history curriculum. How far should teaching be 'research-led', and to what extent should the range of courses on offer reflect staff research specialisms? The recent HEFCE Quality Assessment of History report states that 'History staff are well-qualified and appropriately deployed, teaching in areas related to their scholarship and research interests and enthusiasms.'[8] This supposedly positive statement is really an unsuccessful attempt to resolve some contradictions. It is clear from many of the detailed reports of visits to individual institutions that the peer assessors who took part in the exercise reflected a widespread opinion that the best teaching is research-led. This attitude poses its own problems. While there is universal agreement that historians teaching in higher education should be actively engaged in research and publication, and that research experience ought to be taken into account when appointments are made to academic posts, the precise relationship between staff research interests and the courses they teach is open for discussion.

One of the most striking examples of the primacy of the curriculum over the teaching staff comes from the University of Oxford, where all history students take a heavily source-based special subject in their final year, chosen from a limited range of topics, such as the Italian Renaissance. The staff who teach these special subjects have research interests in these general areas, but the main focus is on opening a substantial range of primary source material up to final-year undergraduates. Teaching of this kind is 'informed by research' rather than 'research-led'. In many institutions staff are appointed or are subsequently asked to teach courses for which their research is at best of tangential relevance. There can be many reasons for this. One of the most common is the need to teach an existing course for which a substantial body of material has been built up in the library. As library budgets dwindle, factors such as these must play a part. The introduction of courses to meet the requirements of modular systems based on semester-length units is also placing pressures on history staff to teach a wider range of topics than ever before. It seems unlikely that they can all be 'research-led', and yet this may well not detract from the quality of education being offered. These considerations are not intended to imply that staff research need not be called upon when designing a curriculum. Without the research experience and enthusiasms of staff, some teaching of the best kind could not take place. It is up to the curriculum designers to decide where such courses are most appropriate.

A Case-study

Identifying areas of debate remains a highly abstract way of approaching the design of a history curriculum. In an attempt to bring them to life, the concluding section of this article focuses on a case-study well known to the writer, the Historical Studies degree at the University of Northumbria at Newcastle, one of the 'new' universities, first introduced in 1993. The planning process took over two years to complete and involved every member of the history staff. Our starting point was an unusual one. After twenty years of teaching history courses as part of a joint degree in English and History, we were invited to design an honours history programme from scratch which could both stand alone and be combined with a range of other disciplines in a new modular structure, organized in semesters. The experience has been described variously by the members of the planning team as 'stimulating', 'liberating', and even 'cathartic'.

A number of principles were established from the start, partly as a reaction to twenty years of teaching courses designed explicitly to meet the need of students of English literature, but primarily in order to take advantage of our existing experience and to make the thinking behind our teaching much more explicit. We wanted to allow students the opportunity to understand the history of Britain in a much broader context, to do so flexibly, and to organize the curriculum progressively in order to develop a wide range of skills appropriate to the study of history. Each aspect of the programme as it emerged was planned to fit in with these three principles, in addition to resolving to our satisfaction many of the areas of debate which have already been outlined. For example, the Northumbria degree has retained two sets of outline courses, one ranging from the eighteenth century to the present day, the other from the Norman Conquest to the end of the seventeenth century, taught at the first and second-levels respectively. Both enable the British experience to be understood in a much wider context, and both recognize that students need to get their teeth into more clearly defined projects for which the general surveys act as a framework.

The balance between the specific and the general is particularly evident in the second-level modules on 'Medieval Europe' and 'Early Modern Europe', in which students are encouraged to study a wide range of primary sources as a means of coming into closer contact with the more distant past.[9] A source-book provides students with selections of primary material for discussion at weekly two-hour seminars. Each group of extracts has been chosen in order to open up a specific area of discussion which, in turn, has been introduced by a more general lecture the previous week. A great deal of attention has been devoted towards making the course practicable in terms of student assignments while leaving each student with an appreciation of the broad sweep of developments. These general surveys are of added significance because they have been identified within the modular structure as the basic minimum to be taken by all students, whether they are following single honours, joint, major or minor programmes.

The degree contains an explicit skills strand which privileges those skills essential to the present-day historian while recognizing that they can be applied more widely. Every attempt is made to enable students to build on these skills throughout the degree programme. The nature and development of the subject are introduced to first-level students as soon as they arrive. This historiographical dimension is then taken up by all second-level courses, before becoming the focus of a third-level course on Issues in Historical Interpretation. The extensive use of primary sources in the second-level outline courses builds on a series of practical workshops on the use of historical sources in the first-level of the programme, and forms in its turn a solid preparation for the final-year dissertation to be written by all students. From the second semester, students are introduced to the basic IT applications used by historians such as databases and spreadsheets, before engaging in the practicalities of learning how to construct a historical database.

Other skills, such as the ability to understand a wide range of historical concepts and use them imaginatively, arise out of a range of more specialized courses. Students choose fairly freely among them, but each course taught at a particular point in the programme belongs to a 'family' of options, all of which are designed to develop students' skills in the same way while exposing them to diverse periods, debates and material.

One such 'family' is the Approaches to History strand offered in the first semester of the second year. Each course focuses on a particular approach to history, such as Urban History, Multicultural History, or Visual History, with the objective of providing students with an introduction to the specific concerns, conceptual frameworks and methodologies of such 'sub-disciplines'. Like the Themes in Historical Interpretation studied at the first level, these Approaches use a broad comparative approach but rapidly focus on a particular period and region. Urban History, for example, uses the towns of early modern Europe as a case-study.

Third-year students also select from 'families' of options. In addition to the traditional special subject, which culminates in a dissertation, each student on the Historical Studies programme selects one of a series of Advanced Options. These paired courses, which last throughout the final year, represent a development of the Approaches. Once again, the emphasis is on the conceptual and the comparative, but through much-more specialized themes such as Intellectual Revolutions in Seventeenth-Century England, Retail History and Consumerism in Modern Europe, and Feudal Societies.

Students are encouraged to acquire additional foreign language skills, both to be able to read primary and secondary material in other languages, and to take the opportunity to travel as exchange students. An alternative route exists for students wishing to develop interests in the local region. This flexibility was built into the degree both to address the diversity in backgrounds and aspirations of potential students, and to build on the strengths of the university's existing links with institutions abroad. Market research and the experience of recruitment to the university's humanities degree programme had shown that many potential recruits were locally based mature students whose domestic circumstances would prevent them from spending three months abroad. It was also widely recognized that throughout the UK higher education system the numbers of applicants for single honours history degrees who had studied a modern language to A-level had been declining for some time. Both pieces of evidence suggested that a programme which was exclusively based on study abroad in a foreign language might have difficulty in recruiting, and would disenfranchise the mature students who were an important part of the university's mission. On the other hand, the team was well qualified in both British and continental history, the university already had links with France, Spain and Italy through the ERASMUS student exchange programme, and new links were rapidly developing with institutions in the United States and Finland. The latter looked particularly interesting because so much teaching in Finnish universities takes place in English, and the location of the university of Joennsuu close to the Russian border offered possibilities for students with an interest in Russian language and history.

Two main possibilities were therefore incorporated in the degree: continental history and local history, with the additional prospect that students might be able to study American history as part of a planned exchange scheme with US institutions. Students wishing to spend a semester in France, Germany, Spain, Italy or Finland follow intensive language courses for three semesters. Students who wish to remain in Newcastle throughout are also offered the opportunity to take courses in modern languages in order to enhance their linguistic skills and apply them to the study of history. The university is increasing its foreign-language book stock to enable students to use their linguistic skills for history courses. As an alternative to courses in modern languages, the university offers students courses in regional history, building on its existing reputation in this field at both undergraduate and postgraduate level.

As part of their commitment to the belief that the skills required to study history are also eminently transferable, the planning team incorporated a period of time at the second level during which students who have chosen to remain in Newcastle rather than to study abroad are placed with a local employer for one day a week. The employers currently working with the university on this scheme were selected from those fields where students of history could apply their skills most effectively: libraries, museums, archives, heritage sites.

The route taken by the history staff at the University of Northumbria requires a variety of teaching strategies which are still under development. The effectiveness of this approach is now being put to the test by its first generation of students. In the end only they can judge if it works, but the planning team anticipate that the three principles upon which their curriculum has been based will leave each student with both an enduring sense and understanding of the past and, above all, a feeling that they have enjoyed the experience.

Conclusion

There is no blueprint for planning a history curriculum. Each staff team begins with its own experiences and resources, which provide a framework within which the student experience takes place. This framework needs to be flexible in order to meet the demands and challenges of existing and future students. It also needs to be shaped by a collective sense of the aims and objectives of a history curriculum within which individual courses can be placed. In the end, there must be a balance between resources, objectives, content, and the ability of individual students to handle what is required of them in the time available. Once this equation has been worked out, it is up to the individual to work out how best to design and deliver his or her own courses. What this chapter has attempted to do is to identify a number of key issues which are still the subject of considerable debate, and to suggest that they should be taken into account when planning a history curriculum:

- the objectives of an undergraduate programme;
- the coherence of such a programme;
- the role of national history;
- the function of outline courses;
- the place of skills and their transferability;
- the role of 'research-led' teaching.

Once the curriculum has been established, the focus shifts to the equally important issues of delivery and assessment.

Notes

I should like to acknowledge the help and advice of Nicholas Reeves of Thames Valley University and Tim Kirk of the University of Northumbria.

1 Source: History in the Universities Defence Group.
2 *History in Higher Education: A Comparative and Analytical Guide to Courses in History in United Kingdom Universities, Polytechnics, Colleges and Institutes of Higher Education*, ed. J. M. Bourne and N. Reeves (Historical Association, London, 1989). See also, A. Cowan, 'History in the United Kingdom Public Sector', *The History Teacher*, 22 (1989), pp. 277–92.
3 Council for Industry and Higher Education, *Towards a Partnership: The Humanities for the Working World* (CIHE, London, 1990).
4 P. N. Stearns, *Meaning over Memory: Recasting the Teaching of Culture and History* (University of North Carolina, Chapel Hill, 1993), ch. 6.
5 An example of this is the humanities programme introduced at the University of Brighton, which was exclusively concerned with the acquisition of skills. See B. Brecher, 'Teaching Skills through History: The New Humanities Degree at Brighton Polytechnic', *PUSH Newsletter*, 1 (1990), pp. 13–30; B. Brecher and T. Hickey, 'A Skills-oriented Humanities Course at Brighton Polytechnic: A Brief Update', *PUSH Newsletter*, 3 (1992), pp. 34–8.
6 G. R. Elton, *The Practice of History* (Fontana, London, 1967), p. 158.
7 Stearns, *Meaning over Memory*, *passim*.
8 Higher Education Funding Council for England, *Quality Assessment of History 1993–94* (HEFCE, Bristol, 1994), p. 6.
9 This approach is discussed in detail in *Course Design for Resource Based Learning: Humanities*, ed. J. Wisdom and G. Gibbs (Oxford Centre for Staff Development, Oxford, 1994), pp. 49–51.

Further Reading

In recent years the changing curriculum has become a pressing issue for historians. In the UK the accelerating move towards modularization, particularly, is forcing a practical re-thinking both of content and how the curriculum relates to the teaching and assessment of the subject in higher education. Whilst progress is being made, there is as yet no significant body of literature specific to history on curriculum matters. However, P. N. Stearns, *Meaning over Memory: Recasting the Teaching of Culture and History* (University of North Carolina Press, Chapel Hill, 1993) is a provocative analysis of the state of teaching and curriculum planning in the United States which ambitiously tackles the problems and opportunities facing the humanities in a mass system of higher education. *Course Design for Resource Based Learning: Humanities*, ed. J. Wisdom and G. Gibbs (Oxford Centre for Staff Development, Oxford, 1994) also contains, in its opening chapters, a very useful review of the general problems facing those engaged in designing humanities programmes in higher education.

There are also useful general texts on curriculum and course design which historians could profitably consult. G. Gibbs, *Problems and Course Design Strategies* (PCFC, Bristol, 1992) provides a useful guide to course design for larger numbers of students. C. and D. Baume, *Course Design for Active Learning* (CVCP, Sheffield, 1992) gives practical advice on developing more student-centred approaches. A. Miller, *Course Design for University Lecturers* (Kogan Page, London, 1987) focuses upon designing undergraduate courses, as does D. Rowntree, *Designing Courses for Students* (McGraw-Hill, New York, 1985). R. M. Diamond, *Designing and Improving Courses and Curricula in Higher Education* (Jossey-Bass, San Francisco, 1989) offers insights from the US system. Finally, for those who wish to explore broader perspectives on curriculum change, an interesting variety of views is provided in *Managing the Curriculum: Making Common Cause*, ed. J. Bocock and D. Watson (Open University Press, Buckingham, 1994).

3

Race in a World of Overlapping Diasporas: The History Curriculum

Earl Lewis and Jeanne Theoharis

Writer Lorene Cary captured in raw eloquence what it means to journey across the United States' racial fault line. In *Black Ice* she recalled her sojourn from the safe bosom of a mostly black world into the fiercely protective and competitive world of an elite 'white' prep school. Using the form that hundreds of African Americans have used to write themselves into being, Cary acknowledged years later how fearful, isolated, anxious, and threatened she felt by this most daring of acts: becoming a racial experiment.

Her autobiography tells another story as well. Once accepted into this elite world of privilege, power, and wealth, she made the world her own. 'I came here, and I went away changed,' she observed. 'I've been fighting that for a long time, to no purpose. I am a crossover artist, you know, like those jazz musicians who do pop albums, too.'[1] As she would remind her successors a decade and a half after her graduation, St Paul's was theirs, just as America was theirs. This kind of self-possession blurred the distinction between the outsider and the insider, between white privilege and black marginalization.

Her place in several overlapping worlds heightened her sense of the contradictions of racial meaning. She recognized the tension in her experience. 'I wondered whether "crossover" was the world I wanted. Did it convey enough tension? I wanted an image of wholeness, inclusion: Moving circles that come together, overlap, drift apart.' At the heart of Cary's questions over identity were dilemmas around the political implications of race. By the late 1960s, a new battle had erupted within the black community over questions of identity, naming, and self-definition. Cary expressed this new development fairly sharply: 'Black American (big B, small b), Afro-American, Afric-American, people of colour, Afro-Caribbean, Anglo-African, people of the diaspora, African-American.'[2]

The connections between Lorene Cary's world and the larger world are brought home by the changing faces of Europe, Africa, Asia, and the Americas. It now comes as no surprise to find a Pakistani in London, a Cape Verdean in Boston, a New Yorker in Johannesburg, a Chinese in Lima, or a Portuguese in Honolulu. This movement is a reflection of the dispersal of various communities, a dispersal that has contributed to the overlapping of racial, cultural, and national diasporas. Ironically, at the precise moment we notice this diversity, we are also confronted with several realities. In some cases, individuals consciously seek the company of those who differ in appearance, religion, ethnicity, or language. At other times, individuals feel openly threatened by the same diversity, they seek the familiar comfort of home, where those around them share a range of similarities. This process is complicated of course; in certain societies at particular times group congregation is the only real alternative to a lack of power. Throughout history, group congregation also became a way for others to secure their power. There is a delicate balance between the history of group empowerment and the history of racial and ethnic persecution. One need only look again at London or Boston or Johannesburg to see that racial and ethnic barriers persist and that racial and ethnic violence seems all too common.

Since the 1960s the academy has looked anew at the teaching of race and identity – often in step with the larger society. In response to the demands of student activists and activist faculty, curricula changed. Colleges and universities developed and codified new fields such as African American Studies, Women's and Ethnic Studies. Many historians shifted their focus from political and economic titans to average men and women who sought to be the architects of their own destinies. Few areas blossomed as much as African American history and the study of race. Yet as we approach the close of this millennium, educators throughout the world struggle to understand the meanings of race. Unable to hear Cary and countless others speak of the multiple meanings of race, too many continue their futile search for race's singular meaning.

The Multiple Meanings of Race

Historians have been teaching about race in one sense or another for the better part of this century. At the beginning of the century, notwithstanding the persistent efforts of black Americans and colonized peoples worldwide, a consensus emerged. Discussions of race became inextricably linked to hierarchical forms of dominance. Those with lighter skins were perceived as the guardians of social progress; with this guardianship came the presumption of racial superiority. Meanwhile, the world's darker-skinned peoples were identified with backwardness and inferiority. Historians of slavery, for example, played a major role in solidifying such notions. U. B. Phillips and other early students of slavery described a child-like, docile people who benefited from their enslavement.[3] These 'historical' narratives were not used solely for the classroom but became part of the means to justify the racial hierarchies of Jim Crow. Thus the teaching of history has long been connected to the construction of race and racial privilege in various societies.

Race is best viewed as a historically situated social construction endowed with multiple meanings. There are few better examples of this than the United States Supreme Court's ruling in the 1923 Thind case. Thind was an Asian immigrant who sought exemption from a new immigration stature barring Asians from US citizenship. He petitioned the court, arguing that as a Caucasian he should be granted citizenship. The court ruled that Thind was indeed Caucasian, but not white. Writing for the majority, Justice argued that 'Caucasian' was a scientific designation and 'white' was status perceived by the common man. In this instance Thind was racially Caucasian but socially other than white. Such decisions underscore the multiple meanings of race in American history.[4]

Race is a category that has been constructed to give 'biological' meaning to social hierarchy and cultural difference. Even though geneticists have demonstrated that genetic differences within racial groups are greater than those between racial groups, people continue to believe in a biological basis for race. Notwithstanding mounting scientific evidence, a new crop of writers persist in linking biology and a number of other human factors. Their work continues to garner a wide audience because it offers a reasonably simple explanation for complex social conditions.

Racial categories and classifications continue to shift based on the social, political, and economic needs of society; one need only look at the dramatic changes in racial classification in the US Census to see that race is not a fixed or impermeable fact. In 1890, for example, two national populations – Chinese and Japanese – appear on the Census as racial categories. In 1930, in the wake of more restrictive immigration legislation and the need to police our southern border, Mexican became a racial category. A decade later, with the abatement of the initial political imperative, this category disappears.[5] Current debates around the Census are as fraught with ambiguity. There is a growing movement to add a new category for mixed-race people, but this movement has encountered political opposition as stalwarts of the civil-rights community raise questions that such a decision will undermine the political gains of minorities.

While race may have been imagined, it is not imaginary. People give meanings to race continually through their actions, and people's lives are daily affected by those meanings. Even while acknowledging that race is a social construction, we continue to make judgements based on race. We often look at someone, decipher their race and believe that knowledge says something meaningful about them. Even when we are in doubt, we feel compelled to guess, to avoid ambiguity at all costs and place them in some socially accepted racial box.

Our need to categorize implicitly acknowledges the multiple ways race functions in our society. Institutions, culture, distribution and access to resources as well as personal identity pivot around race. Moreover, upon closer analysis race has the ability to alter meaning. In the structure of the American railroad industry, for example, Pullman porters rested at the bottom. As service workers they were viewed as inferior to the engineers, brakemen, and others – the majority of whom were white. Thus at work they had a subordinate status and a lower social position. A classical class analysis misses the subtle ways race altered meaning. At home the same men occupied a middle-class status, and such status gave them an important place in the inner workings of black communities. The point here is to emphasize the importance of examining the many ways race functioned in American society.

Race is not only a group designation but an individual one. Examining the racial consciousness of individuals requires us to consider the process of identity formation. Most individuals are multipositional, that is they are not merely racial beings but individuals defined by age, class, gender, religion, and other factors. To understand race requires that we also ask how people construct their identities across space and time. Race then must be viewed in relation to other aspects of the self; it must be viewed as interactive, By doing so, we see how race is constructed in relation to these other factors. For example, Lorene Cary's definition of blackness meant one thing while she was still a young teenager in a predominantly black section of Philadelphia. When she moved to St Paul's, where she was in a decided minority, race came to mean something much different. Moreover, the treatment she received as a racial minority at St Paul's was particular not only because she was black but because she was a black woman.

The Teaching of Race

Teaching race must be about much more than including the triumphs and accomplishments of non-white individuals but fundamentally concerned with showing the role race has played in the unequal distribution of social, political, and economic resources in the United States and throughout the world. It is the study of power, culture, and nationality, as much about how whites became white as how blacks became blacks. We must move beyond ideas about teaching race that can be solved by mere addition, ideas that too often essentialize identity and revolve around static notions about race. The challenge rests on seeing how people are directly related in determining racialized systems of power and privilege. For example, the theft and destruction of the lands of many native American tribes or the trans-Atlantic slave trade are not just scars that American history books must now attest to, but forces and processes that were made and are continually remade by real people.

Teaching race raises fundamental questions about the meanings of fairness and justice, about conceptions of society and the purpose of education. As educators, how do we deal with issues of responsibility throughout history? Do we as a society believe in forgiveness, in revenge, in reparations? Or do we settle by putting the past in the past? And if so, how would we actually do that? Can we imagine teaching the history of all people in the United States by giving the same lessons to whites and blacks? What about Asian-Americans or Latinos or native Americans? And what would those lessons be? If black students identify with the slaves, who identifies with the slaveholders (or should we be trying to avoid this dichotomy)?

Too often, attempts to bring race into the history curriculum have been half-hearted and insufficient. Historical events like slavery or Jim Crow or immigration quotas or the Indian Wars are often seen only as historical events instead of historical processes. In this way, America can still be pluralistic and harmonious. Everyone can decry racism and oppression together, because they happened long ago by people unlike any of us to people like many of us. We can condemn the past but still celebrate our diverse present and future. Diane Ravitch explains, 'the latest generation of textbooks bluntly acknowledges the racism of the past, describing the struggle for equality by racial minorities while identifying individuals who achieved success as political leaders, doctors, lawyers, scholars, entrepreneurs, teachers, and scientists . . .' Believing that sufficient curricula changes may have been achieved, she notes,

> [Children] learn that America has provided a haven for many different groups and has allowed them to maintain their cultural heritage or to assimilate, or as is often the case to do both; the choice is theirs, not the state's. . . . Indeed, the unique feature of the United States is that its common culture has been formed by the interaction of its subsidiary cultures.[6]

Thus multiculturalism becomes a curious combination of individual histories and history for the good of the nation, erasing any tension and conflict in We-Are-the-World togetherness.

Racism, then, is located squarely in the past, an evil that existed long ago; the present is about celebrating the diversity of the human spirit and the triumph of individual achievement. Even those who have pushed to diversify the curriculum tend towards celebration. As Henry Louis Gates writes,

> We need to reform our entire notion of core curricula to account for the comparable eloquence of the African, the Asian, the Latin American, and the Middle Eastern traditions, to prepare our students for their roles in the twenty-first century as citizens of a world culture, educated through a truly human notion of the humanities.[7]

Multiculturalism must move beyond being an additive to history to recasting the whole concept of history. The history of America is not necessarily a history of progress, but a history of contestation and consensus, of accommodation and resistance, continually determined by a variety of peoples. Seeing it this way does not mandate the ritual blaming of white people or men or straight people (or straight, white men) for the evils of America. It means understanding power and greed and xenophobia (and pride and family and individualism) as human forces that allow some to see only progress while others see oppression. It means reconciling that history will not always be pluralistic and harmonious – if that should have been its purpose in the first place.

Some Afrocentric scholars also run into the same problem: in trying to alter the curriculum, they too fall back on ideas of progress and individual success. In showing the triumphs of Africans and African Americans, they sometimes gloss over the hard parts. Molefi Asante writes, 'European domination of Western culture over many years has resulted in the dislocation of Africans both physically and psychologically. . . . Sanity will come only from a conscious relocation of ourselves from the margins of someone else's experience.'[8] But does sanity come in discussions of the Middle Passage, of lynching, of share-cropping, of the Tuskegee Syphilis Experiment? How should one, relocating experience from the margins, come to terms with the more painful parts of the black experience?

One of the hardest parts of teaching race is that it makes students angry, depressed, demoralized, even scared. Teaching race brings one face to face with a system that is neither just nor fair, uncovering a multitude of injustices that we as educators have little response to and often want to stay away from. In the fall of 1994, in an introductory African American Studies course, several students voiced clear anger at the depiction of African Americans in the documentary *Ethnic Notions*. Some black students felt moved to at least temporarily avoid contact with whites; some white students were enraged that such images were in circulation.

The solution to addressing anger does not lie in the remedies offered by scholars and social critics like William Bennett and E. D. Hirsch who worry that the inclusion of multiple perspectives weakens the core. Oftentimes, their argument centres on the issues of standards and excellence without recognizing the time-mediated meanings of excellence. Recall that at the turn of this century many leading universities in the United States debated the need to add courses on American history. At Harvard, Princeton and other schools a classical education assumed that one only needed to learn Latin, some Greek, and basic philosophy.[9] Today we would consider such positions preposterous. Our understanding of what an educated person should know is not as narrowly circumscribed. Yet, in historical context the link between earlier and contemporary debates reminds us of the tenuous nature of curriculum development, and the changing definitions of excellence.

Still, cultural conservatives are right to argue that changing the curriculum is unsettling; even if proponents of curriculum change are disingenuous when they portray it as a feel-good celebration of our nation's diversity. History is dangerous, radicalizing, transformative because it cannot remained trapped in the past. It is transformative precisely because it allows people to make sense not only of where they come from but also of the forces and situations that exist today.

One of the real challenges becomes: where do we leave students? What can we give them in the way of hope, of vision, of political action? Being a teacher means having students look to us for vision, for inspiration, at the very least for judicious opinions. We need to learn not to shy away from this role. This is especially true if the topic is race or ethnicity. Most students write themselves into the subject-matter, they live life in racial and ethnic terms. As a result, the courses are both deeply intellectual and profoundly autobiographical. Negotiating the intellectual and the autobiographical is never easy, however. Recently, a biracial student, who had explored the social construction of race, was still left unglued by a classmate who insisted that she was not black. He later confessed that she did not 'look black'. When she called to ask what she should have done, an appropriate answer was not clear, since the comment said more about her accuser than it did about her own sense of identity and affiliation. One of the challenges we all face is recognizing that we do not have to have all the answers. What is more important is creating a space within our classrooms for students to be angry or demoralized and to begin to work through this in order to find ways to imagine change.

To see history as process, fundamentally, necessitates beginning a discussion of how people create systems that harm people. Racism, sexism and homophobia are continually created by human beings and are not discrete, impersonal forces of their own. People actively benefit from systems that harm others. To see history as process also shifts liberation and social movements away from focusing on a few leaders to understanding the vision and action of numerous individuals who produce such movements. Teaching race is not equivalent (and must be much broader) to teaching racism. People are active agents in the detailing of their own lives. They continually create cultures, traditions, and social movements that are responses to oppression but also live beyond the stare of such racism, building independent and vital community institutions. To interpret everything through the lens of racism is as problematic in the study of race as not seeing racism and power in the first place.

To see history truly as process places the individual squarely in the middle, giving her/him the power of history making.

To do this means seeing the role historians play in creating history as well. History has not been politicized by recent movements of people of colour; history was always political. Often its ideologies were masked because historians claimed objectivity while this objectivity coincidentally and conveniently supported the status quo. Events do not come pre-packaged in linear narratives; historians place value on certain individuals, certain events, and certain explanations for those events. To teach an early American history class and not teach slavery, to mention only black people when teaching slavery or the civil-rights movement, or to reserve a week for people of colour bears little relation to the historical record, yet this is largely the model in American history survey courses. Teaching race must expose those choices, showing not only that choices are made but also that those choices are directly related to power and politics, not some objective standard.

As Howard Zinn explains,

> Objectivity is neither possible nor desirable. It's not possible because all history is subjective, all history represents a point of view. History is always a selection from an infinite number of facts and everybody makes the selection differently, based on their values and what they think is important. Since it's not possible to be objective, you should be honest about that. Objectivity is not desirable because if we want to have an effect on the world, we need to emphasize those things which will make students more active citizens and more moral people.[10]

And this is the crux of the issue: how do we emphasize 'those things' without overly romanticizing how open and democratic this society is? How do we take seriously cultural traditions and local political struggles amidst a system that often belittles them? As educators, how do we teach our students about hegemony, about systems of oppression, and still leave room to teach about agency and social change? Perhaps where we have gone wrong is in distinguishing so heavily between hegemony and agency, that there are individuals acting and resisting and systems and institutions oppressing them. Hegemony or oppression is not produced by impersonal forces, it is produced by individuals. It does not have a life of its own apart from the life that people give it explicitly or tacitly by accepting its workings and assumptions. Zinn continues,

> Teachers should dwell on Shay's Rebellion, on colonial rebellions, on the abolitionist movement, on the populist movement, on the labor move-

ment, and so on, and make sure these social movements don't get lost in the overall story of presidents and Congresses and Supreme Courts. Emphasizing social and protest movements in the making of history gives students a feeling that they as citizens are the most important actors in history.[11]

Again, though, it is easy to fall into the same old histories of America – that the founding of America created in this country a system open and flexible to change, critique, and inclusion of all people and all points of view. If we are to teach social movements, will we also teach about the immense forces of government and business that have usually quashed or co-opted them? How do we best equip students for these realities without resorting to a cynicism and defeatism all too common in the academy?

Teaching race must also move students to see issues in an international context, to push students out of the isolation and parochialism that affects much of American education and see the connections and comparisons between different communities. Race may be nationally specific but it is globally situated. Race in many instances is inseparable from a discussion of ethnicity. In fact, ethnic differences are often framed in racialist language. In Rwanda, despite years of intermixture, the Tutsi were described by western media and Rwandan informants as physically different from the Hutu. Significantly, the populations did have discernible physical characteristics. More than that, each group had its own history of wrongs, slights, and injustices. The rehearsal of these memories worked symbiotically with these physical differences, together enabling each group to position the other as different, the 'Other'.

In such instances, ethnic difference served as a proxy for racial difference, although this construction implodes western conceptions of race. Perceived ethnic differences have torn apart countries from Rwanda to Bosnia to Iraq. While the participants in these conflicts have the same skin colour, these wars arise from a sense of irreconcilable and innate difference. In order to find out what is particular to any individual country, other national contexts must be examined. Often such comparison brings into sharp relief the ways race is manifested nationally. The creation of modern nations has everything to do with current understandings of race and nationality. Racial hierarchies operate on a global level as much as they operate on a national level.

One of the largest difficulties in teaching comparatively and bringing in international counterpoints, however, is being well-versed in both sides of the comparison. Who among us feels equally comfortable with contemporary Latin American, US and African history (let alone colonial and pre-colonial history of these places)? We need not expect ourselves to have mastered all subjects but must rely on colleagues to bring in perspectives we are not as knowledgeable about. Team-teaching is perhaps the most effective way to integrate substantive comparative work. Such collaborative work is not always valued (and not always made possible) in universities; asking for assistance is often viewed as a sign of laziness or lack of rigour or breadth. Yet the danger in not asking is that we simply will not do it or our attempts will be superficial and insufficient. We need to be careful not to repeat the mistakes of adding a book or two and feeling that we have integrated an effective comparison. If we do not admit what we can and cannot do, we send a dangerous message about the seriousness of the study of race and of comparison (that we presume this is all that is necessary).

Teaching race is important, not only because people of colour must be included in the history books but also because teaching history must be about teaching students to look analytically and critically at history. In the focus around identity politics, the more general academic merits of multiculturalism have largely been ignored, leading to the erroneous belief that teaching about race is somehow separate from the steps needed to improve American education. But if we are going to talk about how changing demographics require a change in curriculum, we must also talk about how history must be truthful and relevant. By delving into questions of race, opportunity, equality and resistance, we have produced a class that is far more useful and intellectually sound for all students than it is 'demographically relevant'. If we are going to talk about the need for basics and foundations, we also need to talk about how we motivate students to read, think critically, and analyse effectively. Students become engaged in learning and see the power of their own intellects by allowing them to use them, not by treating them like passive receptacles in need of information deposit. If we are going to talk about how teaching black history gives black students a sense of self-esteem and pride in their culture, we must also talk about how self-esteem rests on students' confidence in themselves. Self-esteem rises not merely by adding information into the curriculum as much as by the curriculum (and the teacher) reflecting that students are important and must be taken seriously. And a multicultural curriculum that engages students in the process of discovering, analysing and critiquing history can do that for all students.

One of the most controversial issues around the teaching of race has focused on who has the right to teach it and what should be said. Can white people teach black history? Must people of colour teach about race? Who should decide? These debates have pushed to the fore issues of authority, authenticity, and expertise. Such controversy is both dangerous and extremely useful. It can reify particular kinds of authenticity, that certain people of colour with certain attributes and ideas should teach about race but not others. This not only limits the intellectual work of people of colour but is based on a narrow (and ultimately self-defeating) idea about what teaching race is all about. African American history, for example, has not and should not become solely the concern of black historians. More important, the study of race should not be reduced just to the study of people of colour. It is as important to talk about white racial identity in a comparative manner as it is to discuss the racial identities of blacks, browns, reds, and yellows. A more expansive discussion also shifts the burden off students of colour, who often are singled out as racial experts whenever classroom discussion shifts to questions of race. Also, by seriously investigating the multiple meanings of race, teachers are freed to teach across the colour line.

Yet, at base, controversies over who can teach what have been extremely useful for they have problematized the relationship between knowledge, power, politics and social position. To encourage students to question their sources of information, to push them to look at what is being said, the context in which it is said, and why it is being said that way, is perhaps the most important lesson we can impart. Sources of information must be scrutinized. Students often come wanting the truth, believing in right answers and the veracity of all things written down. To get them to question their assumptions is necessary if they are to secure their place in a society of critical thinkers. Unfortunately, the degree to which critical thinkers are desired by many is an open question. On this point novelist and essayist James Baldwin writes,

> The purpose of education, finally, is to create in a person the ability to look at the world for himself, to make his own decisions, to say to himself this is black or this is white, to decide for himself whether there is a God in heaven or not. To ask questions of the universe, and then learn to live with those questions, is the way he achieves his own identity. But no society is really anxious to have that kind of person around.[12]

It is humbling, however, to recognize the conflict between one's pedagogical philosophy and the ego gratification that comes from standing in front of a classroom of undergraduates. Even when we say otherwise, we want our students to believe everything we say and to accept our position on all matters. To be questioned or called out publicly is threatening to our own authority and position in the classroom, yet, in the long run, is extremely important in valuing students as independent thinkers. The most important task, however, is not just to get students to question in classes about race but to bring that critical analysis to other classes and other subjects. Often what happens is that scholars of race are seen as political or limited in scope while more-traditional historians retain their broad perspective untainted by politics or bias. This further contributes to the marginalization of ethnic studies programmes and classes at the university level. Seen as political concessions to political correctness, not intellectual strongholds, the history of racial minorities is often not given the intellectual legitimacy of other disciplines.

Teaching race proposes a fundamental rethinking about education and threatens the many hierarchies and traditional suppositions about the university. As theorists like Paulo Freire and Henry Giroux have argued, the educational system has traditionally been structured such that knowledge is given from professors to students. This is problematic because knowledge

> no longer is seen as something to be questioned, analyzed and negotiated. Instead it becomes something to be managed and mastered. In this case, knowledge is removed from the self-formative process of generating one's own set of meanings, a process that involves an interpretive relationship between knower and known.[13]

Teaching race seeks to reform this process of study by fundamentally altering the relationship between the transmission and reception of knowledge.

Classroom Exercises

There are certain strategies and exercises that do this. Of course there are many ways to study race and create a classroom where everyone shares in the process of learning. These are but a few suggestions that have worked well for us. Active participation projects – projects that have students work together to prepare a presentation for the entire class – succeed in getting students to be responsible to the class and to their own educations. Students then become part of creating the course material for the class and of choosing what is important to be taught. It also gets them to see the process of learning as collaborative, to see education as a community project rather than an individual one. Map exercises (particularly handing out a blank map of Africa) are also useful in getting students to see what they do and do not know. Unfortunately, since most students are unable to put more than a few countries on the map, this leads them to question why they do not know basic geography, and to get them to think about why some knowledges are valued more than others (maps of Africa are readily available yet few Americans could locate the countries of Africa). Handing out a map and not providing the right answers later pushes students to take control of their own learning, to see that they need to take responsibility for educating themselves about what they believe is important and not assume that it will be provided.

Autobiographical exercises have proved very useful devices as well. Typically we have had students write autobiographies around themes of identity, race, gender, etc. and then share those autobiographies with the class. Such efforts force students to think through the meanings of self. They are required to explain, if not reveal, what they decided to include or exclude and the decisions for telling one version of their life's story. A spin on this has involved pairs of students writing the biography of a classmate. Here students interview their partner and attempt to place that person's history in a larger context. Both exercises opened the terrain for us to talk about the interrelationship between history, memory, and race.

A final set of exercises involves introducing a range of interdisciplinary texts that discuss the multiple meanings of race in a world of overlapping diasporas. These texts include fiction, films, newspapers, first-person accounts, structural data such as census materials, art, music, and the students' own memories. Using varied materials allows students to see parts of history that are often obscured in more traditional texts and to place themselves in the writing of history. The goal here is to encourage students to take an active role in interrogating race. It was especially powerful when students thought of race as one of the many parts of an individual's identity, and as a concept that varied as one moved from one national community to another.

In sum, this chapter has discussed the importance of thinking of race as a social construction and a material reality. Since race is one of the things that we all believe we know about the other, the suggested dialectic forces us to re-examine the familiar with a heightened sensitivity. As important, we have underscored the need to teach race when we teach history. It must be understood, however, that race is not a natural condition. It is historically situated, relational, and multidimensional – central to a world of overlapping diasporas.

Notes

1 L. Cary, *Black Ice* (Alfred A. Knopf, New York, 1991), p. 233.
2 Ibid.
3 See, for example, U. B. Phillips, *American Negro Slavery* (D. Appleton and Company, New York, 1918).
4 For a description of the case and the historical conditions that contributed to it, see R. T. Takaki, *Strangers from a Different Shore: A History of Asian Americans* (Little, Brown & Co., Boston, 1989).
5 US Bureau of Commerce Department of Census, *200 Years of US Census Taking: Population and Housing Questions, 1790–1900* (US Government Printing Office, Washington DC, 1989).
6 D. Ravitch, 'Multiculturalism E pluribes Pluribes,' *American Scholar* (1990), p. 339.
7 H. L. Gates, Jr., *Loose Canons* (Oxford University Press, New York, 1992), p. 113.
8 M. Asante, 'Afrocentrism in a Multicultural Democracy,' *American Visions*, 6 (1991), p. 21.
9 L. Levine, 'Clio, Canon, and Culture,' *Journal of American History*, 80 (1993), pp. 849–67.
10 H. Zinn, 'Why Students Should Study History,' *Rethinking Schools*, 7 (1992–3), p. 8.
11 Ibid., p. 6.
12 J. Baldwin, 'A Talk to Teachers', in *The Graywolf Annual Five: Multicultural Literacy*, ed. R. Simonson and S. Walker (Graywolf, St Paul, 1988), p. 4.
13 H. Giroux, 'Toward a New Sociology of Curriculum', *Educational Leadership* (1979), p. 250.

Further Reading

In 'A Talk to Teachers', in *The Graywolf Annual Five: Multicultural Literacy*, ed. R. Simonson and S. Walker (Graywolf, St Paul, 1988), the novelist and essayist James Baldwin lays out the challenges of teaching black students in a racist world. The collection of essays, *'Race', Writing and Difference*, ed. H. L. Gates (Routledge, New York, 1993), provides a good foundation into contemporary thinking about race and the need to bring race into the curriculum. Henry Giroux has been one of the foremost voices in connecting power, race, and the production and dissemination of knowledge. His *Border Crossings:*

Cultural Workers and the Politics of Education (Routledge, New York, 1992), offers thoughtful reflection on the roles and responsibilities of educators. G. Graff sorts through the debates around multiculturalism in *Beyond the Culture Wars: How Teaching the Conflicts can Revitalize American Education* (W. W. Norton, New York, 1992). Seeing fear of conflict as the main reason behind opposition to multiculturalism, he believes that teaching conflict is also the key to vibrant education.

Rethinking Schools: An Agenda for Change, ed. D. Levine et al. (The New Press, New York, 1995) offers some of the most incisive thinking on education today. Although predominantly about elementary and secondary education, the issues raised are also applicable to higher education. James Loewen's *Lies My Teacher Told Me: Everything Your American History Textbook Got Wrong* (The New Press, New York, 1995) is an extremely useful book for teachers of American history. Loewen has studied the canon of American history textbooks and effectively outlines the omissions and biases inherent in them. Finally, C. McCarthy and W. Crichlow's *Race, Identity and Representation in Education* (Routledge, New York, 1993), provides a broad-ranging collection of essays from a diverse group of scholars who interrogate race, class and gender and their applications within education.

4

Gender in the Curriculum

Cathy Lubelska

At the most fundamental level, histories which do not consider the experience and significance of gender distort and misrepresent the past. The growing volume of work in this area, especially in recent years, has generated a vast resource, making visible and audible much which had previously been omitted or remained silent in historical accounts, and demonstrating the importance of 'gendered history' to an understanding of the historical process. The historical study of gender also raises fundamental issues about the nature and purposes of history as a discipline. Of central concern in much recent work has been a focus upon gender – and upon the category of 'woman' – as a social construction, and upon history itself as a social product, reflective of and influenced by the material circumstances and discourses in which it is located.

The challenge which much of this work presents to mainstream history provides an opportunity to enrich and possibly to transform our approaches to teaching and research in all historical studies. The assumptions about women and gender which underlie many of the distortions and omissions of gender-blind history reflect the characteristic practices and concerns of the discipline of history regarding matters such as objectivity, structure and agency, and historical significance. In questioning these assumptions a focus upon gender encourages historians both to re-evaluate their sources and methods and to re-define the parameters and nature of historical knowledge.[1] For the student of history the lively debate about what needs to be done, and how, gives access to

a variety of perspectives regarding the nature of the discipline and the
methodologies which it should employ.

   This chapter argues that histories of gender should permeate the
curriculum, informing all analyses. Some recent work on masculinities,
for example, affirms the role of gender in shaping men's as well as
women's histories and, therefore, in renewing the history of both sexes
and, by implication, of all history.[2] The current context of debate about
the relative merits and demerits of gender and/or women as the principal
focus of study provides a topical glimpse, in microcosm, of the larger
political and social climate against which most history is now taught in
higher education, at least in Britain and the USA. In Britain the recent
debates on the nature of history taught under the new National Curriculum in schools have centred upon precisely those areas with which
historians of women, in particular, have been preoccupied. Issues raised
about the kinds and balance of skills and knowledge which should be
taught, the wider educational and political objectives of history teaching
and whose history should be given precedence have been foregrounded
by historians concerned with gender.[3] Concern about the kind of British
history which schoolchildren should learn has centred upon the unequal
representation of the experiences and perspectives of different races and
ethnicities in British society, and accusations of Anglocentric bias, especially in approaches to imperialism.[4] The growth in black women's
history has sharpened the critical focus of gender history upon the
varieties of women's historical experience and the inequalities between
women, in terms of both their different historical experiences and oppressions and their representation within history writing and teaching.[5]
Since the development of social history from the 1960s and 1970s a
concern with oppression and inequality has characterized the work of
many historians, not just those concerned with gender issues. Yet gender
has continued to be overlooked or misrepresented in much of this work,
as in most historical research and teaching.

   The social and political concerns which have shaped debates about the
British National Curriculum and the development of equal opportunities
and affirmative action strategies in Britain and the USA raise issues
about the nature and purpose of history in contemporary society. In
addressing, for example, issues of representation the development of a
gendered curriculum demands that we do more than acknowledge and
rectify the silences and distortions of earlier historians. The fact that,
certainly in Britain now, most history students are women focuses
specific concern upon the methods which we employ in our approaches

to gendered history. Increasing numbers of female students enter higher education from non-traditional educational backgrounds, many bringing with them, and having gained credit for, experiential learning. Students of both sexes may come to history in higher education as the result of stimulating and innovative Access and adult-education courses or with long-standing interests in local and community history. For many mature students, in particular, the relevance and accessibility of the history curriculum depends on the extent to which it acknowledges the resources and knowledge which they have gained from their experiences as women and as men, and seeks to utilize these in the content and delivery of the syllabus.[6] For many, gender is recognized as a crucial category of historical analysis because they have direct experience of its effects. Often, the process of doing history, of transferring and validating their skills and experience through active engagement with historical research, is as important as the content of the syllabus.

The rapid growth of interdisciplinary and vocational courses, many of which cater for predominantly female students, has utilized and contributed to gender history in a number of ways. In addition, gendered perspectives within traditional disciplines have enriched historical analyses. Some of the most challenging and innovative methodological work in gendered history has arisen out of syntheses and adaptations drawing on sociology, anthropology, critical studies, linguistics, and psychoanalysis, to name a few.[7] The topical controversies surrounding post-structuralist approaches within history and the development of ethnographic methodologies within historical research provide two examples of ways in which history can be informed and regenerated by interdisciplinary perspectives. Here, as in other areas, those concerned to gender historical study have been at the forefront of the engagements and innovations. These developments, together with the influence of woman-centred methodologies, feminist theory and the conceptualization of gender as a category of historical analysis, have considerably enlarged the range and nature of historical research and teaching.

Whilst some institutions continue largely to overlook gender issues in the curriculum, probably more common is the tokenistic inclusion of a lecture on women, still often inextricably bound to the family and children as a topic. Many tutors leave it at that, and, satisfied that they have 'done' women, proceed to ignore them and gender issues for the remainder of the course. The effect of such practices is to prevent or stultify the extent to which gender issues are integrated positively into the curriculum. Even where they are present, they too-often remain isolated and disconnected from the main body of historical analysis. Part of the problem here is undoubtedly the tendency to view gender history as the preserve of a minority of enthusiasts, whose work in 'guest spots' on other people's courses and development of separate women's history modules spares other tutors from any engagement with the issues. At the extremes there are lecturers who work to silence and exclude gender issues. Although the situation varies across institutions, gendered history very often remains separate and optional, existing in parallel to 'mainstream' courses. In some institutions such concerns are seen as more appropriately located solely within women's studies or gender studies programmes, which can even lead to the exclusion of women's history from the curriculum, as if it were another subject entirely.

Gender and Women's Histories

In considering both the advantages of a gendered history curriculum and the varieties of current practice, an overview of the historiography of gender history can be illuminating. A glance at what is on offer in different institutions reveals a number of approaches to teaching, informed by a range and mixture of trends within the recent and more distant historiography of gendered history.[8] The influence and relationships (syntheses) of women's history, feminist theory and gendered historical analysis, and the distinctions between these, have been particularly influential in shaping the subject matter and methodologies encountered within a gendered history curriculum. The creative tensions which have characterized the coexistence of gender and women's history within the curriculum and research have generated a diversity of approaches. These reflect not only different emphases in research and teaching but a larger debate about the nature, purpose and politics of history.

Many of those who are committed to woman-centred history remain ambivalent, hostile even, to recent developments in gendered history, which some see as threatening to supplant or suppress women's history.[9] The propensity of many historians of gender to draw heavily on post-structuralist theory has also be seen as problematic. For some, this is indicative of reactionary tendencies. In its focus upon gender through the textual analysis of discourses, which are predominantly elitist and non-woman-centred, post-structuralism may be judged to signal a return to concern with what others say about women, muting the experiential evidence derived from women-centred analysis.[10] It is also argued that post-structuralist textual focus does not amount to doing history, because it fails to take account of material, lived realities. These trends may be seen to undermine and neutralize the feminist exposition of oppression, with its challenge to the politics and practices of history.[11] Critically, it is claimed that approaches centred on women's own histories, as seen through their eyes, demonstrate the ways in which the historical experiences and roles of women and men have been different. Here, women's history is not just another version of men's history, but a distinct subject of enquiry which should not, therefore, be subsumed within gender studies.[12]

The proponents of gender history counter these viewpoints in various ways. For some, gender history is the logical corollary of women's history. If their gender differentiates the historical experiences and roles of women, then men must likewise be affected. Masculinity and femininity are seen as two sides of the same coin, one of which cannot be understood without the other.[13] In moving the primary emphasis from women to the effects of gender upon both women and men, historians of gender argue that their approach stands to be more influential in historical research and teaching than separate and/or woman-centred studies, through its relevance to and permeation of the concerns of the wider history curriculum.[14]

The view that gender history is inclined to be apolitical and disconnected from the feminist concerns apparent in much woman-centred history, is robustly contested, notably by Joan Scott, who argues that in concentrating upon dominant social and political discourses, a post-structuralist perspective on gender continues to address and refresh the feminist concern with power and oppression. In turn, advocates of post-structuralism raise doubts about the validity of both woman-centred and separate women's histories. Criticism has centred on the utility of 'woman' as a category of historical analysis, as it is subject to different and changing meanings within the larger context of the construction and reconstruction of gender. Denise Riley, for example, suggests that woman is not a fixed category amenable to historical analysis but comprises various fluctuating identities conditioned by discourses of gender.[15] Within this framework in order to understand women's history it is upon gender rather than upon women, *per se*, that we should focus. The post-structuralist critique of woman-centred history also raises doubts about the authenticity of experience. The 'deconstruction' of the category of woman and the stress upon changing discourses of gender have led to a sharpened focus both upon the diversities of experience and the extent to which these, rather than being a 'pure', unmitigated source revealing the realities of women's lives, are themselves socially constructed and subject to the wider processes of gendering. In the light of these considerations, it is argued, experience should be studied and appraised as discourse.[16]

Women's History

A loosely chronological view demonstrates both the long and varied genealogy of women's history and its central role in gendering the curriculum. The more recent development of gender history, although in tension with much women's history, is nevertheless heavily influenced and shaped by histories with a distinctively woman-centred focus. These approaches continue to coexist, develop and interact in the research and teaching of gender history.

Although women's history made its presence felt as an integral part of the women's movement from the late 1960s onwards, there was already considerable groundwork on which to build. Earlier, the works of Schreiner, Clark, Pinchbeck and others had focused, in particular, upon the changing roles of women in the processes of industrialization and modernization.[17] Other studies upon which to draw included, for example, a number of suffrage histories, some startling works of retrieval such as Power's medieval and George's eighteenth-century studies, Bland's controversial history of American women and various historical biographies.[18] These works, and others, demonstrated both the existence and importance of women's history and a range of theoretical and methododological approaches directed towards the reclamation and conceptualization of women in history. Much of this early work was influenced by the development of what is often crudely labelled 'first-wave' feminism in Britain and the USA. The political role of women's history, as essential to understanding and rectifying the oppressions of women, provides a clear link of aim between many of these earlier studies and the feminist women's history which has developed since the 1970s.[19] However, the antecedents go back still further: from Christine de Pisan in the late fourteenth and early fifteenth centuries to Mary Wollstonecraft in the eighteenth century, women's history has been explored as part of wider social and political debates about the roles and rights of women.[20]

Although the scope and variety of feminist histories belie generaliz-
ation, feminists share a concern with women's oppression and disadvantage in the past. A central aim of much analysis is to reveal and
understand the experiences, roles, significance, actions and representations of women as part of a wider political project to improve the condition of all women. Of critical importance in most Anglo/American
feminist analysis is the distinction between sex, seen as largely predetermined, and gender, considered as a changing social construct which
plays a pivotal role in the ordering of relationships in all areas of life:
economic, social, cultural and political. Although strongly connected to
the women's movement, feminist analysis has drawn upon and reacted
to a number of influences. It has developed in creative tension with
other histories, to evolve a constructive critique of the omissions and
misrepresentations of gender in historical research.

Gendered Critiques

The aim of establishing the significance and experience of women's lives
to the understanding and shaping of the past remains a central objective
for all concerned with gender history. Whilst it attempts to put women
'on the map', and is relatively visible within the curriculum, much of
this work, certainly before the 1970s, has taken the form of what Gerda
Lerner has termed 'contribution history'.[21] For those who wish to see
gendered and feminist perspectives permeating and informing all historical analysis the value of this approach is ambiguous as it tends to
emphasize the study of women's role in what have been pre-defined as
important events and movements in history, principally within the public domain. Here, women's historical significance is largely measured by
standards appropriate to men. Certainly, in the context of some of the
early suffrage histories such as those of Strachey and Pankhurst, and in
various biographical accounts of the lives of women worthies, the 'heroic'
tales that unfold – of women in public and political life and their contribution to men's histories – underlie women's claims to equality with men
on men's terms.[22] Women are thus accorded historical value by criteria
made by, and appropriate to, men. Received notions of what is or is not
historically significant remain relatively undisturbed. At worst, conclusions drawn from this sort of history can be prejudicial to further engagement with gender, reinforcing rather than questioning assumptions
about women's significance. Heroines are seen to be exceptional, operat-

ing in spheres which women, by definition, did not usually enter, and
exhibiting qualities and behaviour associated with the male and not
the female role. Their presence is seen to count precisely because it
is different to and separate from the histories of the vast majority of
women. As Jane Lewis has pointed out, such accounts implicitly define
women as marginal.[23]

Such work raises legitimate doubts among feminist historians about
the merit of the uncritical pursuit of women's history, where the principal aim is simply to add women onto existing historical narratives rather
than to challenge and change these. As Deborah Thom has commented:
'Without an assumption of value, of political purpose, there seems little
point in simply knowing more and more about women.'[24]

The growth of social history in the 1960s and 1970s, with its primary
emphasis on working-class history, was, like women's history, also concerned with reclamation. As in the feminist history which soon followed,
the study of the underprivileged, powerless, inarticulate and oppressed
was foregrounded; those who, like women, had been largely excluded
from traditional accounts.[25] There was a concern, too, to move away from
stereotyping these groups as 'victims' to look at resistance and agency
and at the conflicts and compromises between oppressor and oppressed.[26] These approaches, together with the influence of Marxist and
socialist theories, challenged prevailing orthodoxies about the nature and
purposes of history.[27] Importantly though, the work on gender within
social history has led to substantive and constructive critiques of what
can be termed the 'gender-blind' nature of much work. The subject
of investigation, the working class, still too-often remains male.[28]
Women's experiences and significance remain largely invisible and
undifferentiated as assumptions about the insignificance of women's
historical role persist. Yet these criticisms are not confined to social
history but apply to common practices across the discipline and the
curriculum. The failure adequately to represent women's role or the
workings of gender is rooted in persistent assumptions about the insignificance of women's and hence of gendered histories. Two assumptions,
in particular, can be noted here. First, the idea that women's significance
and agency in the making of history has been negligible. Second, the
view that women have, in a sense, no history. The common tendency to
locate the study of women exclusively (and separately) in the context of
the family reinforces these notions. Thus marginalized from the concerns of men's history, women's history is apt to be seen as primarily

biologically determined by their maternal and familial roles, and hence relatively unchanging through time.[29]

Feminist Approaches to Gendering History

A key achievement of feminist women's history has been to expose, both empirically and theoretically, the fallacy of assumptions about the unimportance of women, and therefore of gender, to an understanding of the historical process. In so doing, some of the sacred cows of the discipline have been challenged, regarding, for example, the possibility and desirability of objectivity, the authenticity of experience, and notions of historical significance.

Feminists have built upon the work of Clark, Pinchbeck and others on women and modernization. In exploring the concept of the sexual division of labour their studies centre upon the interplay of gender and class, and locate women's history within both the family and the workplace. The inter-relatedness of the spheres of production and reproduction in establishing women's contribution to the processes of modernization as a whole are emphasized.[30] Other studies, particularly in the USA, have centred upon the experience and contribution of women within what were often seen, historically, as their separate spheres: the family and motherhood, women's communities and organizations, sexuality.[31] Here the influence of radical feminism has been marked, with its emphasis on patriarchy, the oppression and control of women's bodies and sexualities, sexual politics and the empowering role of networks and relationships between women. The developing theoretical conceptualization of patriarchy, including, for example, the evolution of dual systems theories which attempt to address the interplay of patriarchy and class in women's history, and the application of psychoanalytic methodologies to the study of its subconscious and psychological underpinnings, illustrates the ways in which different historical and intellectual traditions in feminism continue to be combined in the production of more sophisticated and inclusive historical analyses of women.[32]

The differences and diversities of women's historical experiences have been emphasized by woman-centred approaches. Developments in black feminist perspectives and in the study of sexuality have led to a greater appreciation of the ways in which many variables (class, race, ethnicity, sexuality, etc.) interact in the gendering of the histories both of men and

women in the past.[33] The work of black feminists, in particular, has
sharpened awareness of the inequalities between women and the ways in
which these can be perpetuated by dominant 'white' or Eurocentric
perspectives, both in gender and mainstream approaches, which continue to omit or distort the histories of other races and cultures.[34] Recent
developments in post-structuralism have also had a significant impact
upon gendered and feminist analysis. In its challenge to the notion of a
fixed historical subject and to a social scientific approach, the post-
structuralist focus upon language as discourse, and upon gender rather
than woman, has generated controversies in feminist historical analysis,
particularly regarding the extent to which gender history enhances or
threatens the feminist focus on oppression.[35]

Woman-centred History

Although there were, and continue to be, significant differences in the
concerns of woman-centred analysis it is possible to identify common
themes which have been influential in the development of both women's
and gender history, as well as for different theoretical perspectives within
history.[36]

First, in studying women's roles and experiences and the connections
between these, particularly in the spheres of production and reproduction, the centrality of women's contribution to the historical process is
asserted and demonstrated. The experiential focus also serves to make
visible the role of women's agency in shaping their own and others'
histories. What had been seen as women's history thus shifts from the
wings to centre-stage. Second, the insistence that women should form a
separate category of historical analysis. Third, a focus on woman rather
than on 'women' as a singular, undifferentiated historical entity. The
diversities of women's lives in terms of class, race, ethnicity, sexuality,
age, etc., are a principal focus. In refuting this monolithic stereotype,
woman-centred approaches seek to demonstrate the ways in which
gender, as both a dependent and independent variable, is an essential
constituent of all historical analysis.[37]

Those adopting a woman-centred perspective argue that women's
experiences are inadequately represented by historians and their sources.
Experiential sources are often all that are available; particularly as
woman-centred approaches encourage the asking of new questions
where such evidence provides the richest resource; for example, regard-

ing the material conditions of women's lives. In their principal focus upon the realities of women's lives and upon history 'from women's point of view', woman-centred approaches produce accounts which expose, differ from and challenge the assumptions of those who write 'about' women.[38]

Methodologically, woman-centred approaches focus upon accessing and utilizing sources about women's lives and experiences, which are absent and different from those employed in much traditional history. In their focus upon such sources as oral history, autobiography, personal narrative, diaries, letters and various kinds of collective and community history projects, historians have drawn upon and adapted a variety of disciplinary, theoretical and ethical approaches. Research into women's oral histories, for example, has led to the development of methodologies which reflect the influence of anthropology, ethnography, sociology, and various cultural studies in the exploration and problematization of issues such as the authenticity of experience, the subjectivity/objectivity of researcher and researched, and the relationship between power and representation in determining the nature of the discipline and its curriculum.[39]

Approaches

Critical concern with the validity and authenticity of experience and the evidence which is gleaned from it, raises questions not only about the relative objectivity/subjectivity of traditional versus experiential sources and methods, but also regarding the extent to which it is possible to develop an alternative and new body of historical knowledge rooted in women's experiences. There are clear epistemological challenges inherent in this approach, which take a variety of forms in research and teaching.[40] For some, women's history must remain a separate and alternative history as its subject matter, methodology and theory not only distinguish it from conventional history but also directly confront and undermine orthodoxies.[41] Others want to see a permeation of the distinctive methodologies and challenges of woman-centred approaches across the curriculum and historical research. The aim here is to broaden the historical canvas in a positively inclusive way, to encompass both women's histories and the methodologies which they employ, emphasizing the application of these to the wider study of gender, as well as to the experience of other social groups and to the re-evaluation of other approaches.[42] Where woman-centred study becomes the means by which to gender the curriculum, some synthesis of approaches is implied. The range of positions occupied by historians, regarding both the extent and the relative merits and de-merits of gendered integration or woman-centred separation, is reflected in topical debates about the structure of the curriculum. In stressing the distinctiveness of its concerns and aims through, for example, the provision of separate courses, women's history may occupy a marginal position where opportunities for the permeation of its insights into the core of the curriculum are, at best, limited. Yet there is real concern that the findings and achievements of women's history may be marginalized or re-silenced if they are incorporated into gendered perspectives within an essentially traditional curriculum.

Women's and gender histories may appear, at least at a theoretical level, to be in some ways incompatible, even dichotomous. Yet, in the context of developing and enriching the history curriculum it is possible and desirable to incorporate both approaches, and to explore their potential complementarity as well as their creative tensions. Both share a concern with making gender visible as a key variable in all historical analyses, which helps shape differences amongst women as well as between men and women. In drawing upon methodologies and theoretical perspectives, particularly within feminism, which distinguish their concerns and approaches from those of traditional history, both gender and women's histories challenge prevailing orthodoxies about the nature and practices of the discipline.

A key achievement of both women's and gender histories has been to expose and interrogate the assumptions about women and men, past and present, which many historians continue to make, and to demonstrate how these are themselves rooted in historical constructions of gender and of womanhood. The re-reading and reappraisal of conventional sources, in the light of both experiential evidence and post-structuralist perspectives, help to reveal the omissions and distortions which such accounts contain as well as to illuminate the role of gender in shaping these sources and the histories 'about' women. Certain familiar themes and assumptions about women commonly emerge from such critical analysis of the sources: the view of women as historically inconsequential or unchanging, as passive, as victims, as problems, and as objects of male intervention and concern. Such perceptions are influenced by, and closely related to, essentialist and ahistoric perspectives on women and, by implication, on gender. Women's condition needs no substantial analysis since it is natural, biological and hence immutable through time. Here, for example, the sexual division of labour is seen as simply a natural determinant of sex, whereas woman-centred and gendered approaches both reveal the extent to which it is an ever-changing part of the construction and reconstruction of gender as a historical process, central to an understanding of the histories of both sexes.[43]

In centring upon the assumptions and myths about women that continue to prevail in much historical research and teaching, both the historical constructions of gender and their influence upon subsequent histories become revealed. In looking, for example, at constructions of motherhood, woman-centred and gendered perspectives together reveal the extent to which essentialist accounts, which flavour the more orthodox sources on the subject, such as Parliamentary Papers (where evidence is frequently gleaned from scientists and professional experts), also colour the historian's approach and conclusions. History and the biological sciences emerge as recognizable disciplines from the same historical and social context of the late nineteenth century. Here, a preoccupation with the social implications of Darwinist theory in the context of international imperialism and perceived national decline is reflected in the growing importance accorded to the objective scientific knowledge of the experts, particularly such groups as the medical profession and the burgeoning civil service.[44] The material on motherhood which can be gleaned from these sources resonates with these influences.[45] Recurrent themes emerge in the constructions and discourses of gender which are echoed, rather than critically appraised and explained, by most historians concerned with this issue: the naturalness of motherhood and of the sexual division of labour of which it is a part; mothers as social problems and objects of social policy, as evinced, for example, by the ongoing focus upon working women as bad wives and mothers, and the increased intrusions of the state in women's lives in the cause of good mothering; the national and imperial duties of the mother in producing healthy males to work and fight for their country; concern about birth control, spinsterhood and the unnatural 'feminist' woman, who is out of her predetermined role and a 'traitor to her sex'.[46] A woman-centred account can produce a different but complementary focus, where the stress is upon material realities, social conditions, attitudes, the experience of childbearing and childrearing. Such accounts frequently challenge the apparently more objective versions derived from conventional sources. Explanations for the perceived shortcomings in the maternal role differ, the blame now shifting from individual women to extraneous social and political factors.[47] The interplay of gender, class and race becomes more visible as the difference in experiences amongst and between women and men become apparent. Critical study of the gendering of motherhood in turn-of-the-century Britain highlights the complementary social constructions of femininity and masculinity. The other side of motherhood is revealed in the gendering of men as, variously, the father and provider, protector and head of the family, patriotic soldier and defender of the Empire and, for the white man, occupant of the highest point on the evolutionary ladder.

The syllabus/course outline which follows indicates some ways in which the curriculum can be gendered. The themes and case-studies here invite comparison and integration of the concerns of conventional history with those of both gendered and woman-centred approaches. In this outline the concern with both gender and class is foregrounded, shaping as well as permeating the whole syllabus. The objectives are twofold: to make gender visible in the curriculum and to demonstrate the centrality of gender as a key variable within all historical analyses. The contents of such a syllabus are underpinned by methodologies reflective of the different influences at work in shaping contemporary teaching and research. Through practical evaluation of the range of sources, methods and theoretical perspectives available within a gendered curriculum, students become familiarized with key debates within history. The tensions which exist between these approaches are explored with reference to areas such as experience, discourse, structure and agency, objectivity and subjectivity, interdisciplinarity, epistemology. Students are thus encouraged to engage in the re-readings, redefinitions and subversions of conventional historical knowledge which characterize the contribution of gendered historical research to the reconceptualization and renewal of the discipline. Through the recognition of gender as a key constituent of the histories of both sexes the curriculum can be transformed to become more varied, relevant and accessible to both students and tutors, making its own contribution to the continued vitality of the discipline.

Gender, Class and Society in late Victorian and Edwardian England

Key: (a)   Focus of syllabus.
        (b)   Themes.
        (c)   Indicative topics, case-studies

1 (a) Sex, gender and social history: a conceptual overview.
  (b) Industrialization.
  (c) Production, reproduction and the sexual division of labour; separate spheres: rhetoric and reality; nature, culture and agency: the sexual dynamics of history.
2 (a) Women's roles and men's roles: social constructions and social realities.
  (b) Education and socialization.
  (c) Educational reform for middle-class women and girls; gendering and the elementary schoolcurriculum; public schools; sex, destiny and education: debates on the physical and intellectual education of girls.
3 (a) Gender at work: 1.
  (b) Occupational differentiation.
  (c) Theory in context: the sexual division of labour, the 'family wage' and the domestic labour debate; gendering the census: gendered patterns of employment.
4 (a) Gender at work: 2.
  (b) Women, men and paid work.
  (c) Case-studies, e.g., job segregation in the textile industries; domestic service; sweated and dangerous trades; professions and semi-professions; occupational mobility and the lower-middle-class.
5 (a) Family and household: 1. size and structure.
  (b) Demographic trends; gendering the census.
  (c) Family size and birth control; marriage rates; the marital role and status of women and men; the 'plight' of the single woman.
6 (a) Family and household: 2. production, reproduction and the sexual division of labour.
  (b) Concepts of domesticity; household management and responsibilities; 'man the provider' and the male 'breadwinner' role.
  (c) Making ends meet, with reference to, for example, pawn-broking, credit, patterns of employment; standards of living.
7 (a) Social issues and policies: 1.
  (b) Social conditions: rural/urban/regional comparisons.
  (c) Case-studies, e.g., poverty, standards of living, low pay, under-employment and unemployment; public health; other health issues.
8 (a) Social issues and policies: 2.
  (b) Social policy and the state.

   (c)   Debates about state intervention and 'collectivism'; phil-
         anthropy and social reform; comparing the role of central and
         local government in social policy formation; imperialism and
         social reform with reference to motherhood and to race, gender
         and 'degeneration'.
 9 (a)   The labour movement and industrial politics.
   (b)   Developments in trade unionism: representation and involve-
         ment in the labour movement.
   (c)   Case-studies chosen from particular unions, industries and oc-
         cupations reflective of old/new, single-sex and mixed unions.
10 (a)   Political participation and activism: the spectrum of involve-
         ment in local and national politics.
   (b)   The suffrage campaigns; the range of extra-parliamentary
         politics.
   (c)   'Universal', 'adult male' and 'women's' suffrage: differences
         and alliances; feminism, anti-feminism and women's suffrage;
         concepts of citizenship.
11 (a)   Sexuality and conformity.
   (b)   Marriage, morality and conformity.
   (c)   The spinster: image and reality; lesbian women, feminist pol-
         itics and marital reform; prostitution and the campaign against
         the Contagious Diseases Acts; 'Vice and Vigilance' campaigns;
         the Criminal Law Amendment Act and the criminalization of
         homosexuality.
12 (a)   Leisure and popular culture.
   (b)   Consumption, commercialization and the development of mass
         entertainments; work, play and 'time to spare': gendered con-
         structions of leisure.
   (c)   Case-studies of spectator and participant sports: music
         hall; cycling; drink and 'pub culture'; women's 'spare time'
         activities.

Notes

1   K. Offen et al., *Writing Women's History* (Macmillan, Basingstoke, 1991).
2   Forum, 'Gender and Masculinity', and D. Morgan, 'Men Made Manifest:
    Histories and Masculinities', *Gender and History*, 1 (1989), pp. 87–92.
3   C. Chitty, 'Central Control of the School Curriculum, 1944–87', *History of
    Education*, 17 (1988), pp. 321–34.
4   Various contributors, 'History, the Nation and the Schools', *History Work-
    shop*, 30 (1990), pp. 239–43.

5   On these issues see E. Brookes-Higginbotham, 'Race in Women's History', in *Coming to Terms: Feminism, Theory, Politics*, ed. E. Weed (Routledge, London, 1989), pp. 122–33; A. Davies, *Women, Race and Class* (Random House, New York, 1981) and *Women, Culture and Politics* (Random House, New York, 1989); D. Dennis, *Black History for Beginners* (Writers and Readers Publishing, New York, 1984); B. Hooks, *Talking Back: Thinking Feminist, Thinking Black* (South End Press, Boston, 1989); and the special issue on new developments in black women's history: *Women's Studies Quarterly*, 16 (1988).

6   A. Karach, 'The Politics of Dislocation: Some Mature Women Students' Experiences in Higher Education', *Women's Studies International Forum*, 15 (1992), pp. 309–17.

7   S. Alexander, 'Feminist History and Psychoanalysis', *History Workshop*, 32 (1991), pp. 128–33; J. Okeley and H. Callaway, *Anthropology and Autobiography* (Routledge, London, 1992); L. Stanley and S. Wise, *Breaking Out Again: Feminist Ontology and Epistemology* (Routledge, London, 1993).

8   Women's History Network (North), *Courses in Women's History in the North of England* (Women's History Network, York, 1992).

9   J. Hannam, 'Women, History and Protest', in *Introducing Women's Studies*, ed. D. Richardson and V. Robinson (Macmillan, Basingstoke, 1993), pp. 303–24.

10 L. Stanley, 'Rescuing Women in History from Feminist Deconstructionism', *Women's Studies International Forum*, 13 (1990), pp. 151–7.

11 L. Gordon, review of J. Scott's *Gender and the Politics of History*: *Signs*, 15 (1990), pp. 853–8.

12 A. John, *By the Sweat of their Brow: Women Workers in Victorian Coalmines* (Routledge, London, 1984).

13 S. Humphries's contribution to 'What is Women's History?', in *What is History Today?*, ed. J. Gardiner (Macmillan, London, 1988).

14 J. Scott, *Gender and the Politics of History* (Columbia University Press, New York, 1988).

15 D. Riley, *Am I That Name?: Feminism and the Category of 'Women' in History* (Macmillan, Basingstoke, 1984).

16 J. Scott, review of L. Gordon's *Heroes of their Own Lives*: *Signs*, 15 (1990), pp. 848–52.

17 O. Schreiner, *Women and Labour* (Fisher Unwin, London, 1918); A. Clark, *The Working Life of Women in the Seventeenth Century* (Routledge, London, 1982 [1919]); I. Pinchbeck, *Women Workers and the Industrial Revolution, 1750–1850* (Virago, London, 1981 [1930]).

18 E. Power, *Medieval English Nunneries* (Cambridge University Press, Cambridge, 1922), and 'The Position of Women', in *The Legacy of the Middle Ages*, ed. C. G. Crump and E. F. Jacobs (Clarendon Press, Oxford,

1926), pp. 401–33; D. George, *London Life in the Eighteenth Century* (Penguin, Harmondsworth, 1966 [1925]): M. Bland, *Women as a Force in History* (Macmillan, New York, 1946).

19 S. Rowbotham, *Hidden from History: Three Hundred Years of Women's Oppression and the Fight Against It* (Pluto, London, 1973).

20 C. de Pisan, *The Book of the City of Ladies* (Penguin, Harmondsworth, 1985 edn); E. McLeod, *The Order of the Rose: The Life and Ideas of Christine de Pisan* (Chatto and Windus, London, 1975); M. Wollstonecraft, *A Vindication of the Rights of Women* (1792).

21 G. Lerner, 'Placing Women in History', in *Liberating Women's History*, ed. B. Carroll (University of Illinois Press, Urbana, 1976), pp. 357–79.

22 R. Strachey, *The Cause* (Virago, London, 1978); E. S. Pankhurst, *The Suffragette Movement: An Intimate Account of Persons and Ideals* (Longmans, London, 1931).

23 J. Lewis, 'Women Lost and Found: The Impact of Feminism upon History', in *Men's Studies Modified: The Impact of Feminism on the Academic Disciplines*, ed. D. Spender (Pergamon Press, Oxford, 1981), p. 59.

24 D. Thom, 'A Lop-sided View: Feminist History or the History of Women?', in *Critical Feminism: Arguments in the Disciplines*, ed. K. Campbell (Open University Press, Buckingham, 1992), p. 49.

25 E. P. Thompson, *The Making of the English Working Class* (Victor Gollancz, London, 1963).

26 L. Gordon, *Heroes of their Own Lives: The Politics and History of Family Violence* (Viking, New York, 1988); S. Rowbotham, *Women, Resistance and Revolution* (Penguin, Harmondsworth, 1972).

27 J. Kelly, *Women, History and Theory* (University of Chicago Press, Chicago, 1984).

28 J. Scott, 'Women in the Making of the English Working Class', in *Gender and the Politics of History*, ed. Scott, pp. 68–90.

29 P. Hilden, 'Women's History: The Second Wave', *Historical Journal*, 25 (1982), pp. 501–12.

30 M. Barrett, *Women's Oppression Today: Problems in Marxist Feminist Analysis* (Verso, London, 1980); S. Walby, *Patriarchy at Work* (Polity, Cambridge, 1986).

31 See N. F. Cott, *The Bonds of Womanhood: Women's Sphere in New England, 1780–1835* (Avon, New Haven, 1977); K. Millett, *Sexual Politics* (Avon, New York, 1969); M. Ryan, *Cradle of the Middle Class: The Family in Oneida County, New York, 1790–1865* (Cambridge University Press, Cambridge, 1981); C. Smith-Rosenberg, 'The Hysterical Woman: Sex Roles and Conflict in Nineteenth Century America', *Social Research*, 39 (1972), pp. 652–78; M. Vicinus, *Independent Women: Work and Community for Single Women, 1850–1920* (Virago, London, 1985).

32 Alexander, 'Feminist History and Psychoanalysis'; J. Mitchell, *Psychoanalysis and Feminism* (Vintage Books, New York, 1984); R. Tong, *Feminist*

Thought (Westview Press, Colorado, 1989); S. Walby, *Theorising Patriarchy* (Blackwell, Oxford, 1990).

33 See P. Hill Collins, *Black Feminist Thought: Knowledge, Consciousness and the Politics of Empowerment* (Routledge, New York, 1991); B. Hooks, *Ain't I A Woman?: Black Women and Feminism* (South End Press, Boston, 1981); *Black Women in White America: A Documentary History*, ed. G. Lerner (Vintage Books, New York, 1972); Lesbian History Group, *Not A Passing Phase* (Women's Press, London, 1989); *The Sexuality Debates*, ed. S. Jeffries (Routledge, London, 1987).

34 J. Little and S. Rai, 'Between Feminism and Orientalism', in *Making Connections: Women's Studies, Women's Movements, Women's Lives*, ed. M. Kennedy, C. Lubelska and V. Walsh (Taylor and Francis, London, 1993); V. Ware, *Beyond the Pale: White Women, Racism and History* (Verso, London 1991).

35 See L. Gordon and J. Scott's reviews of each other's books in *Signs*, 15 (1990), pp. 848–58, and Hannam, 'Women, History, and Protest'.

36 Lewis, 'Women Lost and Found'.

37 L. Davidoff and C. Hall, *Family Fortunes: Women and Men of the English Middle Class, 1780–1850* (Hutchinson, London, 1987), p. 29.

38 S. B. Gluck and D. Patai (eds), *Women's Words: The Feminist Practice of Oral History* (Routledge, New York, 1991); M. Llewellyn Davies, *Life as We Have Known It: By Co-operative Working Women* (Hogarth Press, London, 1931); E. Roberts, 'Oral History and the Local Historian', *The Local Historian*, 13 (1979), pp. 408–16.

39 K. Borland, '"That's not what I said": Interpretative Conflict in Oral Narrative Research', in *Women's Words*, ed. Gluck and Patai, pp. 63–75; S. Harding *Feminism and Methodology* (Open University Press, Buckingham, 1987); L. Stanley, *The Autobiographical I* (Manchester University Press, Manchester, 1992).

40 *Feminist Epistemologies*, ed. L. Alcoff and E. Potter (Routledge, London, 1993).

41 Editorial, *Women's History Review*, 1 (1992), pp. 5–8.

42 N. Zemon Davis, contribution to 'What is Women's History?', in *What is History Today?*, ed. Gardiner.

43 Walby, *Patriarchy at Work*; W. Seccombe, 'The Construction of the Male-breadwinner Norm in Nineteenth Century England', *Social History*, 11 (1986), pp. 53–76.

44 G. Bock, 'Women's History and Gender History: Aspects of an International Debate', *Gender and History*, 1 (1989), pp. 7–30; H. Perkin, *The Rise of Professional Society: England since 1880* (Routledge, London, 1989).

45 A. Davin, 'Imperialism and Motherhood', *History Workshop*, 5 (1978), pp. 9–65; J. Lewis, *The Politics of Motherhood: Maternal and Child Welfare in England, 1900–1939* (Croom Helm, London, 1980).

46 *Maternity and Gender Policies: Women and the Rise of European Welfare*

States, ed. G. Boch and P. Thane (Routledge, London, 1991); *Mothers of a New World: Maternal Politics and the Rise of Welfare States*, ed. S. Koven and S. Michel (Routledge, New York, 1993); S. Jeffries, *The Spinster and Her Enemies 1880–1930* (Pandora, London, 1985).

47   M. Llewellyn Davies, *Maternity: Letters from Working Women* (G. Bell, London, 1915).

Further Reading

For those who want some basic guidelines, *Genderwatch: Self-Assessment Schedules for Use in Schools* (Schools Curriculum Development Committee Publications, London, 1987), designed for use in secondary schools, provides a practical checklist, and D. Beddoe's *Discovering Women's History: A Practical Manual* (Pandora Press, London, 1983) still stands as a useful introduction, with many case-studies which can easily be applied within a teaching context. *Writing Women's History*, ed. K. Offen et al. (Macmillan, Basingstoke, 1991) discusses the methods employed by historians of women. In exploring the range of work in the field, *Studies on Women Abstracts* (UK) and *Women Studies Abstracts* (USA) detail much relevant material, as do many journals, especially *Gender and History*, *Journal of Women's History* and *Women's History Review*, where current issues and debates can be followed.

For consideration of the various approaches to gendering the history curriculum: on women's history, see G. Lerner, 'Placing Women in History', in *Liberating Women's History*, ed. B. Carroll (University of Illinois Press, Urbana, 1976), pp. 357–79; J. Lewis, 'Women Lost and Found: The Impact of Feminism on History', in *Men's Studies Modified: The Impact of Feminism on the Academic Disciplines*, ed. D. Spender (Pergamon Press, Oxford, 1981), pp. 55–72; and the anthology *What is History Today?*, ed. J. Gardiner (Macmillan, Basingstoke, 1988). Some key features of structuralist and post-structuralist approaches to gendering history can be gleaned from G. Bock, 'Women's History and Gender History: Aspects of an International Debate', *Gender and History*, 1 (1989), pp. 7–30, and J. Scott, 'Women's History', in *New Perspectives in Historical Writing*, ed. P. Burke (Polity, Oxford, 1991), pp. 68–90, whilst J. Hoff, 'Gender as a Postmodern Category of Paralysis', *Women's History Review*, 3 (1994), pp. 49–69, provides an accessible critique of post-structuralism in gendered historical analysis. Different perspectives on feminist history can be found in J. Bennett, 'Feminism and History', *Gender and History*, 1 (1989), pp. 251–72, and D. Thom, 'A Lop-sided View: Feminist History or the History of Women?' in *Critical Feminism. Arguments in the Disciplines*, ed. K. Campbell (Open University Press, Buckingham, 1992), pp. 25–51. S. Rose, 'Gender History/Women's History: Is Feminism Losing its Critical Edge?', *Journal Of Women's History*, 5 (1993), pp. 89–128, casts a critical eye over recent developments.

5

Teaching History Theory: a Radical Introduction

Keith Jenkins

Not only is it sometimes considered difficult for students to understand 'history theory',[1] but, from the perspective of those practical, 'professional,' robustly commonsensical empiricists who still dominate our 'history culture', it is often deemed to be unnecessary or even positively harmful to do so. But let us say that we want to do it. Let us say that, just as first-year undergraduates reading literature, politics, sociology or linguistics are introduced to literary, political, sociological or linguistic theory almost as a matter of course, so young historians should be similarly introduced to history theory.

Of course, it is not just a matter of introducing any old theory, and certainly not some sort of metanarrative of the kind that too-often passes for it, for the last few years have seen both traditional, anti-theoretical history and old metanarratives become increasingly cut adrift from some very particular approaches to discursive knowledge; namely, approaches of a textualist, post-structuralist and post-modern type. Consequently, it is these perspectives which I would argue history students now need to know if they are to understand anything of that general intellectual milieu within which they actually live, and which has serious implications for any considerations on the 'nature of history' that they may today undertake. In which case the question arises as to what sort of theoretical content and what sort of organizing structure a course introducing these kinds of discussions to students could have.

Working the Past/History Distinction

Let us start from the assumption that history theory today can best be entered by drawing a radical distinction between 'the past' and 'history', rendering the *idea* of history – as the various accounts constructed about the past by historians and those acting as if they were historians – by the term 'historiography'. And let us assume that we do not just want to recognize this past/historiography difference and then pass on quickly to 'do' some history. We want to dwell on it, to make it the centre of our concerns and suggest to students that they might make it the centre of theirs if they are to understand the theoretical nature of history via some of today's most prominent debates. And let us take as our entrée into these debates some ideas about history as articulated by Bennett, White and Ankersmit.

For Bennett, it would appear that characterizing history as historiography (as writing, as texts different to the past – which, whilst not itself a text, must be 'read' through its remaining 'textual traces') *theorizes* both the notion of 'the past' and the 'writing up' of it. For, given that the past exists (by definition) only in the modality of its current historiographical representations, this means that the issues traditionally involved in discussions about the nature of historical scholarship may be 're-thought in a manner which allows a break with the ways in which they have traditionally been posed as part of a general epistemological problem concerning the nature of our access to the past *as such*'.[2] As Bennett says, that is not the point of historical enquiry and never has been. Consequently, since historians never access 'the past as such', problems formulated along the lines of, 'How can historians truly know the past?', or, 'If historians cannot access the "real past" then how can there be any "real" checks on their accounts as opposed to just further "interpretations"?', are beside the point. For what is at issue in historiography – and indeed what can only ever be at issue – is what can be derived from the 'historicized' record or archive. And it is the 'historicized' nature of the records/archive which historians access that must be stressed here. For such records and archives are, as Bennett explains, highly volatile and mutable products of complex historical/social processes in that, apart from the considerable amount of organized labour (by librarians, archivists, curators) which goes into their production (preserving, cataloguing, indexing, 'weeding out', etc.) the composition and potential of such records/traces of the past vary considerably

over time. Witness, says Bennett, 'the influence of feminist historiography in expanding the range of what now counts as the historical
record'.[3]

In this way, then, we can think of 'the past as such' as being simply an
absent object of inquiry, its presence (its *absent presence*) being signified
by its remaining traces, which is the only 'real past' we can ever have.
Here, such traces function not as the historian's referent in the sense of
actually being some kind of extra-discursive reality, but *as if* they were
such a referent in that they constitute 'the last court of appeal for historical disputes, the point of which, so to speak, they hit base – but a base
within discourse'. On this account, history is therefore simply the discipline through which historians working at the level of what Bennett calls
the public historical sphere (as, say, salaried workers in higher education)
come into contact with the historicized record or archive as currently
existing in order to 'intervene' in it (to interpret it). From this perspective, historiography may be regarded as a

> specific discursive regime, governed by distinctive [historicized] proce-
> dures, through which the maintenance/transformation of the past as a set
> of currently existing realities is regulated . . . the discipline's special pro-
> ductivity consist[ing] precisely in its capacity to reorganise its referent and
> thus transform 'the past' – not as it was but as it is. Understood in this
> way the cogency . . . of historical inquiry may be admitted without the
> question of its relations to 'the real past' ever arising.[4]

This is not to doubt for a moment that the past actually existed, but it is
to say that in respect to what is at issue in historiographical debates and
the manner in which they are actually conducted, 'it may be allowed to go
its own way – as it surely has'.[5] In this straightforward way of seeing
things, we can thus appreciate that the real past doesn't enter into the
practices of historians except rhetorically – except theoretically – so that
we can accept in quite a matter-of-fact way Derrida's (in)famous remark
that, so far as our understanding of the past is concerned, there is
'nothing outside of the text'.

These kinds of argument from Bennett mean, in short, that 'the past
as existing traces' is always apprehended/constituted *textually* through
the sedimented layers of previous interpretations and through the reading habits and categories developed by previous and current methodological practices. Consequently, the status of historical knowledge is not
based on its correspondence with the past *per se* but on the various
historicizations of it: historiography always 'stands in for' the past. Such

arguments undercut traditional historiography in so far as it depends upon that correspondence between the past and historiography as actually being between historiography and a separate, accessible, non-historiographically constituted past. And here some interesting arguments by White and Ankersmit develop what is meant by such 'undercuttings'.

Although White occasionally expresses his definition of what he thinks history is in different ways, the understanding he usually works with is that the historical work is a 'narrative discourse the content of which is as much *invented* – or as much *imagined* – as found'.[6] And it is White's stress on the invented/imagined element that might be profitably explained and developed at this juncture. What does White mean?

He seems to mean two things. First, in order to make sense of events or sets of events which occurred in the past, in order to make 'the facts' of the past 'significant', White argues that such events/facts *always* have to be related to a context; to some sort of 'whole', 'totality', 'background' or even to the notion of 'the past itself'. And here the problem is that whilst the historian can certainly 'find' the traces of past events in the historicized archive and so (selectively) establish (some of) the facts about them in, say, a chronicle-type form, no historian can *ever* find the whole context, totality or background against which 'the facts' can become 'truly' significant and meaningful. What this means is that any such context which is constructed to contextualize precisely the facts just has to be ultimately invented or imagined: unlike the facts, the contexts can *never* be definitively found. Therefore, because all historical accounts have to involve part-to-whole or whole-to-part relationships (that is, all accounts to be meaningful involve the tropes of metonymy or synecdoche),[7] then at least three conclusions can be drawn at this point. First, that all interpretations of the past are as much invented (the contexts) as found (the facts), and that, on this first argument alone, White's definition seems plausible. Second, because of the imagined (fictive) element in *all* histories (i.e., histories in both the upper and lower case), no history can be literally 'factual' or completely 'found' or absolutely true. Third, that because of the inevitable troping of parts-to-whole and whole-to-parts, then all historical accounts are ultimately metaphorical and thus – because of their inescapable troping – metahistorical.[8]

This is the first thing which White seems to mean by his statement that the historical work is as much invented/imagined as found. The second is this: he thinks that most historians consider the characteristic form in which they represent the past to their audience – that is, the narrative form – as the actual content of the past (namely, 'narrativity'), then going on mistakenly to treat narrativity as an essence shared both by the historical representation and by the sets of events in the past alike. This is perhaps a difficult point to grasp when stated so curtly, so it might be worth taking a few sentences to spell it out. White's argument goes roughly as follows.

Since its 'invention' by Herodotus,[9] traditional western historiography has featured predominantly the belief that it consists of congeries of lived stories – both individual and collective – and that the principal task of the historian is to discover these stories and retell them in narrative form, the truth/accuracy of which would reside in the degree of correspondence of the story told to the story lived. However, the point to be made here is that, unfortunately for this traditional view, people in the past did not live stories either individually (at the level of 'real life' stories) or collectively (at the level of, say, metanarratives which give purpose and meaning to the past 'as such', as in Marxist or Whig theories of history), so that to see people in the past or the past as such in story-form is to give to the past an imaginary series of narrative structures and coherences it actually never had. To see the content of the past (i.e., what actually occurred) as if it were a series of stories (of great men, the rise of labour, the emancipation of women, of 'Our Island Story', of the ultimate victory of the proletariat . . .) is therefore a matter of imaginative projection. To read the past in the *form* of stories, therefore, is to invent the *content* of the past (i.e., to see the myriad events of the past as really having stories 'in them' which historians somehow 'discover'), caused by mistaking the narrative form in which historians construct their knowledge of the past as actually being the past's own. Accordingly, the traditional idea that the truth/accuracy of history as told in narrative is evidenced by its degree of correspondence to the lived stories of the past is undercut when it is recognized that there are no stories in the past to ever correspond to; that the only stories the past has are those which historians confer on it by their interpretive emplotments. Thus, any theory of correspondence which goes beyond the level of the singular statement or the chronicle – and historians' interpretations by definition always go beyond the statement and the chronicle – is ultimately self-referencing. For, ultimately, any correspondence is not between the historian's story and the story the past itself would (if only it could) tell, but between the historian's story and the putative past's story as put into narrative form in 'the past tense' by historians themselves.

This point is reinforced a little differently by Ankersmit.[10] For Ankersmit, the history text consists of many individual statements, most of which claim to give an accurate description of some state of affairs in the past. Historians formulate these statements on the basis of the sources they work on in archives, and it is these sources – as evidence – that will decide the truth or falsity of the statements in question. But – and this is Ankersmit's point – because the sources available to most historians will allow them to write many more 'true' statements than are actually to be found in their texts, then out of all the statements they could have made, the ones actually made are carefully selected, distributed, 'weighted' and so on, the result being that a certain 'picture of the past' (an 'impression' or an icon) is fabricated. Consequently, says Ankersmit, we can make two points about the text's statements: (1) they individually refer to and describe a fragment of the past and can either be true or false; (2) they collectively define the 'picture of the past' which cannot be said to be either true or false but simply an 'iconic' impression/interpretation. For whilst it is generally the case that individual discrete statements (facts) can indeed be checked against the discrete source to see if they correspond, the 'picture of the past' can never be so checked because there is no 'real' picture of the past save that which the historian has himself/herself put together to check it against. And since all that is essential in the writings of historians is not to be found at the level of the individual statement but rather at the level of the 'pictures of the past' (in that it is these pictures which, for example, most stimulate historiographical debates and thus determine the way we 'see' the past), then historiography is again as much invented/imagined as found. I mean, says Ankersmit, saying *true* things about the past at the level of the statement is easy – anybody can do that – but getting the picture 'straight', that's not only another story but ultimately an impossible one . . . for you can always get another picture, you can always get another context.[11]

Four Implications

As has already been suggested, these ways of theorizing and working the past/historiography difference have some serious implications, especially for traditional historiography, in that once we see the impossibility of any literal representation of the traces of the past as the past *per se*, then all such representations, being ultimately as much imagined as found, become a series of ideas (theories) which historians have about ways of making the *past* 'historical', all of which are problematic. Such problematical areas are legion, but in order to see how this sort of theorizing affects especially the sort of traditional history most students will be familiar with, four examples of such problematicizations can be briefly outlined before going on to outline the sort of course where such areas can be examined. They are: ideology, historicism, interpretation and truth, and empiricism.

Ideology

At the level of historiography (as opposed to the level of the statement/chronicle) and in terms of epistemology, the conviction that the past has no meaning *in it* stands, in our postmodern days, at the same level of conviction as that it has; that is, the matter is undecidable. Consequently, as White for example argues, any claim which is made to suggest that history has to be considered in one specific way because that way embodies or reflects what the past and/or historiography 'really are', must be ideological. And such claims are ideological whether they are made at the level of the upper case, as History (that is to say, a view of the past which purports to assign past events their objective significance by identifying their place and function within a general schema of development as might be claimed by any metanarrative, such as Marxism), or at the level of the lower case (that is, the view that the proper study of the past is a study of it for 'its own sake', eschewing metanarrative for an ostensibly disinterested, objectivist, and generally empirical approach); this lower-case variant being seen by White as 'bourgeois'. For having had their own use of history in the upper case (for example in Whiggism), the bourgeoisie, now having nothing else to 'become', have no need for a historical trajectory which has not reached its destination. Consequently, at this point in time, what could be more 'natural' (i.e., ideological) to them than understanding history as a non-worldly (academic) discipline allegedly 'above politics'; the conclusion to be drawn being that *all* histories are suasive. History is always history for someone, and that someone cannot be the past 'itself' for the past doesn't have a 'self'. Any history which therefore considers its particular type of discourse (its species) as identical to history *per se* (its genus) is not only ideological (and thus 'theoretical'), but ideological (and theoretical) nonsense.

Historicism

The second problematic is related to the first, and for convenience we can again draw on White. He sees all histories as equally historicist; that is, the dichotomous view held particularly by 'proper' historians (i.e., by bourgeois, lower-case 'academics') that historicism is an improper use of the past in so far as it illegitimately uses it to illuminate present-day problems or, worse still, predict future developments, can be rejected on the ground that every historical representation, 'however particularizing, narrativist, self-consciously perspectival and fixated on its subject matter "for its own sake" – contains most of the elements of . . . historicism'.[12] All historians have to shape their materials somehow *vis-à-vis* what constitutes narrative in general at the time of writing, so that in the very language historians use they subject the past to the kinds of 'distortions' that 'historicists' are said to impose upon their materials. Consequently, those old dichotomies between 'proper' history and historicism, and between 'proper' history and 'ideological history' – those dichotomies so beloved in the seminar room – obscure more than they illuminate about historical representation. For in 'proper' history, the element of overt construction is simply displaced to the interior of the narrative while the element of 'found' data is made to occupy the position of prominence in the (imagined) story-line, whereas in upper-case history the reverse takes place: these are two sides of the same coin.

But it is not only that, for at this particular juncture of the 'postmodern condition', the remarks made under 'Ideology' (above) are pertinent. For to argue in the context of historicism that the study of history should have nothing to do with projecting the past into the future, is precisely as present-centred and ideological (historicist) as the argument that it should. That is to say, whilst upper-case history is quite explicit that it is present-centred in its use of the past as a basis for a trajectory into a different future, the fact that the 'bourgeoisie' doesn't want a different future and therefore doesn't want a past-based scenario – the fact that at this point the past can be neutralized and studied not for 'our' sake but for 'its' own – is precisely what is needed in 'the present'. Thus, to pretend not to be present-centred – and to declare such present-centredness to be illegitimate – is what actually constitutes its own present-centred (historicist) needs.

Interpretation and truth

The above two arguments underline the point that all history is interpretative and never literally true – a 'true interpretation' being oxymoronic beside anything else. As we have seen already, in history discourse narrative serves to transform into stories past events (as 'facts' etc.) that would otherwise be only a series of singular statements and/or a chronicle. Consequently, to effect this transformation the events, agents, dates, etc., represented in the statements/chronicle, must be encoded. And here the obvious point to be made is that this encoding is not of the type which means that the narrative explains more fully the statements/chronicle, but rather, as White argues, that narration produces a meaning quite different from the statements/chronicle, transforming them into patterns no literal representation of them as facts could ever produce. Consequently, given that no set of events/facts are intrinsically anything (i.e., they're not intrinsically tragic, heroic, comical or whatever) but can only be constituted imaginatively as such within a fabricated story-line which endows them with a meaningful form, then it is narrative *per se* that endows real events with the kind of meaning found otherwise only in myths and literature. This means, according to White, that we are therefore justified in regarding all histories as allegorical. Indeed, he concludes, 'a narrative account is always a figurative account, an allegory', it being only a modern empirical prejudice 'in favour of literalism that obscures this fact to many modern analysts of historical narrative'.[13]

Empiricism

Because a narrative account is always a figurative (allegorical) account, history cannot have a true correspondence in ways traditionally seen as mimetic and/or empirical. Even in the most chaste prose (that is, history texts intended to represent things as they were without rhetorical adornment), 'every such mimetic text can be shown to have left something out of the description of its object or to have put something into it that is inessential to what *some* reader, with more or less authority, will regard as an adequate description'.[14] Thus, every mimesis can serve as the occasion for another description of the same phenomenon, one claiming to be 'more faithful to the facts', and so on *ad infinitum*: this is the world of

endless deferments . . . Derrida's world . . . our world. And thus by extension from mimesis, empiricism, with its obsession about getting the
facts and 'getting them straight', also succumbs to the charms of
emplotment. For where empiricism is most flawed is where, as White
again argues, it refuses to see how narrativity constitutes the grounds
whereon what counts as a 'fact' is decided upon in the first place. This is
not to say that facts do not exist, but rather that the most they can offer
are the elements which can be made into a story by emplotment, troping,
and so on, so that how a given situation from 'the past' is to be plausibly
configured depends on the historian's skill in matching up a specific plot-
structure with the events/facts he or she wishes to endow with meanings
of a certain kind, the resultant 'account' being made up not only by the
constituted facts but also intertextually *vis-à-vis* what passes for a recognizable history within any given culture and, more narrowly, within any
given 'history culture'.

On the Narrative and other 'Turns'

As already suggested, these sorts of theories and these sorts of implications do tend to undermine traditional notions of what history is and
what constitutes historical knowledge, such *textualist* arguments
problematicizing the 'real foundations' on which to define history as such
and on which to 'ground' (and thus be able to adjudicate between)
different versions of the past. Consequently, much has been heard recently from Lawrence Stone and Gabrielle Spiegel, Geoffrey Elton and
Arthur Marwick, and others, that history as 'we' have known it (i.e.,
history as 'they' have known it) is in danger, in that the slippery slopes
opened up by the eradication of the 'reality' of the past in favour of
endless textualist/allegorical redescriptions ushers in the spectre of a
hapless relativism or even nihilism.[15] Yet it seems to me that these sort of
worries are largely beside the point in that those taking up positions
similar to those of Stone and Spiegel in particular, have misunderstood
the nature of the 'textualism' they attack, defending a 'traditional'
history on grounds that have, in fact, never been available to it.

   The point here is that Stone and the others would only be identifying
a problem with the idea of the past as textuality if the past had ever been
accessed (or could logically ever be accessed) outside of textuality. If the
past had ever been or could be accessed or appropriated directly, then
textuality would indeed deform or distort it. But given that direct access

has never been possible, that the past is always known through its representations, that the only past the historian has ever had access to is Bennett's historicized archive, and that in practice historians have pretty much to a man and a woman had no problems whatsoever in accepting this *as if* this was exactly what studying the past historically meant (i.e., going to the record office, surveying a site, reading other historians, etc.), then the objections to textuality seem to be taken on behalf of a practice no historian has ever achieved: you cannot have a non-textual history.

This raises the point that those who are fearful of textuality – that is, those who have similar fears to Spiegel when she argues that the 'dissolution of the materiality of the sign signals the dissolution of history' (as does Elizabeth Fox-Genovese when she worries that such textualism undercuts the basis for a materialist, structural Marxism, for fears of textualism run across the whole political spectrum in so far as any position clings to realist and objectivist types of historical knowledge) – just do not understand what textualism actually is.[16] Textualism does not prevent Stone, Spiegel and Fox-Genovese doing the kind of history they have long been doing in any way whatsoever. For textualism is not, of course, a way of 'doing history' at all. All that textualism does is to draw attention to the textual conditions under which all historical work is done; under which all historical knowledge is produced. What textualism does is thus to allow all the various methodological approaches, be they Marxist, empirical, phenomenological or whatever, to continue exactly as before but with one proviso: that none of them can continue to think that they can ground their interpretations in a past reality appropriated plain. It is therefore no good for traditional historians of whatever position attacking textual practices or 'history as textuality', because they are attacking themselves: for all histories – to repeat – are textual. Here is Hayden White pulling all this together:

First, it should be said that every approach to the study of the past presupposes or entails some version of a textualist theory of historical reality of some kind. This is because, primarily, the historical past is, as Fredric Jameson has argued, accessible to study 'only by way of its prior textualisations', whether these be in the form of the documentary record or in the form of accounts of what happened in the past written up by historians themselves on the basis of their research into the record. Secondly, historical accounts of the past are themselves based upon the presumed adequacy of a written representation or textualisation of the events of the past to the reality of those events themselves. Historical events, whatever else they may be, are events which really happened or are believed really to have happened, but which are not longer directly accessible to perception. As such, in order to be constituted as objects of reflection, they must be described . . . in some kind of . . . language. The analysis or explanation . . . that is subsequently provided of the events is [therefore] always an analysis or explanation of the events as previously *described*. . . . On this basis alone, one is justified in speaking of history as a text.

This is, to be sure, a metaphor, but it is no more metaphorical than Marx's statement that 'all previous history is the history of class struggle' or the statement by Fox-Genovese that 'History, at least good history, is inescapably structural'. More importantly, the statement 'History is a text' is in no way inconsistent with these other statements about the nature of history. On the contrary, it is or at least can be so considered for methodological purposes, if anything, a qualification of these other statements. As thus envisaged . . . textualism . . . has the advantage of making explicit . . . the textualist element in any approach to the study of history.[17]

In that sense, then, contemporary 'textual' theory – of the type I am arguing that students today should be introduced to so that they might be participants in the general intellectual milieu within which historiography is now situated (whether some historians like it or not) – stems from that manifestation of our 'post-modern condition' which might be conveniently summarized by referring to it as the narrative or the linguistic or the discursive or the deconstructionist or some other type of 'textual turn'. Here, to draw this section together with the first and second, is a quotation by Raphael Samuel who registers the impact of the 'deconstructionst turn' on historiography.

The deconstructive turn in contemporary thought . . . puts all of history's taken-for-granted procedures into question, both as an intellectual discipline and as a literary (or writerly) mode. By placing inverted commas . . . around the notion of the real, it invites us to see history not as a record of the past, more or less faithful to the facts, nor yet as an interpretation answerable to the evidence even if it does not start from it, but as an invention, or fiction, of historians themselves, an inscription on the past rather than a reflection of it, an act of designation masquerading as a true-life story. It asks us to consider history as a literary form, on a par with or at any rate exhibiting affinities to, other kinds of imaginative writing. Our continuities are [therefore seen as] . . . storyteller's devices to give order and progression to the plot. The periodisation, by which we set such store, is a strategy of narrative closure. Events are singled out for attention not because of their intrinsic interest, but because of the logic of the text; they are not material realities but the organising units of historical discourse, 'highly coded tropes that "read" or allegorize the past'.[18]

Constructing a Theory Course

These are some of the theoretical debates currently being discussed in 'the literature', the argument of this chapter being that undergraduates should be introduced to such debates so that they can think about the nature of history/historiography for themselves. And what this arguably means in practical terms is that an introductory course would need to take students from what might be called 'old' formulations on the nature of history (formulations typically expressed through a series of dichotomies; of content *vs* skills, facts *vs* interpretation, objectivity *vs* subjectivity, arts *vs* science, truth *vs* opinion, etc.) to a 'newer' vocabulary of, say, self-referentiality, absent-presences, signifiers-signifieds-referents, metaphorical tropes and so on; and against manifestations of a textualizing postmodernism (post-structuralism, deconstructionism, anti-foundationalism, new pragmatism, new historicism, post-Marxism, post-feminism, etc.). In this respect, the popular mainstream texts generally recommended to students (such as those by Carr, Elton, Geyl, Marwick, Plumb and Tosh) need to be set alongside works by writers such as White, Montrose, Rorty, Fish, Derrida, Foucault, Ricouer, Kristeva, and Bhaba.

Now, all this is not to say, of course, that existing undergraduate courses do not sometimes have introductions to the nature of history. But the point I am making is that whilst some are highly theoretical and critical, a study of prospectuses and discussions with colleagues suggest that many courses (with titles like 'The Historian At Work', 'The Skills of the Historian' or 'Study Skills for History') centre on agendas springing from old empirical/documentarist concerns, peppered with suggestions that students become information-technology literate and start word-processing their essays. And whilst most undergraduate programmes conclude with a 'special subject', relatively few of these are on theoretical issues.

How might the sort of things I have been talking about here under the label of 'theory' be organized in an introductory course, a course which we will say has three hours contact-time per week over twelve weeks, to be assessed by a conventional 3,000-word essay?

I think such a course could begin – after some preliminary input by lectures which 'set up' the course in the way I have tried in the first three sections of this chapter – by a discussion of Carr and Elton. For although students may not actually be familiar with either of them, there is a reasonable chance – given their mainstream status – that students will see what Carr is saying and why Elton may well object to it. There is also a good chance that students will be able to cope with the vocabulary and concepts Carr and Elton use and so will not find themselves out of their depth. At the same time, the fact that it will have been made clear to them that Carr and Elton are only the orthodox starting points for the course, should be enough to retain the interests of those students who have 'already done them'; the thrust of the course being *away* from Carr and Elton and towards Bennett, Richard Rorty and White.

Now, whilst the choice of Carr and Elton to hang part of the course on may raise few eyebrows, the choice of Bennett, Rorty and White may not be so 'self-evident'. Besides, if the course is to organize its 'theories' around 'theorists' (as opposed to concepts, movements, schools, controversies or whatever) then one could produce a list of these, say, E. P. Thompson, Althusser, Popper, Foucault, Habermas, Oakeshott, Perry Anderson, and so on. So, why Bennett, Rorty and White?

The choice of Bennett is based on his formulation of what history might arguably best be seen as, as in chapter 3 of his book, *Outside Literature*, wherein Bennett re-thinks the question of what is history in a post-Marxist way.[19] This is not, it has to be said, the only thing that Bennett is concerned with in *Outside Literature*. At least since the publication of *Formalism and Marxism*,[20] Bennett has been addressing, in various articles and papers, the interconnected areas of literary theory, literary value, the historicity of texts and more general questions related to ways of reading popular culture from a critical Marxist perspective. And in *Outside Literature* he re-visits these areas in thought-provoking ways. But, as I have indicated, in addition to these old preoccupations, Bennett also examines for the first time in any substantial way, the problems that have arisen around the possibility of gaining, in these 'postist' days, some secure grounds on which the claims we make about the status of historical knowledge can be assessed. Bennett is therefore useful as a transition from the relative certainties of Carr and Elton to the anti-foundationalism and ironic scepticism of Rorty and White.

The choice of Rorty may also need a little justification, no least because, although he has written extensively on the history of ideas, he is not really a historian at all but a philosopher. But the reason for choosing

Rorty is based on 'the fact' that over the last thirty years or so, Rorty has moved from being a fairly ordinary analytical philosopher to blending deliberately a 'personalized' pragmatism to readings of Nietzsche and Freud, Heidegger and Wittgenstein, Foucault and Derrida, Davidson and Quine. Rorty has absorbed and worked aspects of semiotics, post-structuralism, deconstructionism, feminism and post-Marxism, and declared himself an occasional postmodernist. Quite deliberately he has crossed and collapsed the borders of philosophy, history, literature, science, aesthetics and linguistics to emerge, bricolage-like, on the 'other' side, with an original and seminal position which can, for now, be described as an anti-foundational, ironic, rhetorical, conversationalist style of philosophy, which holds within it so many current debates. Rorty thus seems to be the embodiment of the contemporary, a baro-meter, perhaps, of intellectual pressures across so many discourses, all of which, like history, have the problems of meaning and representation in focus. Rorty's work therefore arguably constitutes the best single guide to what is going on in general, so that on this course he is used to 'contextualize' history within a wider intellectual field into which White can be inserted.

In 1973 White published his controversial *Metahistory*, followed by *Tropics of Discourse* in 1978 and *The Content of the Form* in 1987. More recently he has written on Proust and penned an incisive Afterword to *The New Historicism* edited by H. A. Veeser. In these and other works, White has ranged critically over a host of historians/theorists – Hegel, Marx, Nietzsche, Barthes, Foucault et al., while his footnotes refer to some of the most vibrant debates in contemporary thought: literary theory, linguistics, narratology, hermeneutics, post-structuralism and so on, White applying these and other approaches directly to his-toriography, historical method and the status of historical knowledge in thought-provoking ways. Moreover, Elton, in his conservative *Return to Essentials* (1991) signals all that is wrong in the way of current theorizing via a heavy critique of post-structuralist, deconstructionist and other postmodern fads, picking out White as the arch-exponent of such 'rub-bish'. In this way, the old Carr–Elton debate is explicity linked up to those practices variously engaged with by Bennett, Rorty and White, thus lending a polemical tone and coherence to the course which might therefore be structured as follows:

Week 1: *Introduction*, including video footage of Elton, Rorty and White.

Week 2:	*Overview of 'History Today'*. A introductory overview of the type discussed in the first three sections of this chapter.

Week 3:	*On E. H. Carr*. A general analysis of Carr's *What Is History?* situating Carr in the midst of other early 1960s developments to stress the impact of Carr's (alleged) relativism on historiography.

Week 4:	*On Geoffrey Elton*. A general examination of Elton's defence of what was – and still is – the *doxa* of the 'historical profession'; texts to be drawn on are Elton's *The Practice of History*; *Political History: Principles and Practice*; and *Return To Essentials*.

Week 5:	Student-led seminars on chapter 1 of Carr's *What Is History?*, Elton's chapter on 'Research' (in *The Practice of History*), and the first three chapters (on post-structuralism, etc.) of *Return To Essentials*.

Week 6:	*Student-led seminar* on Tony Bennett's chapter ('Literature/History') in *Outside Literature*.

Week 7:	*On Richard Rorty*. An overview of Rorty's position, based on his chapter 'Pragmatism, Relativism and Irrationalism', in *Consequences of Pragmatism* (where Rorty outlines his sort of pragmatism in an accessible, general way), and the early chapters of *Contingency, Irony and Solidarity*.

Week 8:	*On Hayden White*. Overview of White's work, drawing especially on 'The Historical Text As Literary Artifact' in *Tropics of Discourse*, and the essays, 'The Question of Narrative in Contemporary Historical Theory', and 'The Politics of Historical Interpretation: Discipline and De-Sublimation' in *The Content of the Form*.

Week 9:	*On Hayden White*. Overview of *Metahistory* based upon its 'Preface', 'Introduction' and 'Conclusion'.

Week 10:	*Seminar on Rorty*. Based on 'The Contingency of Language' in *Contingency, Irony and Solidarity*.

Week 11:	*Student-led seminar* on White's *Metahistory*, especially the 'Introduction' and 'Conclusion'.

Week 12:	*Resumé of the course*. General discussion and comments on the essays submitted at the end of Week 11.

Essay Title: 'What is History?' What seems to be an appropriate answer to Carr's old question today?

Such a Course will have a bibliography, divided into three sections:

1	Books by Carr, Elton, Bennett, Rorty and White.[21]
2	General background.
3	Selected, relevant articles.

The above course is, very obviously, just one attempt to try and get undergraduate historians interested in and involved in some of the particular, 'radical', textual-type debates which are currently in the literature, and which connect up to some of the wider currents ebbing and flowing around the fairly conservative discourses of history. It is not, of course, some definitive model, but I have developed and run courses based on the sorts of arguments presented here, and with the same sort of structure, assignment title, bibliography, etc. It is therefore presented as a 'workable sketch' in the hope that it might be useful to others.

Notes

1   In this paper I use the phrase 'history theory' throughout, even though it looks and sounds odd. But this oddness is significant I think, indicating just how unusual it is to even think of 'history theory'.

2   T. Bennett, *Outside Literature* (Routledge, London, 1990), p. 50.

3   Ibid., p. 49.

4   Ibid., p. 50.

5   Ibid., p. 51.

6   White defines history throughout his works, but most precisely in *Tropics of Discourse: Essays in Cultural Criticism* (Johns Hopkins, Baltimore, 1978), p. 82, and in *Metahistory: The Historical Imagination in Nineteenth Century Europe* (Johns Hopkins, Baltimore, 1973), p. ix.

7   On tropes, see especially the 'Introduction' to White's *Metahistory*.

8   There is sometimes a confusion between metahistory and metanarrative. For White, metahistory refers to the formal structures *all* histories have in both the upper and lower case. Thus, it is no use 'proper' historians attacking metahistory as if it has nothing to do with them: their histories are as much metahistorical as everyone else's; therefore they are attacking themselves. Metanarratives, are simply histories in the upper case.

9   H. White, 'Preface' to *The Content of the Form: Narrative Discourse and Historical Representation* (Johns Hopkins, Baltimore, 1987).

10   F. R. Ankersmit's reply to P. Zagorin, *History and Theory*, 29 (1990), pp. 174–96.

11   Ibid., p. 278.

12   White, *Tropics of Discourse*, pp. 101–20.

13   White, *Content of the Form*, p. 48.

14   White, *Tropics of Discourse*, p. 3.

15   L. Stone, 'History and Post-Modernism III', and G. M. Spiegel, 'History and Post-Modernism IV', *Past and Present*, 135 (1992), pp. 189–94, 194–208. See also, P. Joyce, 'History and Post-Modernism I', and C. Kelly, 'History and Post-Modernism II', *Past and Present*, 133 (1991), pp. 204–9,

209–13; G. Elton, *Return to Essentials: Reflections on the Present State of Historical Studies* (Cambridge University Press, Cambridge, 1991), *passim*; A. Marwick, 'A Fetishism of Documents?: The Salience of Source-Based History', in *Developments in Modern Historiography*, ed. H. Kozicki (St Martin, New York, 1993), pp. 107–38.

16   E. Fox-Genovese, 'Literary Criticism and the Politics of the New Historicism', in *The New Historicism*, ed. H. A. Veeser (Routledge, London, 1989), pp. 213–24.

17   H. White, 'New Historicism: A Comment', in *New Historicism*, ed. Veeser, p. 297.

18   R. Samuel, 'Reading The Signs II', *History Workshop*, 33 (1992), p. 220.

19   Bennett, *Outside Literature*, pp. 41–77, *passim*.

20   T. Bennett, *Formalism and Marxism* (Routledge, London, 1979).

21   Books in this first section would be T. Bennett's *Outside Literature* (London, 1991); E. H. Carr's *What is History?* (London, 1961); G. Elton's *The Practice of History* (Sydney, 1967) and *Return to Essentials* (Cambridge, 1991); R. Rorty's *Philosophy and the Mirror of Nature* (Princeton, 1980), *Consequences of Pragmatism* (Princeton, 1980) and *Contingency, Irony, & Solidarity* (Cambridge, 1989); H. White's *Tropics of Discourse* (London, 1978) and *Metahistory* (London, 1973).

Further Reading

The further reading suggested here does not include any of the books and articles already noted, but gives titles which might be useful to complement them.

Since the chapter was written, J. Appleby, L. Hunt and M. Jacob have published what promises to be a best-seller: *Telling The Truth About History* (Norton, New York, 1994). Radical and feminist in intent but anti-postmodernist, their text ranges over the rise and fall of 'proper', positivistic, scientific histories, the 'fall' being caused by the (for them) interrelated phenomena of mass university education in the USA and postmodern tendencies. It can be highly recommended as an introduction to contemporary debates. J. Baudrillard's *The Illusion of the End* (Polity, Oxford, 1994) is a brilliantly suggestive set of 'speculations' on the notion of the 'end of history'. J. W. Scott's *Gender and the Politics of History* (Columbia University Press, New York, 1988), though now a little old, is still the best introduction to feminist history and postmodernism in general. More difficult, and drawing increasingly on Derrida, two books by D. Elam mix postmodernism and feminism in thought-provoking ways: *Romancing the Postmodern* and *Feminism and Deconstruction* (Routledge, London, 1992 and 1994). *Objectivity, Method and Point of View*, ed. W. J. Van der Dussen and L. Rubinoff (E/J. Barill, Leiden, 1991) critiques postmodern approaches by way of analytical philosophy amongst other approaches.

Over the years, the journal *History and Theory* has often and critically addressed the issues of post-structuralism, postmodernism, 'narrative' and the work of Hayden White. Articles particularly relevant to the discussion in this chapter are F. R. Ankersmit's 'The Dilemma of Contemporary Anglo-Saxon Philosophy of History', 25 (1986), pp. 1–27, and 'Historiography and Postmodernism', 28 (1989), pp. 137–53; D. Carr's 'Narrative and the Real World: An Argument For Continuity', 25 (1986), pp. 117–31; and C. Strout, 'Border Crossings: History, Fiction and Dead Certainties', 31 (1992), pp. 153–62. In a similar fashion, *Social History* has recently been discussing the impact of postmodernism on history. A recent article by P. Joyce, 'The End of Social History?', *Social History*, 20 (1995), pp. 73–91, summarizes much of the discussion which has been taking place and includes ideas for a new 'postmodern history' after those so closely connected to modernity are seen as increasingly moribund. The journals *Gender and History*, *Economy and Society*, *The Oxford Literary Review*, *New Left Review* and *Textual Practice* also regularly carry articles extending the arguments introduced in this chapter.

PART II

Reviewing Traditional Methods

6

Teaching and Learning in Lectures

Peter N. Stearns

Lecturing – delivering prepared remarks to a group of students – is one of the oldest forms of teaching, dating back, in the western tradition, to medieval universities where it was the principal means of conveying information. It is by the same token an archaic form in certain respects, as it antedated the easy availability of information through printed books (and more recently other media). Lecturing is widely criticized as a means of teaching, both because it establishes a hierarchy of authority between lecturer and students and because it enjoins a rather passive learning mode on the audience. Since the student upheavals of the 1960s, blasts at the political implications and potential mindlessness of lecture attendance have been quite popular. At the same time, lecturing remains widespread in higher education. This may reflect sheer inertia, and some teachers' preference for seizing centre stage and manifesting their knowledge and authority. It also reflects financial realities, particularly in underfunded disciplines like history where large classes help universities earn money. In the United States, freshman history classes of several hundred students are quite common, at both public and private institutions, and popular lecturers or topics even in upper-level history courses also draw considerable crowds. Finally, lecturing can be more than a fallback, traditional teaching mode; properly done, it can encourage effective learning. Lecturers face real options in method and subject matter, and sensible decisions reduce the boring routine that can unquestionably creep into the large classroom.

Virtually any history tutor has encountered stultifying lectures, delivered in a monotone, sometimes read outright from notes yellowing with age or even from textbooks, droning endlessly on while students fidget, doodle and think about other things. Even lively lectures are sometimes badly planned in relation to other teaching options. But a good lecture can be an artistic gem, and at the risk of displaying my own authoritarian streak I must confess a real pleasure in preparing and delivering lectures (which I have done for years in a 300-student freshman world history class). This brief discussion of the lecture form seeks to pick up on the frequent criticisms, towards offering some guidelines against bad usage. At the same time, it presents lectures as something more than an outdated, unfortunate necessity; good lectures can stimulate students' understanding of history and historical analysis.

Various proposals have been offered, and occasionally acted upon, to eliminate lecturing from the teaching armamentarium of most tutors in disciplines like history. At one extreme, reformers advocate televising the best lectures of the best lecturers, thus utilising the formal presentation while taking advantage of modern technology to drain away all but the cream of the crop. Televised or filmed lectures have gained a place in off-campus distance learning, while deliveries taped on cassettes have won some popularity among adults who advance their education while driving or engaging in other activities. Occasionally, televised lectures are presented in college classes. The option has not swept away ordinary, day-to-day classroom lectures, however, in part because tutors defend their turf against high-tech, elite incursions, and also because personally delivered lectures, even if rather formal, permit some human contact that watching film or reading textbooks cannot. Seeing a live instructor, able usually to ask questions at least after the lecture, students gain some momentum that even the best filmed offerings cannot provide.

At the other extreme, recent critics of the lecture mode have been experimenting with what might be called anti-lectures, even in fairly large classrooms. The purpose here is to develop active student participation and to reduce or eliminate any special teacher authority. Some of this experimentation relates not only to hostility to the lecturing mode but also to recent attacks on conventional history in the name of relativism. If history is in large part the personal creation of any given historian, students should not be exposed to artificially reinforced truth claims. Rather, they should develop their own truths, in ways the conventional structure of a lecture inhibits. Experimental classrooms often encourage student group-work with subsequent presentations. Or, in place of lectures, source materials are offered, through slides and overheads, which students can then develop into historical accounts. Instead of lecturing, the tutor becomes a facilitator and co-ordinator, carefully avoiding any special claims to expertise. Experimentation of this sort has been limited to date. Properly done, it demands extensive preparation by the tutor and also, frequently, a considerable staff of teaching assistants to support the student groups. It may gain ground in future, but thus far it does not even rival the televised lecture as an alternative to more conventional lecturing modes.

Within the conventional history classroom, lecturing takes many forms, depending on tutor preference and class size. Formal, hour-long lectures fill many survey courses. In smaller classes, full lectures are a rarity but teachers often break into a lecture mode for at least part of the class period, when student discussion cannot appropriately get at the goals being sought or where student preparation is too deficient to permit intelligent discussion in the first place. Whether formal or not, lectures benefit from certain guidelines, some of them fairly obvious, some the fruit of more subtle experience. For the fact is that lectures can be mishandled, not only by poor delivery but by inadequate planning and goal-setting. Lecturers do have authority, and this may encourage them to ramble on without much attention to audience needs. Their authority is also fragile. Students may come to class but their attention needs to be elicited and sustained; it cannot be mandated save very indirectly, and often incompletely, through examinations that call upon lecture coverage. Lecturing is a cost-efficient mode of teaching, in that an instructor can 'handle' dozens, even hundreds of students (supplemented perhaps by some graduate students paid even less to grade tests and papers). At a private university in the United States, a lecture (room and utilities aside) may cost well under 1 per cent of what students are paying in tuition for the course. But this very efficiency demands some correctives. Lecturers must be given time to prepare well and must be monitored and evaluated. Their considerable impact on large numbers of students ought to necessitate careful planning.

There is no form of teaching so easily abused as lecturing, for there is no other form where it is so easy to fall in love with one's own gifts – regardless (almost) of student reactions. Teachers who lead discussions, whatever their fascination with their prowess or their ability to blame students' poor preparation for failures, can scarcely escape some recurrent feedback. Even choices of reading elicit student comment as well as being reflected in performance on tests. But the lecture is so much the creation of the instructor that miscalculations are perilously easy, with student inattention, sleeping, or non-attendance either not noticed – for it is easy not to see the audience while speaking – or blamed on the students themselves. Students (including teachers themselves, on occasions such as summer training institutes when they turn back into students) often value lectures simply because they allow them to park, without thought, or be entertained, or accept authority unconditionally.

Few historians choose to go into history teaching because they know they love to lecture, much less because they have any particular skill at lecturing. Few graduate students receive explicit training or experience in lecturing. Many – and I was once among them – never give a lecture until, doctorates in hand, they are thrown in front of their own class, which may number in the hundreds. Most learn by doing, and some become extremely adept. Some, gifted speakers and dramatists by nature, do well from the first; others improve more gradually. Almost all would benefit by fuller awareness of some general rules of the game, flexibly interpreted to allow for diverse settings and skills.

Lecturing should not monopolize a history course, which does not mean that the genre is to be condemned. Classes that are small enough to permit discussion should insist on discussion, spiced only occasionally with formal lectures. In the United States, the most common current complaints about unnecessary lecturing involve high-school history classes, where size readily permits interaction but where some teachers prefer simply to talk at the students, reducing the latter's involvement and enhancing a sense that history consists of little but a litany of facts, drily presented. At the college or university level, large classes where lecturing is essential should be subdivided at least once a week for discussions where student participation is featured – and no lecturing permitted. Because lectures do encourage passivity, they must not consume the teaching process, in history or in any other subject. Few instructors would want them to, but economics, in the United States, occasionally dictates nothing-but-lecture classes in which students' morale, predictably, plummets as their captivity grates. This said, it remains possible not only to have lectures work when no other options are available, but to make them positive assets in a history teaching programme.

Bringing Students In

The first enhancements to the lecture mode involve combating student passivity. Student involvement is crucial, for this is really what elevates the standard lecture over a masterpiece lecture series on television. Involvement includes making sure the lecturer stays around for questions after a session, and insisting that these are welcomed. Availability for further questions or clarifications in office hours or (increasingly) through electronic mail is also important.

Student involvement also occurs through raising questions during the lecture itself. Except in rare instances when I have a certain amount of material to get across or when I know student preparation will be inadequate (e.g. right after a test or paper), I routinely address questions to a student audience of two to three hundred. The result is not a real discussion, and typically the same 10 per cent among the audience do most of the talking. But there is real exchange, and the passive mould is broken not only for participants but for at least some others who are thinking through their own responses even if the setting inhibits their explicit involvement. Some lecturers go further, by deliberately asking questions of students at random, to encourage better participation and to gain feedback from the more reticent. The lecture-jewel, presented to an audience silent until question time, remains a valid contribution, but it should not and need not be regular fare in a history course. Learning to bring in the audience is a vital addition to standard lecturing skills.

In fact, again to use a personal example, I regularly schedule about a fifth of my lectures to my World History audience of two hundred in terms of a collective pursuit of only one or two basic questions. An early lecture thus asks students to help me think through the basic advantages and disadvantages of an agricultural economy, compared to its 'hunting-and-gathering' predecessor. A later entry focuses almost entirely on the issue of whether, in a world history context, the United States should be thought of as a separate civilization – American exceptionalism – or as an extension of West European civilization. I provide brief context for the discussion, and a brief conclusion, but that is it – everything else is up for grabs, and I never know exactly what topics the discussion will evoke. The result spills over into more orthodox lectures in which questioning is more sporadic, for students know there is a participatory intent.

Student involvement, finally, occurs through various other techniques designed to break the routines. Several initiatives are designed to grab student attention during the lecture itself. Students may be asked periodically to produce a summary of the lecture, during the last five minutes of class; these can be spot-checked, not actually graded (or graded only on pass – fail basis) as a means of ascertaining the effectiveness of the lecture and pulling students into greater alertness. Or

students may be asked to list the three most important questions the
lecture has raised – again, not for a grade but for a fuller sense of
participation; a subsequent lecture might then address some of the leading issues these responses have established. Or students may be polled
about their responses to key questions – how many believe that Germany
caused the First World War, or that women rather than men governed
the adoption of new birth-control techniques in the nineteenth century.
Questions students generate at the outset of a lecture – What do you
know about topic X? – reproduced on a transparency, may be used to
guide the subsequent, quick-on-the-feet lecturer comments, with students drawn in because they had helped orchestrate the show. Obviously,
if a standard lecture – discussion mix is employed (a small-group class
once a week, combined with two larger lectures; the standard routine in
freshman history courses in the United States), discussion sections ought
routinely to pull in some questions about previous lectures, helping to
relate them to other materials being analysed, again to encourage active
use of lecture content.

   The most important attempts to experiment with greater student
involvement, including such simple techniques as asking some open-
ended questions, need to be timed with attention spans in mind. Research indicates that the middle 20–30 minutes of an hour-long lecture
require the greatest enlivening, where interruptions can most benefit
learning. Lecturers in some problem-focused disciplines, as in the sciences, are increasingly inserting some quick group-work into this period.
They let students cluster in twos or threes to solve a problem, with
results quickly reported back and then integrated into the next lecture
segment. This technique can be used in history lectures as well. Take, for
example, a lecture early in a World History course, designed to help
students understand comparative analysis by looking at major features of
Han China and Gupta India. It is fairly simple actually to break for five
minutes, with students (clustered in small groups where they sit) asked
to produce short lists of two major political similarities, two major political differences. A few of the lists can be collected and then worked into
the next phase of the lecture. As computer facilities spread in lecture
halls – admittedly, a dream still for many history lecturers – these
response exercises will become even more routine. And some problems
can simply be set to students for five minutes' worth of work on their
own, in the context established by the preceding lecture segment with a
follow-up on the lecturer's own resolution of the problem bridging to the
next portion of the class. The goal always is a variation in presentation

style designed to make lecture segments more assimilable, while drawing students into the same kind of problem analysis that the lecture itself undertakes.

All of the techniques designed to enhance involvement require the history lecturer to be alert and inventive. The superficial convenience of canned, read-from-the-notes monologues is abandoned, or at least limited. But the enjoyability of the session, from the lecturer's own standpoint, may go up in the process, and this too can increase effectiveness.

Student participation, finally, also means providing opportunities for lectures to be evaluated, and not simply at the end of a course when remediation can only benefit a subsequent audience. Course evaluations have become standard in most lecture courses in the United States. An early or at least midway assessment is even more useful in giving students a sense that the lecturer cares about their reactions and is willing to modify in their light. The resultant atmosphere seems particularly desirable in the current collegiate climate, where students like to be able to sound off and to feel that authorities are responsive, but the evaluation produces more explicit benefits as well. A simple early questionnaire, for example, can ask students to rate such issues as the lecturer's speed of speech and audibility, the quality of lecture organisation in terms of note-taking, whether too much or not enough information is being provided and the extent to which the lecture unduly repeats established material or races too fast ahead; students can respond on a three-point scale of good, a bit of a problem, and bad. Midpoint questionnaires can raise these performance issues but also ask about topics students would like to expand or curtail in the next set of lectures.

Organization and Structure

Organizing a lecture well forms the most obvious precondition for this mode of history teaching. Novice lecturers quite properly worry about how to present their material effectively, and even old hands have to consider whether their organization properly meets the needs of a student audience. While styles vary, the structure of a lecture should be clearly established in advance, and it should be conveyed to students by means of a 'table of contents' on a chalkboard or an overhead projector. Students need this framework in order to follow the course of a lecture and to take good notes. Solid organization does not preclude the occasional excursion, sometimes in response to a student comment or question, but the lecturer must be responsible for sticking to the plan fairly clearly and relating any deviation to that plan.

Lecturers should not attempt to make too many separate points. Three or four basic points, diversely illustrated and sometimes subtly repeated, are all that a fifty-minute span really allows. An extremely detailed lecture with hosts of subtopics simply cannot be followed save by an expert audience at a professional conference. In a really oral culture, memory for spoken remarks is much better than it is in the literate culture in which students participate; covering a few basic points well is preferable to a more ambitious reach that leaves most of the audience groping for coherence. Earnest, well-informed novice lecturers most frequently err in trying to cover too much.

It is also important, again, to heed student attention span. Students remember best in the first and the last five-to-ten-minute segments of a fifty-minute lecture. This means that the first portion of a lecture should not be wasted by summing up a previous session or covering minor details (including excessive announcements). Here is the chance to get at least one of the main points across, or possibly to anticipate all three. The final portion (until students become restive because they must get to another class; good timing is part of appropriate organisation, so that the lecturer does not overstay a welcome) can drive home the third point. A lecturer may, by the same token, alternate delivery somewhat during the middle of the session. Here is an ideal time to introduce some discussion, or to provide a particularly dramatic illustration of the first or second basic point, or to drive home the first two points by some careful summary – any combination of which may improve student alertness and retention.

Careful organization of a lecture should combine with student involvement by means of some attention to student notetaking abilities. Many American students, coming to a large lecture class from relatively undemanding secondary school backgrounds, really do not know how to take effective notes. The distinction between what is important and what is nonessential or supportive illustration may escape them. Good organization in the lecture itself, including some repetition, will help deal with this problem; it is particularly important to signal basic points clearly in the early portion of a history course. Students can be guided in using the lecture outline as the structure for their own notes. But it is often worth while to go further. Some historians use a segment of one of the first discussion sections to review notetaking, or at least to indicate clearly to students that tutors are available in office hours to discuss techniques. Some review an early set of notes, offering non-judgemental comments. Existing knowledge about notetaking should certainly be available to students as part of their orientation to undergraduate study, including the desirability of reviewing notes soon after a lecture to improve both outright memory and an ability to separate highlights from the less essential materials. Some tutors distribute a copy of 'good' notes after an early substantive lecture, in a freshman course, to further appropriate mechanics.

Students more frequently complain about poor lecture organization that they have trouble following than about any other point. While organization is not in fact the most important aspect of effective lecturing, none the less it is vital. Historians who begin a lecturing career frequently feel compelled to write out elaborate notes for themselves, lest they lose their way in their own nervousness. While outright reading is to be discouraged because of its deadly effect on an audience, obviously any tutor has to experiment with what works best. Most lecturers with experience reduce the elaborateness of their notes or learn to lecture – even to deliver brand new lectures – with no notes at all. Minimal notes, so long as good organization is preserved, facilitates eye-contact and other desirable interchange with students. While experience helps a lot, lecture preparation can also be eased by remembering the injunction to stress a small handful of basic points. Again, aside from lectures at formal academic conferences, the lecture is a poor place to introduce a vast array of factual material where detailed notes might be essential. Students get information better and more quickly from reading – the average lecturer requires two minutes to cover the material equivalent to a single printed page, which might be read far more rapidly by most students. And the lecture itself will benefit from a more streamlined organizational framework that stresses, in script and in delivery, the real highlights.

Many novice lecturers, and some old hands, will also wish to pay attention to techniques beyond good organization. Audibility (often a key issue) and rapidity of speech or distracting (or ridicule-provoking) gestures or mannerisms sometimes merit concern. Having colleagues comment on these issues, or watching one's own televised performance, are painful experiences but they are preferable to student disdain or disinterest. Student evaluations may signal the need to return to some form of feedback in these areas. Students will poke fun at even the best of lecturers, for this is a means of coming to terms with their authority; too much sensitivity is unwise. Obviously, however, lecture delivery should be effective even if occasionally and unwittingly amusing, which is where recurrent self-appraisal comes in.

Special Effects

Lectures may be spiced by a variety of eye-catching techniques. Some historians love to be remembered for lectures which they deliver in costume, or for other efforts at narrative dramatization. Some lecturers are adept at humour, using both prepared jokes and spontaneous repartee to help establish a conducive atmosphere and (in some cases) to further their reputation for showmanship. Slides legitimately bring artistic materials in for comments, and the slide lecture is something of a special form of the genre. Overheads may provide the outline of a lecture and possibly some other specific information, such as statistical data. Computer aids may provide background materials as well as outlines, along with e-mail for questions; here is a lecture enhancement that is bound to expand. And the inventive historian can easily imagine other special features that would embellish a lecture presentation.

Some caveats apply, however. Special effects may be remembered better than the material they are meant to emphasize. A joke (and this is the special effect to which I am most addicted) that draws a great laugh may distract from the next point. Slides may require so much specific discussion that they distract from any sense of overall structure, particularly when too many are crammed into a single session, in a darkened room that may encourage more somnolence than aesthetic appreciation. Overhead outlines may sometimes lure both lecturer and audience into needless oversimplification, as one set of 'bullets' after another is placed on the screen and then read aloud, with little variance, by the lecturer – an insult to audience intelligence that is happily more common in presentations by businessmen or academic administrators than in those offered by practising historians.

The rule of thumb is clear: special effects should be chosen carefully, and not overextended so that they overwhelm the real message. Relief of dry lecturing is fine, particularly in the middle portion of a session, but it is possible to shift unduly into an entertainment syndrome that makes for popularity but little learning.

Basic Purposes

This last set of points is far and away the most important, for without careful consideration of the reasons for giving a lecture in the first place all the organization, student involvement and cheerful distractions in the world cannot justify the genre as a means of history teaching. History lectures really have three purposes, in my judgement, if they are not merely to be time-fillers for instructors and students alike. First, as already suggested, they present an educated human being to students, for some potential contact and guidance. Second, they may provide a certain amount of information. Third, and most fundamentally, they aid students in the difficult process of historical analysis.

Here, I do take issue with some otherwise-sensible recent comments on the lecture form (not specifically addressed to historians). Graham Gibbs, for example, emphasizes the utility of lectures in helping students remember specific facts, while shying away from using lectures to help students 'synthesize or put together information in new ways'. It is true, of course, that a history lecture that repeats some data students have already encountered, or will encounter, in reading will help drive home memory-retention. And it is also true that students remember some good stories told in a lecture. Overall, however, the evidence on deriving tremendous mnemonic benefits from history lectures is disappointing. In contrast, the experience of using lectures to help students learn how to analyse historical data, to identify and begin to help solve conceptual problems, is quite encouraging. Lectures that spend time breaking down the process of comparing societies in the past, or identifying periodization and explaining the criteria used to arrive at it in terms of change and continuity, or discussing causation, promote student abilities to accomplish these same goals in their own work.

This means that, in history lecturing at least, the informational purpose of lectures should be kept within rigorous bounds for, as I have already suggested, the lecture is not really the best way to present data, given the time and the difficulties of memorization involved. (College students retain about 60 per cent of lecture data on average, and they usually cannot go back to check for gaps or garbling). Almost any history teacher will need to convey factual information through lectures at some point because of a particular blend of enthusiasm and expertise about some historical passage or because of a lacuna in available reading that can be efficiently filled no other way. But these should be occasional uses.

Lectures should never be substitutes for textbooks or other reading, and if a historian finds her/himself moving towards that mode s/he should really consider writing up some segments for distribution to the class, even if outright publication is a distant prospect.

As a rule, lectures should play off the assigned reading, in order to highlight major analytical issues, at whatever level is appropriate to the students involved. In the process, students will gain a better understanding of the kinds of facts a course is emphasizing, and the uses to which these facts should be put – but not because the lecture introduces new data so much as utilizes materials initially encountered in the reading. Lectures are ideal spots, for example, to deal with problems of periodization or causation, to enhance students' grasp of how historical analysis proceeds. Lectures can grapple with conflicting interpretations, helping students see what the crucial issues are and what options are available to emerge from dispute with a defendable choice or resolution. In world history, an increasingly common genre for lecture-based teaching, comparisons among civilizations constitute another conceptual focus for recurrent lectures. The lecture, in sum, exhibits historical thinking at work, defining and resolving or elaborating problems of interpretation while relying primarily on factual materials the students should already have addressed. Even if students lag in their reading, a not uncommon phenomenon in an imperfect world, such that the lecture serves as an advance organizer allowing them to approach their subsequent work more intelligently, the goal of furthering analytical sophistication can be met. The lecture, in sum, is the ideal spot to move a history course from a purely factual parade – one damned thing after another – to its proper position as an exercise in which facts are employed towards greater understanding of the past.

Lectures in this sense serve history in much the same function, though with radically different trappings, as the science or mathematics session in which an instructor works through equations. Good history lectures efficiently, but with a flexible, personal touch, guide students through the process of thinking problems through. Analytically centred lectures blend well with attendant discussion sections, where students are asked to perform some of the same tasks more directly. They also relate to the open-ended, participatory qualities that a lecture should strive for, as the interpretive focus encourages questions to and comments from the student audience.

Finally, lectures devoted primarily to issues of analysis offer the greatest potential for commanding the enthusiasm of the lecturer her/

himself – a vital ingredient in making the lecture a successful teaching instrument. Lectures command no small amount of energy. Part of this goes into simple showmanship, offering the gestures and changes of pace that keep the presentation lively. Most, however, goes to conveying the sense of excitement about the historical issues that the historian wishes students, at least periodically, to share. The lecture is the place where, in the most direct form available, students glimpse a historian at work, and if this work is not performed with relish, students will quickly grasp the message: the whole enterprise is a compulsory waste of time. To keep enthusiasm high, lecturers need to feel the importance of the basic points they are trying to convey. They need to use the lecture to establish and justify the significance of the materials the course is presenting, which is why, as a rule, the focus on analytical concerns, where facts are used to deal with problems, works best. Enthusiasm also requires periodic reworkings of established lectures. Redoing a number of lectures annually allows the lecturer to keep up with new findings and to cast aside some approaches that have not worked optimally, but above all the renewal works to give the lecturer her/himself the challenge not of offering cut-and-dried summaries but of answering serious questions.

Using lectures to work through historical problems maintains the distinctiveness of the genre as a teaching form. No longer routinely useful to convey information, requiring careful controls to assure student involvement, the lecture provides a class with a hands-on analytical experience more immediate and dramatic than reading or even televised talks can offer. The experience is also more sophisticated than student discussion can be, thought it should help prepare participation in the same kinds of analytical tasks. Sound organization, appropriate techniques, and flexibility, when combined with an explicit and enthusiastic sense of purpose, make the lecture more than an unfortunate necessity in the teaching of history. A good lecture joins tutor and students in a joint effort to make sense of a historical problem, in a way no other form quite permits.

Further Reading

For those who wish to explore the process of lecturing in some detail, see G. Brown, *Lecturing and Explaining* (Methuen, London, 1978) and J. McLeish, *The Lecture Method* (Cambridge Institute of Education, Cambridge, 1968). There are also succinct accounts of the research contained in some general texts on teaching and learning in higher education, and particularly worth mentioning here are G. Brown and M. Atkins, *Effective Teaching in Higher*

Education (Methuen, London, 1988); J. Beard and J. Hartley, *Teaching and Learning in Higher Education* (Harper Row, London, 1984), and E. Fenton, *Teaching in Colleges and Universities* (forthcoming).

The problem of teaching large classes is a growing one in the UK. Here, G. Gibbs, *Lecturing to More Students* (PCFC, Bristol, 1992) offers practical guidance, as does G. Gibbs, S. and T. Habeshaw, *53 Interesting Things to do in your Lectures* (Technical and Educational Services, Bristol, 1989), and *53 Interesting Ways to Teach Large Classses* (Technical and Educational Services, Bristol, 1992). P. Cryer and L. Elton, *Active Learning in Large Classes and with Increasing Numbers of Students* (CVCP, Sheffield, 1992) suggest ways of increasing student involvement.

In the United States and Australia there is much expertise in teaching large groups of students. Particularly useful are *Teaching Large Classes Well*, ed. M. G. Weimer (Jossey-Bass, San Francisco, 1987); L. W. Andresen, *Lecturing to Large Groups: A Guide to Doing it Less but Better* (Tertiary Education Research Centre, University of New South Wales, Kensington, 1988), and R. Cannon, *Lecturing* (HERDSA, Kensington, 1988).

7

Seminars for Active Learning

George Preston

The term 'seminar' is a brief and convenient term that frequently appears on timetables but often covers a diverse range of activities. In the author's experience, and within the published research on seminars, dissatisfaction is often expressed both by students and tutors as to the effectiveness of what takes place during these sessions. For example, staff often comment on the fact that students are not willing or are not sure how to contribute to discussion or do not appear to have done the necessary preparation. Students comment about the fact that the seminar turns into a mini-lecture with the tutor indicating that it is the only way that she/he can cover all the work. Another complaint from students concerns fellow students who say little or nothing in seminars but concentrate on taking notes and then gain high marks for subsequent assignments, having given nothing to other group members. The purpose of this chapter is not to lay down a prescriptive recipe of what should take place in seminars but to discuss some important issues which can affect the quality of what happens, and to offer some suggestions for action.

It would be possible to devote the whole of this chapter to a discussion of what a seminar is and how it differs from other activities in which small groups of students and tutors are involved on history courses. Some writers on learning and teaching methods use the term 'seminar' to describe only one particular set of activities. Habeshaw, for example, defines a seminar as 'a session in which a student presents a prepared paper to a group and is then expected to lead the discussion based on it'.[1]

To avoid the difficulties attendant upon such a precise definition, other writers prefer to refer simply to 'small group work'. Such definitions offer useful insights into some of the things that might be taking place in seminars; for example, that students may lead activities and that it is a group activity. For the purpose of this chapter I am going to use the term 'seminar' to cover the whole range of activities that may take place when working with small groups of history students.

As a starting point it is perhaps helpful to list some of the key attributes of seminars, as mundane aspects, such as location, can often have a significant effect on what learning actually occurs.

- the group meets at a prescribed time;
- the group meets in a prescribed location;
- the session has a fixed duration;
- one or more tutors are usually present;
- the number of students is usually eight to fifteen;
- there is a free exchange of ideas between all members of the group;
- tutor(s) and students may all provide the stimulus and responses for the session.

A key aspect of most history seminars is the free exchange of ideas between all members of the group, and it can be quite illuminating to analyse what is going on in a seminar by sketching diagrams of the interaction between participants and any group leader if one is appointed. Observations of this nature are best undertaken by an impartial observer who is not involved in the seminar. Later we shall consider how such things as seating arrangements can influence the exchange of ideas.

Why Seminars?

Research on learning in groups indicates that some aims of higher education in general can most effectively be achieved through seminars. Abercrombie and Terry see the distinctive feature of seminars as being the vehicle through which students can develop autonomy,[2] or, in the words of Boud, 'the ability to learn more effectively without the constant presence or intervention of a teacher'.[3] Jaques makes a useful distinction between what he calls the 'intrinsic' and 'extrinsic' aims of learning in groups.[4] He suggests that the outcome of a discussion, say, on the causes of the First World War, may be seen as being extrinsic to the process and might be achieved in some other way. He suggests that through the process of discussion students develop the more highly prized aims of higher education, including the development of:

* imaginative and creative thinking;
* a critical and informed mind;
* an awareness of others' interests and needs;
* a sense of academic rigour;
* a social conscience;
* a willingness to share ideas;
* an ability, and sense of enjoyment, in lifelong learning.[5]

A moment's reflection on the above reveals that none of the highly prized aims relate to specific subject knowledge. They all describe those human qualities that are highly valued by most people in all walks of life. The majority of students studying history in higher education will not become professional historians, but enter a wide range of careers, many not calling upon the subject content of the students' higher education at all. In the current economic climate, employers require an adaptable workforce able to work in collaboration with others. Most people's careers are likely to change direction several times during their working life. The above qualities are equally important to people in their personal and social life if it is to be fulfilling. Tutors and students also have more specific objectives in seminars, such as being able to check that a lecture has been understood and to answer students' questions. The purpose of this chapter is not to overlook these more specific objectives but to consider issues that inhibit groups from achieving the more highly prized aims and to offer some strategies for enhancing the quality of seminars.

Approaches to Learning

Before discussing the ways seminars can enable students to achieve the prized outcomes of learning it is necessary to consider the relationships between approaches to learning, learning outcomes and course design.

One of the most seminal concepts on student learning in the last twenty years has its origins in the work of Ference Marton and Roger Säljö in Sweden.[6] Their original research focused on the way students learnt from written texts but has since been developed in numerous ways to explore the approach students take to learning in many subject areas and in differing contexts. This body of research has established that some students set out on a new learning task with the intention of making connections with previous learning and experience, question what they are doing, search for personal understanding and tend to be self-motivated. It is interesting to note that this set of intentions has many affinities with the highly prized aims of higher education. These students are said to have adopted a *deep approach* to learning. At the other end of the spectrum, some students tend only to memorize facts considered important for immediate assessment purposes, fail to make connections to previous learning and experience, do not search for personal understanding and tend to be driven by the external demands of the assessment system. These students are said to have adopted a *surface approach* to learning. In reality, learners may adopt a whole range of approaches between these two extremes.

While the evidence suggests that students tend to have a favoured style of learning it is important to appreciate that students may frequently switch between approaches depending on the demands of the situation. If a student adopts a deep approach in a particular learning situation it is a result of the interaction between that student and the learning experience rather than an attribute of the student. It follows from this that if a tutor wishes to bring about a change in a student's approach to learning, from a surface to deep approach, it is necessary to address the design of the whole learning experience. In particular this has important implications for modes of assessment which are well documented as having a significant influence on learning outcomes. It is also important to appreciate that it is the *intention* of the student that is most important, so this does not preclude a student from engaging in rote learning if this will be subsequently used to come to a greater understanding of the subject matter. Evidence shows that what comprises deep approaches to learning differ from subject to subject.

Gibbs summarizes the course features associated with students adopting surface approaches; a heavy workload, high contact hours, excessive course material which is covered superficially, lack of student choice and a threatening assessment system.[7] Research indicates that reducing workload and contact hours, providing a clearly ordered knowledge base, creating learning contexts in which the motivation comes from the student rather than being externally imposed and providing opportunities for students to work collaboratively will all contribute to a learning environment that encourages a deep approach to learning. An inspection of these course characteristics reveals the need to address aspects of course design, course presentation and assessment to bring about the desired changes.

So far the relationship between approaches to learning and course characteristics has been explored but not the relationship between approaches to learning and learning outcomes. Ramsden reviews the literature that demonstrates a positive link between a deep approach to learning and the more highly prized learning outcomes.[8] He argues that while a surface approach prevents effective learning, a deep approach does not guarantee it as other factors must also be taken into account. He highlights the need for vigilance in developing assessment schemes, even at degree level, as many only require the adoption of surface approaches for success. Various instruments have been devised which can be used to investigate the approach to learning being adopted by students. Gibbs, uses a questionnaire, derived from a much longer one, which provides an insight into three aspects of the approach to learning adopted by students. Students who achieve a high score on the 'achieving orientation' tend to be well organized in their study and competitive. Students who attain a high score on the 'reproducing orientation' adopt a surface approach to learning. They tend to be driven by the requirements of a course, follow the syllabus closely and memorize material largely to pass course components. The third group of questions explore 'meaning orientation'. Students who score well in this part have a desire to make sense of a subject and are prepared to explore beyond the boundaries defined by the course assessment. They adopt a deep approach to learning.[9] The following sections explore ways in which the learning context in seminars can be modified to encourage students to adopt a deep approach to learning.

Product or Process?

Seminars provide a valuable opportunity for students to share ideas with other students and members of staff, but this requires communication and group skills which students may not necessarily possess. My experience of working with history tutors is that there is sometimes a tension between devoting time to the subject matter of history, and to the processes, in this case 'the seminar', by which the subject is explored. Tutors do not always see it as part of their job to help students develop skills such as being able to express an argument verbally in a coherent manner, or planning to lead a discussion. Talking to students reveals that many have not had experience of this type of activity through their former educational experience and feel inhibited about contributing to group discussions, at least in the early stages of their studies. It would seem important that early in an undergraduate programme some time is devoted to a sharing of what is understood by a seminar and what responsibility each participant has to ensure that it will be a valuable learning medium for all parties. My own research, at least, suggests that time devoted to these non-subject-oriented aspects will be repaid many times over in the later parts of the course.

Tutors often feel that there is insufficient time to devote to aspects of process, or think that another colleague will be explaining and developing issues and skills of the type required. Problems increase with multi-disciplinary programmes where students tend to meet more staff and be members of more varied student groups during the course of their studies. Some institutions have implemented strategies for providing help through study-skills courses, but these seem a poor substitute for each group developing its own approach over an extended period of time.

Hidden Agendas

Have all the tutors' (and students') intentions been made explicit? Course documentation and introductory sessions may indicate that seminars are an opportunity for students to explore and consolidate ideas, but are there also other issues that have not been made explicit? Examples of these implicit agenda items that the author has come across are the expectation that students will be required to demonstrate a range of communication and group skills such as leading a discussion and working as a member of a team. While it is impossible to identify every activity a student may be involved in, it is helpful for both students and tutors if course documentation makes it explicit that a student will be expected to undertake, for example, a group presentation. This signals to students that they will have to think about how work will be apportioned to team members, how they will ensure that the resulting presentation is coherent, and how they will involve other group members. For tutors it should signal where, in their experience, advice will be most appropriately given to help students acquire what are, often, new skills. Making issues such as these explicit is even more important if students are going to be formally assessed for their contribution to presentations.

Authority

However relaxed and informal a tutor may seem, the issue of authority is one that needs to be considered by all students and tutors. Jaques and Stenhouse raise some interesting issues on this topic.[10] The tutor is 'in authority' by virtue of the position she or he holds within the institution and may use this in a 'democratic' or 'authoritarian' manner. Unfortunately, the authority is frequently used in an authoritarian, unilateral manner in an area that looms large in most students' lives: assessment. The tutor may behave in an authoritarian manner in other ways such as deciding what students will learn and the way in which it is learnt. The tutor is also 'an authority' as a result of her or his knowledge of the subject: 'He is familiar and at home with both academic institutions – conferences, journals, personnel – and the criteria and norms accepted in his field.'[11] It is important for the tutor to be aware of the authority issue and thus try to speak in a manner that leaves real openings for students. Some tutors find it quite difficult to make this change from being a director of student learning to being a facilitator of student learning. The following suggestions are examples of things you may wish to try in order to enhance the quality of seminars. All have been tried by the author and his colleagues. It goes without saying that not all the suggestions will work in all situations and for all people, but you can experiment and build on the things that you and your students find effective.

Icebreakers

If the sort of interaction referred to above is going to develop quickly it is imperative that students and staff get to know each other early in a course. It is often assumed, incorrectly, that students know each other because they are all studying history. Very often students may take other subjects for the rest of the week, live in different places and have different leisure activities so that the *only* time they come together as a 'group' is when they attend the seminar. It is therefore important that group members get to know each other. Games and tasks that have this objective are often referred to as icebreakers. Sometimes these are regarded as time wasters or 'silly games', whereas in fact they are examples of time devoted to process rather than product. An important, and sometimes overlooked, aspect of icebreaking activities is that they give individuals an opportunity to let group members know how they wish to be addressed. For example, some individuals prefer not to be addressed by the shortened forms of their name.

An activity that can be used to help with learning names involves the group sitting in a circle and throwing a soft ball to one another at random. To begin with, the person throwing the ball gives their name, but, after a short time the rules are changed so that the person in possession of the ball has to say the name of the person they are throwing it to. An alternative strategy is to ask each member of the group to introduce themselves to the group. It is often helpful if guidelines are agreed beforehand so that each member of the group is offering similar information about themselves. A variation on this activity involves each group member 'interviewing' her or his immediate neighbour for about two or three minutes and introducing that person to the rest of the group. This activity has the advantage that the initial interaction can be less threatening for some, as it takes place between just two students.

The introduction to the whole group can be dispensed with altogether and each person asked to introduce themselves to just two or three members of the group that they have not previously met. An activity that can be usefully combined with many icebreakers is to draw a plan of where group members are currently sitting. This can be done either as an individual or group activity. The act of writing down names can help in associating names with individuals even if the seating arrangement is only short lived.

Ground Rules

Early in this chapter I indicated that dissatisfaction with what takes place in seminars sometimes arises from members of the group not knowing what is expected of them. These difficulties can often be overcome by having a set of explicit rules of which everyone is aware. Developing these rules is another activity that is best started in one of the early sessions with a new group. The rules need not be set in concrete and can be updated as and when appropriate. Many of the rules may be arrived at by discussion within the group, or a tutor may suggest certain basic rules and give everyone a chance to discuss them. Examples of some ground rules which I have used are:

• each member of the group is expected to prepare for a seminar;

- each member of the group is entitled to make a regular contribution to discussion;
- group members will not interrupt other group members when they are speaking.

Group Size

The ideal size for seminar groups probably lies between eight and fifteen students. Within the present climate in higher education, groups are tending to grow in size so that seminar groups frequently exceed fifteen. The larger the size the more likely it is that one or more members will be reluctant to contribute. There are various ways of temporarily reducing the effective group size to make the situation less threatening to group members, but one of the most effective and easiest to operate is 'pyramiding'. The general procedure is as follows.

- Students work on their own for five minutes. This can give the more reticent an opportunity to prepare their contribution.
- Students discuss an issue in pairs for ten minutes. This provides a safe environment in which ideas can be explored.
- Two pairs share their findings with each other for a further ten minutes or so.
- Finally there is a plenary session with the whole group.

The whole process is represented in figure 7.1.

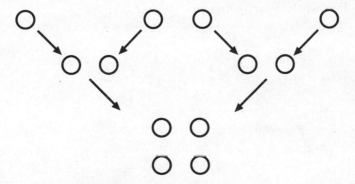

Figure 7.1   Pyramiding
Students work on their own for five minutes.
Students work in pairs for ten minutes.
Groups of four work for a further ten minutes.
Plenary.

Seating Arrangements

Many rooms used for seminars leave rather a lot to be desired, having fixed or unsuitable furniture. Spending some time considering how the furniture can most effectively be arranged can enhance the interaction of group members to a considerable extent. Figure 7.2 shows three of many possible seating arrangements.

Figure 7.2a shows the arrangement in which there is the best opportunity for a balanced exchange of ideas between all members. Research confirms that the most frequent communication (both verbal and non-verbal) takes place between individuals sitting opposite each other. The arrangement in figure 7.2b makes it difficult for those members sitting down one side of the table to communicate with one another. Figure 7.2c shows a common arrangement and it is easy to appreciate that most of the communication is likely to take place through the individual sitting alone. It is interesting to surmise where students who want a quiet hour will position themselves once they have established the usual layout of the room.

As indicated earlier, there are other issues that interact with seating that will influence the overall pattern of interaction.

- Do you, as the tutor, always sit near the board – an influential position?
- Do you surround yourself with books and papers before the students arrive?
- Is your style authoritarian?

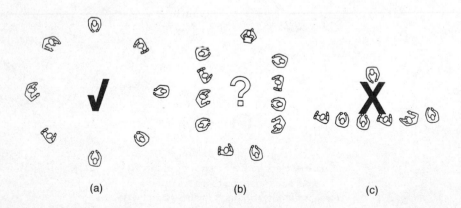

(a)   (b)   (c)

Figure 7.2   Seating arrangements

It can be quite interesting to watch how a room fills up if students think they know where you are going to sit, and even more interesting when you sit in a place that the students did not expect.

Planning for Participation

Students often admit to not preparing adequately for participation in seminars unless it is their turn to lead a seminar. This frequently leads to a read paper by the student, followed by an inquisition of that student by the tutor with other group members taking a relatively minor part in the proceedings. There are a number of strategies that can be adopted to improve this situation.

Prescribed readings

During the previous week the tutor spends some time dealing with reading material that will inform the following week's discussion. Readings are then allocated to students. Some weeks all students may be asked to read the same text while on other occasions students will be given a variety of reading so that different perspectives are brought to the discussion. The material reviewed need not be limited to the printed word as usually there is a wealth of audio and video material to draw upon. This procedure works most effectively if students are given guidelines as to the type of contribution it would be helpful to make. For example:

- a list of the key points made by the author;
- points with which they personally agree/disagree;
- comparison with previously read/studied accounts of events;
- criticisms from a particular historical point of view.

An alternative approach which I have found particularly useful is to discuss the topic during the preceding week but leave students to find something relevant to the topic themselves. This has a number of potential benefits. Students may bring perspectives to the topic which you, as the tutor, had not anticipated. It is also one way of encouraging students to take more control over their own learning and can help them to explore the whole range of materials that are available within the library resources centre.

Topic web

This is a term used to describe the method of structuring seminars suggested by Wilson as it seems to bear some similarity to the procedure often used by primary school teachers when planning a topic.[12] Wilson

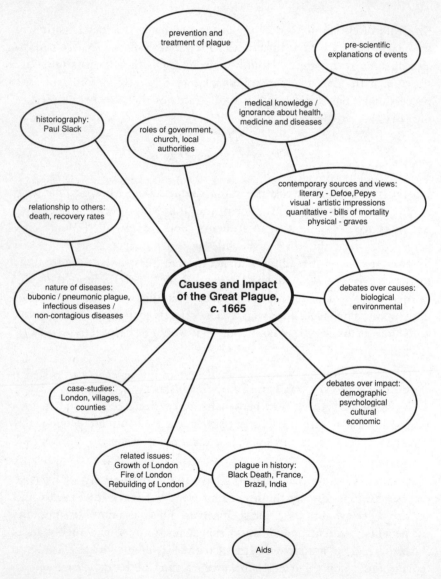

Figure 7.3   Topic web

asked students to read anything relevant and be prepared to say a few words about it. Following this, a topic web (see figure 7.3) is constructed on a board or overhead projector with the discussion title at the centre. Around this topics are written in, but the discussion begins as students try to decide whether an item is a new topic or a subheading of an existing group. Students are then asked if any of the items form natural subgroups and, if so, lines are drawn around them. A discussion of the issues follows.

The important aspects of this process are that the students are involved in deciding:

- what the important issues are;
- in which order they are to be discussed;
- the time which can be allocated to each topic;
- further issues which will not be covered.

Students also have a succinct visual record of the discussion to take away with them. It is interesting to note that this method has many similarities with Buzan's 'mind map' method of taking notes in lectures.[13] Other approaches to keeping a record of what takes place in seminars will be considered later.

Student-led seminars

There are one or two people who come with a list of points and discuss those but a lot of people don't have the confidence to do it and so they read out a long paper, and consequently the rest of the group loses interest after the first ten sides . . . well you do switch off.[14]

Habeshaw's definition of a seminar clearly indicates that a student or students may be involved in initiating the activities in a seminar.[15] Both staff and students have indicated that very often this results in the student reading a paper, followed by questions, as in the quotation above. Why is it that students read from a prepared paper? There appear to be a number of contributing factors. Sometimes the seminar contributes to the assessed work of the student but it is the written paper and not the seminar itself that is marked by the tutor. This leads students to see it as yet another essay-writing exercise. Another difficulty is that students do not always have the confidence to talk from notes or the expertise to involve the rest of the group. Some of their anxieties can be alleviated by providing help in preparing appropriately for a seminar. There is not space in this chapter to develop all of these ideas, but the following list indicates some issues which it might be useful to discuss with students preparing to lead seminars.

- Content should be written in note-form to prevent reading and encourage eye-contact.
- Plan for group activity. In addition to being a good teaching strategy it provides a breathing space for the facilitator. Consider whether they will split the group into subgroups or not.
- Include approximate timings for each section of the seminar.
- Decide whether quotations are written out in full or reference made to a book/journal at the appropriate point. The simple task of referring to a book can alter the pace, direction and atmosphere.
- Be selective.
- Have plenty of tasks and questions for the seminar group even if they are not all used. Students will need help in devising tasks and questions and understanding the difference between open and closed questions.
- Be prepared to set reading/preparation in advance of the seminar.
- Guidance in the use of support aids such as the overhead projector. There is nothing more demoralizing for a student than to realize all-too-late that their preparation is incomprehensible to the rest of the group.

Group seminars

In my opening remarks I indicated that two of the attributes of seminars were that they take place in a prescribed location at a set time. Both of these can be constraining influences, so how can these disadvantages be overcome? One strategy that can be used is to ask students to prepare for seminars in groups. This approach is derived from the syndicate approach of Collier.[16] Groups of three or four students work together over a period of several weeks to investigate a topic. They then have to report back the results of their work to the whole of the group. This process is enhanced if the groups have access to the tutor for advice, and the way in which I have achieved this is to free one or more sessions from other commitments. This approach provides students with an opportunity to develop team skills and learn how to draw upon each other's strengths. So, for example, it is possible for someone who feels apprehensive about giving a verbal presentation to make their contribution to the team effort in some other way. This need not mean that the individual will always be able to avoid verbal presentations completely, but that they can be introduced to the process in a gradual and less intimidating way. This approach also has other practical advantages for course organization. It is often very difficult to fit in the opportunity for each member of a group to facilitate a seminar without the time allocated becoming impossibly short. Groups of students can be allocated a much longer period of time, which allows them to develop ideas with the rest of the group.

Absent friend

Students often feel inhibited by the tutor being present, so it can sometimes be valuable to leave the room and let the group work on their own. Jaques coined the rather apt term 'absent friend' to describe this approach.[17] For tutors the biggest problem, in my experience, seems to be a feeling that they are abdicating their responsibilities. Occasionally, students who perceive education as being given by tutors and received by them also object on the grounds that they are there to be taught. This approach does require preparation, however, as the students need to have the necessary skills to be able to organize themselves and a clear idea of what they have to achieve.

Responding to contributions

It is imperative that all members of groups are sensitive to the way in which they respond to the contributions made by others. Students in particular can be inhibited from making contributions if the tutor dismisses their initial responses out of hand. An approach I always try to adopt is to say 'Yes and . . .', rather than 'Yes but . . .', when having to encourage a student to think further about her/his response. It is also important that individuals are sensitive about the time at which they respond, and avoid interrupting the speaker. These are issues that can usefully be discussed when drawing up the ground rules for sessions.

Recording proceedings

Students are often concerned about having some record of what has taken place in seminars. If they are concentrating on taking notes then they will be less able to become involved in the discussion. The following are some strategies which can be adopted to alleviate this conflict.

• The seminar facilitator can provide a synopsis of points raised after the seminar in note form, and this might also be reckoned to contribute to their overall assessment.
• If it is a group seminar, one member of the group can be assigned to provide a synopsis.
• If groups have been working on different tasks they can provide a synopsis of their findings for the facilitator to collate. I regularly use this approach and it can be made very easy if groups all provide their notes on disk.

Conclusion

In the preceding paragraphs I have raised awareness of some key issues that affect what happens in seminars and have provided some practical ideas. It has not been possible to consider in depth all the skills that are needed to work effectively in groups or discuss all the possible strategies that can be drawn upon. The references given in the text and the additional readings suggested in the further reading list will allow the reader to explore the subject further.

Notes

1 G. Gibbs, S. and T. Habeshaw, *53 Interesting Things to Do in Seminars and Tutorials* (Technical and Educational Services, Bristol, 1984).
2 M. J. L. Abercrombie and P. M. Terry, *Talking to Learn: Improving Teaching and Learning in Small Groups* (SRHE, Guildford, 1978).
3 *Developing Student Autonomy in Learning*, ed. D. Boud (Kogan Page, London, 1988 edn).
4 D. Jaques, *Learning in Groups* (Croom Helm, London, 1984).
5 Ibid., p. 65.
6 F. Marton and R. Säljö, 'Approaches to Learning', in *The Experience of Learning*, ed. F. Marton, D. Hounsell and N. Entwistle (Scottish Academic Press, Edinburgh, 1984), pp. 36–55.
7 G. Gibbs, *Improving the Quality of Student Learning* (Technical and Educational Services, Bristol 1992).
8 P. Ramsden, *Learning to Teach in Higher Education* (Routledge, London, 1992).
9 Gibbs, *Improving the Quality of Student Learning*.
10 Jaques, *Learning in Groups*; L. Stenhouse, 'Teaching Through Small

Group Discussion: Formality, Rules and Authority', *Cambridge Journal of Education*, 2 (1972), pp. 18–24.

11   Stenhouse, 'Teaching Through Small Group Discussion', p. 20.

12   A. Wilson, 'Structuring Seminars: A Technique to Allow Students to Participate in the Structuring of Small Group Discussions', *Studies in Higher Education*, 5 (1980), pp. 81–4.

13   T. Buzan, *Use your Head* (BBC, London, 1982).

14   G. Preston, 'A Review of the Teaching and Learning Strategies used in the Teaching of History at Bath College of Higher Education' (Unpublished M. Ed. dissertation, University of Bath, 1987), p. 180.

15   Gibbs and Habeshaw, *53 Interesting Things to Do in Seminars and Tutorials*.

16   G. Collier, 'Syndicate Methods Placed in Context', in *The Management of Peer-Group Learning: Syndicate Methods in Higher Education*, ed. G. Collier (SRHE, Guildford, 1983), pp. 3–12.

17   Jaques, *Learning in Groups*.

Further Reading

D. Jaques, *Learning in Groups* (Croom Helm, London, 1984) provides a comprehensive exploration of group work covering research into group behaviour, communication theory, practical techniques, evaluation of group work and a number of workshop activities. Concomitant with introducing small-group work is the transfer of responsibility for learning to the student. *Developing Student Autonomy in Learning*, ed. D. Boud (Kogan Page, London, 1988 edn) explores a whole range of issues which have to be addressed if students are to be successfully given this autonomy, often in the face of resistance from those whose only experience is of traditional higher education.

P. Denicolo, N. Entwistle and D. Hounsell, *What is Active Learning?* (CVCP, Sheffield, 1992), and S. Griffiths and P. Partington, *Enabling Active Learning in Small Groups* (CVCP, Sheffield, 1992) are two of twelve volumes on *Effective Learning and Teaching in Higher Education* that contain theoretical insights, a wealth of practical ideas and examples from many disciplines on teaching and learning, produced by the Staff Development and Training Unit of the CVCP. R. M. Beard and J. Hartley, *Teaching and Learning in Higher Education* (Harper and Row, London, 1984), and G. Brown and M. Atkins, *Effective Teaching in Higher Education* (Methuen, London, 1988) both cover the whole spectrum of teaching and learning. G. Gibbs, *Improving the Quality of Student Learning* (Technical and Educational Services, Bristol, 1992) does not include examples of learning in history, but it does provide valuable insights into the way course design can influence the way students learn. G. Gibbs, S. and T. Habeshaw, *53 Interesting Things to Do in Seminars and Tutorials* (Technical and Educational Services, Bristol, 1984) provides a wealth of practical ideas that are readily accessible.

8

Measuring and Improving the Quality of Teaching

Paul Hyland

Most historians are naturally resourceful, critical and even adventurous in their professional research and writing, but it would not be easy to sustain the claim that such intellectual curiosity and a constant willingness to test and challenge orthodoxies is equally characteristic of the way in which most teaching and learning methods for history are maintained in British universities and colleges.

Of course, in recent years there have been great public debates among historians and others about the schools' curriculum and the role of history in higher education, as well as less conspicuous but probably no-less-heated discussions within departments about the introduction of courses that reflect and build upon the many new fields of interest and research that have emerged within the discipline. These are important developments, but for the most part they have been concerned with defining the aims and content of the curriculum, the skills and knowledge that students should acquire, and the kinds of history that should be offered to a rapidly diversifying student population. Thus, much attention has been given to the aims and learning outcomes of individual courses and degree programmes but, as yet, few review and validation documents have as much to say about how approaches to teaching and learning have been developed, except in relation to specific and unusual courses or in the general context of preserving traditional methods in the face of growing student numbers. In recent years, many history departments have also 'modularized' their course provision in a process that appears to have been driven as much by institutional concerns to increase cost-effectiveness, accountability and managerial authority as by the educational merits of increasing student choice of courses and modes of study. Thus great investments have been made in modular and credit-accumulation schemes, though how these systems might be expected to affect the quality of history teaching and learning has seldom been the subject of investigation. Even where radical and demonstrably successful new teaching strategies have been designed, as for the 'history' courses of the Open University, such striking innovations as this kind of distance learning have not usually been matched by a corresponding shift in methods of assessment. So, almost everywhere in British higher educa-tion, the standard fare for history students is still a staple diet of lectures, seminars, essays and examinations.

The conventional wisdom is that this system is well tried and tested, but a moment's reflection suggests that this is rather wishful thinking. Historians are not generally renowned for the enthusiasm with which they read and digest the findings of educational research, much of which clearly challenges the assumed effectiveness and universal value of tradi-tional practices such as lecturing and essay-writing. Many reasons for this can be cited, including a lack of confidence in the objectivity and vocabulary of educational research; a belief that as it is seldom empiri-cally based in history, its findings are largely inappropriate to the distinc-tive needs and character of the discipline; and a recognition that the lessons of education research are often a matter of contention. Such misgivings are not confined to history, but they would bear greater scrutiny if we were agreed about what constitutes 'objectivity', eschewed subjects of controversy and, most important, regularly conducted our own research and analysis into the effectiveness of our teaching and learning strategies. In this last respect, the complaint that the first na-tional HEFC Quality Assessment for History was flawed due to some historians' lack of instruction and experience in the art of writing self-critical reports, is not reassuring. Yet it is symptomatic of much deeper problems. The lack of a scholarly journal devoted to promoting research and development in the teaching and learning of history in higher education; the explicit refusal of the British government's Research Assessment Exercise to admit and support 'scholarship' that consists of 'the development of teaching materials' (as if 'proper' history books and articles serve some other function); and the reluctance of most institutions and departments, even those which espouse the parity of teaching and research, to act upon their missions (as in staff appoint-ments and promotions), cannot be expected to advance teaching research and publication within the discipline. So it is not surprising that when asked about the effectiveness of their teaching, many historians fall back upon a stock of customary responses.

What Are We Measuring?

One of the most common assertions is that teaching effectiveness is largely measured by the final achievements of students in terms of their degree classifications, awards and certificates; and there are many variations on the use of this kind of 'exit performance' as the vital indicator. So for example, a history department that normally only admits students with high A-level scores (based largely upon traditional examinations) emphasizes the high proportion of its students who attain a 'good' degree (largely by examinations) or who go on to postgraduate work. Similarly, a department that sets minimal entrance requirements or that enrols many non-traditional candidates measures its success in terms of the academic 'value added' to students between their apparently limited abilities at entry (whether measured traditionally or notionally) and their much greater performances at exit. Such yardsticks have their uses, particularly in the politics of higher education, but they cannot measure what are often critical components of good teaching, such as the extent to which a tutor can enthuse and motivate all students, or, the extent to which students have passed a course regardless of (and in some cases even despite) the quality of teaching. Moreover, when equally applied as measures of ineffectiveness they are often greeted with dismay. So, in both cases, when large numbers of students fail to attain a good degree, it is not the quality of their history teaching that is most readily called to question, but a host of other factors such as student motivation, prior abilities and institutional resources, as if these factors only played a peripheral role in the records of success.

As the exit performance of each history student is invariably constructed from a particular combination of grades or marks awarded on a variety of courses, the extent to which the final data are an accurate measure of each student's learning (even before they are altered by the judgements of boards of examiners, as in cases of compensation) must obviously depend, among other things, upon the validity of each course's methods of assessment. Yet it is not uncommon to find whole programme aims and course objectives, such as 'the development of oral skills' and 'the ability to problem-solve in groups', that are either never tested or, if so, make no contribution to the summative performance. As with the testing of traditional essay-writing and examination skills, even where some abilities are repeatedly assessed, the extent to which each student's achievements can be attributed to the effectiveness of teaching as against a range of other factors, such as prior knowledge and experience or learning facilities and opportunities, raises many questions. This is not to say that some forms of teaching are not generally more likely to produce greater levels of achievement in terms of students' critical understanding or deep learning than are others, but that overarching confidence in output or input–output data (such as withdrawal or completion rates) as the sole measures of good teaching is generally mistaken. It may well be that the predominant forms of assessment used in history, a combination of essays and essay-examinations, are neither as reliable nor as valid in terms of stimulating and measuring deep learning as is generally supposed. But however valid and reliable these methods may be reckoned, the data that they yield should only be regarded as one among many kinds of information that are needed in order to evaluate the quality of teaching.

Closely related to the faith in output information is the view that 'peer' review in the form of external examiners' reports is the most telling measure of the quality of education; a view that is explicitly endorsed by the special prominence afforded to the receipt and processing of reports in the Quality Assurance systems of most institutions. This too is generally more comforting than convincing, for apart from advising and adjudicating on such matters as the setting of examination papers and the marking of essay and examination scripts, the principal focus of most examiners' attention is upon student achievement, rather than the effectiveness of teaching. Thus, aside from standards of marking and supervision, any comments that examiners may make about the quality of teaching are inferences, drawn almost invariably without any direct observation or analysis of teaching sessions. The same is true when, in the name of equity, some examiners occasionally offer to 'moderate' the marks of students in the hope of ironing out differences in their learning experiences at the hands of different tutors, for any relationship that this suggests between student performance and teaching effectiveness must be largely a matter of conjecture. Even when examiners do attend some teaching sessions in order to assess, say, student marking of student seminar presentations, a lack of training combined with the unconventional nature of such work means that most historians are unable to draw upon comparative evidence or their own experience in reaching their conclusions. Just as it is not the function of output data or external examiners' reports to measure the quality of teaching, so too they are not well suited to the task of demonstrating the merits or limits of innovations.

What is Good Teaching?

In order to measure and improve the quality of history teaching, it is necessary to consider how each and every aspect of the teaching process affects and helps to promote the kind of student learning that tutors are aiming to produce. Every aspect of teaching, from the design of the curriculum to the setting of assignments, sends signals about the kinds of learning that tutors are expecting, so it is clearly important that these signals are in fact in keeping with the tutor's real intentions.[1] Yet what is often signalled by some elements of history teaching, such as a curriculum that is too voluminous to be studied deeply, or assessment methods that produce anxiety and answers based on memory, is usually a surface approach to learning. It is unlikely that many historians see their teaching function as limited to the transmission of an agreed body of knowledge and interpretations about the past, which students then absorb in ever-increasing amounts according to their personal capacities. But this naïve view of learning is commonly associated with the delivery of a series of didactic lectures or seminars which casts students in the role of passive recipients of teaching. It is equally unlikely that most historians' views about how to improve the quality of student learning are confined to the acquisition and deployment of rules of instruction or techniques that aim to increase the effectiveness of the tutor's communications, or the abilities of the student to receive them. Yet much staff development and training in the use of new technologies, from overhead projectors to computers, and on topics such as 'Lecturing to Large Groups', may well give this impression. If, as in other disciplines, the goal of history teaching is to facilitate deep learning, in which the knowledge, concepts and skills of history are generated, embraced and applied by students for a multitude of uses, then it is the extent to which tutors promote this kind of learning that must be the central yardstick for measuring and improving the quality of teaching.

Working with a definition of good teaching as that which cultivates deep learning, there can be no single indicator of the quality of teaching. Many different sources of opinion and methods of investigation are needed to measure how any particular element of teaching, or combination of elements, is likely to affect the kind of learning that is undertaken. Thus even in making an apparently straightforward decision, say, about what book or books to recommend for student reading, the tutor is faced with a complex process of evaluation. Sources might include the tutor, students, colleagues, examiners, reviewers and librarians, whose opinions about such matters as the price, availability, scholarship and level of difficulty of each book in relation to the needs and achievements of past and prospective students might only raise more pressing questions about how the book is to be used in relation to the teaching. A few of the methods of investigation, such as the analysis of questionnaires and student records, might yield statistical information. But as with most other common but important elements of teaching, neither the reasons for the tutor's final choice of books nor the wisdom of that decision could be determined by quantification. Clearly, the value of different sources and methods of investigation will depend upon the nature of the host of questions and decisions that tutors can and do examine. Thus traditionally, through validation and review, specialist historians have played a vital role in contributing to judgements about a tutor's knowledge and expertise in a given field, the content and organization of the syllabus, and the setting of course objectives. However, if we wish to understand the relationship between teaching and learning, both in general and in any particular situation, we will have to listen carefully to what students tell us about their own experiences.

In general, we know from many kinds of studies in Britain, North America and Australia that undergraduates are remarkably consistent in what they regard as the characteristics of good teaching.[2] Broadly, these may be summarized as the following: good teaching

- stimulates students' interest and intellectual curiosity in the subject matter;
- provides clear and understandable explanations, and highlights what is most important;
- shows real interest in and respect for students, and is responsive to their needs and problems;
- is well prepared and well organized, and makes good use of course material;
- expresses a genuine knowledge and love of the subject, and enthusiasm for teaching it;
- has clear goals and high expectations for student learning;

- fosters independent thought and a spirit of enquiry;
- enables students to develop a sense of independence and control over their learning;
- provides opportunities for students to consult tutors outside the classroom;
- uses fair and appropriate methods of assessment;
- provides high quality feedback on student progress and assignments;
- recognizes and allows for individual differences in student learning.

Many of these and other properties of good teaching are well known to tutors. But whereas much research and student opinion about good teaching emphasizes the importance of tutors continuously learning about their students and looking for ways to help them learn both in and outside the classroom, much of the culture of teaching in higher education seems impervious to this way of thinking. So it is not hard to find evidence of tutors who use teaching to proclaim their own achievements, courses that are overburdened with content and that create few opportunities for students to exercise control over their own learning, forms of assessment that seem to value recitation, departments that regard attempts to help students as evidence of 'spoonfeeding', and teaching methods that are unresponsive to student problems. Such attitudes and practices cannot be expected to facilitate deep learning.[3] Yet they appear often to be driven by the notion that students become deep learners through the absence or denial of assistance, and that in higher education they are and should be 'on their own' when it comes to the nature and quality of their learning. The latter view clearly parallels how many tutors feel about their teaching, and in this respect it is worth noting that when tutors describe what they regard as the properties of good teaching, their most distinctive addition is to emphasize the importance of a tutor's personal record of research and publication.[4]

Though much can be learned from general studies of student opinion, it would be extraordinary if the views of history staff and students about what constitutes good teaching or deep learning were identical to those in all other disciplines. Were the research to be undertaken, it would be equally surprising if history students' views were entirely different from those summarized above. Yet, though general studies may offer guidance in planning and preparation, no amount of reading or external research can determine what is good teaching in terms of the content, methods, assignments and so forth that ought to be adopted in any actual situation. To do this, as individuals and departments we need to engage in a constant process of evaluation that is based not only upon knowledge of the ever-changing needs and levels of understanding possessed by every group of students, but also an appraisal of the particular strengths and talents of ourselves as tutors working within and under what are often far from ideal conditions. Thus, in the course of lecturing or leading a seminar discussion, if we change the pattern and direction of our teaching in response to student learning, we do not abandon the goals of good teaching but take an important step towards their realization. It is not difficult to deliver the whole transcript of a lecture almost regardless of what if anything the audience is learning, or to spend an hour answering our own questions under the guise of holding a discussion. In this way a great deal of material may be covered, and many important questions brilliantly answered, by the tutor. Equally, it is not difficult to keep most history students busy by getting them to 'do' things, such as working in small groups or with computers, out of fear that the so-called 'passive' activities of listening and reading cannot generate the kind of enthusiasm, critical insights and understanding that we associate with deep learning. However, whatever activities we or students are engaged in, to prevent them from becoming rituals in which we find ourselves going through the motions of pretending to be teaching, there is no alternative to listening at every opportunity to what our students tell us about their learning.

What Are We Evaluating?

In addition to the traditional means of enabling students to participate in review and decision-making processes, through representation on various boards and committees such as staff/student groups, in recent years most history departments have instituted some form of student evaluation of course provision. Typically, at the end of its delivery, each course or module is evaluated anonymously and individually by students in a questionnaire (see figure 8.1), though there are many variations as the views of whole enrolments or distinctive groups such as part-time students can also be documented in this way.

Although often introduced in response to student demands that their views about the relative merits of different courses and tutors be taken seriously and made available to future students (as in ranking tables),

Please complete the following evaluation by circling the number which you feel most accurately describes your course, and return it, unsigned, to the Faculty Office.

Course Title:..Code: ....

Year/Level: .... Semester: .... Lecture Group: .... Seminar Group: ....

1 = strongly disagree; 2 = disagree; 3 = don't know; 4 = agree;
5 = strongly agree.

1	The aims of the course were clearly explained	1	2	3	4	5
2	The course was well designed	1	2	3	4	5
3	The aims of the course were achieved	1	2	3	4	5
4	The explanations and discussions were understandable and useful	1	2	3	4	5
5	The course material was well organized and used effectively	1	2	3	4	5
6	The course was presented enthusiastically	1	2	3	4	5
7	The important material was clearly identified	1	2	3	4	5
8	There was good factual coverage of subject matter	1	2	3	4	5
9	Lecture/seminar/fieldwork/and practical work were well linked	1	2	3	4	5
10	The pace of the course was adjusted to the needs of the class	1	2	3	4	5
11	The course allowed for the feelings and problems of individual students	1	2	3	4	5
12	The course stimulated independent thought	1	2	3	4	5
13	The course stimulated an exchange of views between tutor and students	1	2	3	4	5
14	The contact time was satisfactory	1	2	3	4	5
15	The tutors were accessible to students outside teaching sessions	1	2	3	4	5
16	Additional tutorials were available on request	1	2	3	4	5
17	Collaboration between tutors was satisfactory	1	2	3	4	5
18	Sufficient time and information were given concerning coursework	1	2	3	4	5
19	Coursework was marked fairly and promptly	1	2	3	4	5
20	The examination(s) was a fair test of the course	1	2	3	4	5
21	The library resources for the course were satisfactory	1	2	3	4	5
22	Overall, the course was satisfactory	1	2	3	4	5

Please indicate the reasons for your final answer:

What changes would you introduce?

Figure 8.1   Student course evaluation

most course evaluations are now usually designed, administered and owned by tutors for departmental uses. Thus, much information that is usually verifiable, quantifiable and amenable to various kinds of comparative analysis is collected for what are often several purposes: to inform and assure students about the quality of courses; to assist in the formal evaluation and appraisal of all tutors; to provide individual tutors with information that can be used to increase the effectiveness of their teaching; and to help academic leaders decide what improvements can be made in the management of a range of resources, courses and degree programmes. It is not surprising, therefore, to find that questionnaires commonly call for student responses to many aspects of course delivery and provision, from the utility of lectures to the availability of books and journals, and that while this information helps various bodies to identify the most pressing needs and problems of students within the general context of their educational experience, in terms of producing demonstrable improvements in the quality of teaching the impact of such staff-directed student questionnaires is often reckoned to be disappointing.[5] This is particularly true when student responses are scored or aggregated to produce some form of annual reckoning which is then laid before each tutor as an authoritative statement of the quality of her or his performance. For in such cases, no matter how conscientiously student opinion has been solicited and documented, what exactly is being measured, by whom, for whom, and for what purposes, is invariably uncertain.

However students, academic leaders and staff appraisers choose to exercise or divest their rights and responsibilities to gather information about teaching and course provision, the use of student opinion for formative purposes, such as to improve the effectiveness of teaching, needs to be considered as a largely separate and distinctive function.[6] Clearly, tutors can benefit from knowing students' answers to many kinds of questions such as those concerning the size of classes or the methods of assessment, as these can significantly affect the way in which tutors would like to deliver their courses in the future. But unless these kinds of factors are largely under the control of individual tutors, it is neither fair nor useful for individual diagnostic purposes to confuse them with questions that are designed to gather information about those aspects of teaching which are almost invariably within each tutor's responsibility and capacity to alter. While summative evaluations may or may not be accompanied by various forms of feedback to the tutor (say, through course committees or staff appraisers), where student views are used for diagnostic purposes such feedback is obviously essential. Moreover, whereas traditional course-evaluations seldom include any elements of self-description by the tutor(s), are easily beset with problems about the reliability and validity of the evidence collected, and can easily become cosmetic exercises in which tutors actually try to hide their shortcomings, none of these factors is likely to help improve the effectiveness of teaching. Nor are these the only differences between formative and summative practices. Most summative evaluations are normally designed and directed by a figure of authority, are administered annually or bi-annually after or towards the end of a teaching programme, and (due in part to the need to make historical and other kinds of comparisons) often continue for many years without revision. But none of this is a natural or inevitable aspect of the use of student opinion by tutors whose sole intention is to improve their teaching and the quality of student learning.

Among historians who have regularly used course evaluations, there appear to be few doubts about the benefits and insights to be gained from these relatively formal mechanisms, though much less agreement about the extent to which student opinion should direct the pattern of teaching and course provision – let alone be made public as in some North American institutions. Part of the problem here can often lie with fear of being dictated to by the vagaries and limitations of student experience, and in particular an understandable resistance to being subjected to what, if misapplied, can easily become a competition for the best 'consumer satisfaction' rating – as if this were the universal hallmark of good teaching. But if the relationship of staff and students is one of partnership in the constant search for ways of improving the quality of teaching and learning, and course evaluations are seen as the natural points from which to initiate rather than to terminate such work, the criticisms that they raise can be an excellent means of stimulating more discussion and research.

How Can We Improve Individually?

Although there are many ways of using student questionnaires to explore and increase the effectiveness of teaching, one obvious place to start is with a group of tutors who can advise and support one another in the design, administration and analysis of questionnaires that are focused upon one part of teaching, say, what happens in the seminar classroom.

Please circle the number which you feel most accurately describes your tutor's teaching.
1 = not at all true, 2 = rarely true; 3 = sometimes true; 4 = generally true; 5 = very true.

1	Discusses points of view other than his/her own	1	2	3	4	5
2	Contrasts implications of various theories, where appropriate	1	2	3	4	5
3	Discusses recent developments in the field, where appropriate	1	2	3	4	5
4	Gives references for more interesting and involved points	1	2	3	4	5
5	Emphasizes the conceptual understanding of subjects	1	2	3	4	5
6	Explains clearly	1	2	3	4	5
7	Is well prepared	1	2	3	4	5
8	Gives lectures that are easy to take notes from	1	2	3	4	5
9	Summarizes major points	1	2	3	4	5
10	States objectives for each class session	1	2	3	4	5
11	Tests the extent to which objectives have been achieved	1	2	3	4	5
12	Identifies what he/she considers important	1	2	3	4	5
13	Encourages questions and class discussion	1	2	3	4	5
14	Invites students to share their knowledge and experiences	1	2	3	4	5
15	Invites criticism of his/her own ideas	1	2	3	4	5
16	Knows if the class is understanding him/her or not	1	2	3	4	5
17	Asks students to apply concepts to demonstrate understanding	1	2	3	4	5
18	Knows when students are bored	1	2	3	4	5
19	Has a genuine interest in students	1	2	3	4	5
20	Gives personal help to students having learning difficulties	1	2	3	4	5
21	Relates to students as individuals	1	2	3	4	5
22	Has an interesting style of presentation	1	2	3	4	5
23	Is enthusiastic about his/her subject	1	2	3	4	5
24	Varies the speed and tone of his/her voice	1	2	3	4	5
25	Has interest in and concern for the quality of his/her teaching	1	2	3	4	5
26	Motivates students to do their best work	1	2	3	4	5
27	Keeps students well informed of their progress	1	2	3	4	5
28	Gives students some opportunities to help determine the curriculum	1	2	3	4	5

Figure 8.2 Student description of teaching – seminars

Source: Based upon K. O. Doyle, *Evaluating Teaching* (Lexington Books, Lexington, Mass., 1983), p. 32.

At first, standardized forms (see figure 8.2) can be issued and compared with tutor responses to the same questions, thereby helping to identify any differences between how tutors view their style and methods and how students actually describe them. The purpose here is not to draw comparisons with other classes, or to see how high or low student expectations are according to a norm or to their previous experiences and ideals about what constitutes good teaching. So the extent to which students are positive or negative in their ratings of any particular aspect of instruction is best considered principally in relation to other items and to the tutor's own perception. Of course, there may well be differences between what tutors and students believe to be the most important questions, but where major discrepancies appear between their descriptions, there is at least a prima facie case for some further investigation. In one history department where two colleagues (chosen by the tutor) were used to discuss the findings of several 'Student Description of Teaching' questionnaires and to offer guidance about the kinds of changes that might be introduced, it became clear that the aggregation of the student ratings was of little diagnostic value, and that in relation to any single question the range of student responses was as interesting as the mean or average position. These historians also soon decided that the standardized questionnaire was often too general to help each tutor to determine what action (if any) should be taken, and that more individualized or highly focused forms were needed. After the creation and analysis of these, and depending upon how long each tutor needed in order to feel confident that he or she had changed some aspect of instruction, the questionnaires were re-issued both to the original (experimental) group of students and wherever possible to a similar (control) group who had not been previously questioned, so as to permit comparisons. What emerged from this procedure was not only that in most cases staff and students could perceive some notable improvements, but that both were now eager to explore the extent to which the effectiveness of other aspects of teaching, such as the tutoring-back of course assignments, could be enhanced by the use of similar methods of investigation.

Because the scope of most traditional course-evaluations is so broad, almost any single question or comment about teaching and learning can be used as the foundation for more progressive studies; either by further questionnaires, by interviews, by providing opportunities for groups of students to construct their own statements about their learning patterns and the quality of teaching, or by many other kinds of work involving various degrees of staff–student input and interaction.[7] So, in a department where it is the responsibility of every tutor to design and lead each year at least one project that critically examines some aspect of her or his own teaching, a great range of strategies is produced. For example:

Assessment options   Rather than requiring students to write three essays for each of his courses, a tutor agreed with students that they could undertake a 'negotiated assignment' that would be equivalent to one essay. Each student would propose a topic, method of research, form of submission/presentation, and criteria for assessment to be approved in consultation with the tutor. Projects included the production of a video, a public lecture, a review article, an edited collection of correspondence, and a search for primary sources. At the end of the course, self-assessment forms were used to evaluate the extent to which the option had promoted student learning.

Course content and materials   Towards the end of her courses, a tutor allocated time for students to assess her lecture and seminar programmes, course handbooks and bibliographies (150–230 pp.) with a view to improving them for future students. Working in small teams, students were asked to select and explain what they had found the most/ least stimulating topics and teaching sessions, what materials in the handbook (documents, reviews, etc.) had been most/least helpful in developing their understanding of the course's themes, what books and articles could/could not be recommended for various reasons, and what changes they would make to the general design and content of the course. The courses were revised in the light of student comments.

Dissertation supervision   Following a staff/student meeting, a tutor and group of third-year students agreed that part of the stress and difficulties that some students experienced in working on their dissertations might be relieved by more effective supervision. Together, they created a brief Dissertation Log (held by students) to record the date and duration of each tutorial, what progress the student was making, what problems he or she was experiencing, what advice and assistance had been given, and what targets would be set for the following meeting. At the end of the year, the practice was evaluated by holding group interviews to compare the views of students who had kept a log with those who had not participated.

Seminar management   To examine the effectiveness of his management of seminar discussions, a tutor audio-recorded ten sessions and analysed his comments and interactions in terms of positive/negative criticisms, open/closed questions, tutor – student/inter-student exchanges, etc. The views of students about how and why they contributed, what deterred them and what might have facilitated their participation were taken from brief end-of-seminar questionnaires. The project was evaluated in the following year when the tutor repeated part of the exercise to consider what aspects of his management he had improved.

Seminar presentations   To improve student seminar presentations, a pro forma was devised both to enable students to select the criteria under which they wished to be assessed, and to enable the marking tutor and seminar group to record their most important advice and criticisms at the end of each presentation. The pro forma (figure 8.3) was used by several groups of students, presenting many types of papers on a range of courses. A supporting document was distributed by the tutor to explain and illustrate the new procedure, and to suggest ways in which each group might determine its own conventions for contributing to the marking. The innovation was evaluated by the tutor in discussion with each group of students, and with the assistance of other historians who had been invited to attend the sessions.

Such projects are not costly, nor are they inordinately time-consuming. Yet they are a vital means of generating and testing new ideas and practices, particularly in relation to those aspects of teaching and learning whose effectiveness we are apt to take for granted. Where projects are thought to be successful and are potentially applicable to the work of other tutors, further studies can be conducted to check initial findings, and maybe allay misgivings, before a general decision is taken about whether or not a particular innovation should be more widely introduced. Moreover, even in debating that recurrent question, the whole department could be expected to review the evidence on which beliefs about the effectiveness of current practices are based, and the kind of evidence that would be required to persuade tutors of the merits of a proposed improvement.

Although the findings of these sort of projects may easily be dismissed as parochial, this is precisely why they are so useful, for not only is the great majority of history teaching and learning conducted within a distinctive educational context and location, but for all the differences

To be completed by the student(s)

Name(s): ....

Course Code: .... Course Title: ....

Seminar Group: .... Date of Seminar: .... Tutor: ....

Seminar Title: ....

Tick 20 Assessment boxes (5% each)	**To be completed by the marker(s)**	Mark Awarded	Total Mark	COMMENTS
	PRESENTATION			
[ ]	Introduction of the topic and agenda			
[ ]	Clarity of aims and objectives			
[ ] [ ]	Communication skills (oral)			
[ ] [ ]	Communication skills (written)			
[ ] [ ]	Use of IT resources and skills			
[ ] [ ] [ ]	Quality of teamwork			
[ ]	MANAGEMENT OF THE SEMINAR General design and management of the session			
[ ] [ ] [ ]	Level of group interest/participation/ interaction			
[ ] [ ]	Responsiveness to group needs and issues			
[ ] [ ]	Relevance of discussions and responses			
[ ] [ ]	Imaginative use of the group			
[ ] [ ]	RESEARCH AND ANALYSIS Depth and breadth of secondary reading			
[ ] [ ]	Search and use of primary sources			
[ ] [ ]	Explanation and use of concepts			
[ ] [ ]	Understanding of historical controversies/ historiography			
[ ] [ ]	Evidence of critical abilities			
[ ] [ ] [ ]	Development of logical argument			
[ ] [ ] [ ]	Originality of thought and judgement			
[ ] [ ] [ ]	OTHER CRITERIA (e.g. statistical analysis) Specify:			
[ ] [ ] [ ]	Specify:			
[ ] [ ] [ ]	Specify:			
[ ] [ ] [ ]	ACHIEVEMENT Attainment of objectives			
[ ] [ ] [ ]	Value of seminar to the course			
	TOTAL		100	

Summary of observations and assessment: ....

....

....

Tutor's Signature: ....

Figure 8.3 Seminar-presentation assessment form

within and between departments, responsibility for the design and delivery of a course or module is still largely held by individuals. Thus where there appear to be striking similarities in the aims and content of the curriculum at various institutions, as many provide, say, a module on the English Civil War, differences of tutor experience, student enrolment, teaching objectives, library resources and so forth, combine to ensure that much of the character of each course is unique in far more than just a nominal sense. This is not to deny the importance of identifying and investigating common teaching needs and problems, but as most historians probably regard their teaching styles and methods as highly personal, however radical or conventional they appear on paper, much can be built upon that platform. Moreover, although it may be tempting to believe that the keys to more effective teaching are always in the hands of others – if only they provided bigger libraries, smaller classes, less committees, more resources – to bemoan these perceived deficiencies without self-critical reflection is both to displace the locus of responsibility for students' learning and to fail to seize the opportunities for improvement that even small and subtle changes can make to the effectiveness of teaching in any institution. What individual self-critical work may seem to lack in theoretical sophistication may be more than compensated by the diversity and practical orientation of the empirical research that is undertaken, and by the fact that it cannot very readily be used to draw superficial and invidious comparisons. Moreover, by democratizing the approach to improving the quality of teaching, staff are empowered both to develop their own talents and to resist the growing tendency for members of internal bodies and external agencies to direct the pace and pattern of change according to other interests.

How Can We Improve Collectively?

In departments where there is broad agreement about the pertinence of student criticism or a shared perception of the need to improve some common aspect of the teaching, there are many kinds of collaborative diagnostic work that can be undertaken without either jeopardizing the sense of active participation in and ownership of research by staff as individuals, or raising intractable problems about the validity and reliability of evidence that is used principally for the purposes of formal or external evaluation.[8] One approach that has proved successful involves the agreement of staff and student to review the effectiveness of teaching and learning by recording and discussing interviews and teaching

sessions under the supervision of an independent counsellor and researcher. Each tutor is asked to select several lectures, seminars and
documentary workshops from their normal teaching schedules and to
have these observed and criticized by staff and students at various inter-
vals throughout the year. Notes on the recorded sessions, briefing papers
and progress reports are provided by the independent counsellor and
facilitator who also conducts all confidential interviews with students.
Thus a rolling programme of action research is opened, in which all
tutors have several opportunities to observe, discuss and modify their
teaching styles and methods, both in the light of direct criticism from
staff and students and according to their own perceptions of the strengths
and weaknesses of teaching strategies adopted by their colleagues. A
simple model of the cycle of research is expressed in figure 8.4.

Like any research, the difficulties of planning and conducting this
kind of work are multiple, not least in securing the necessary technical

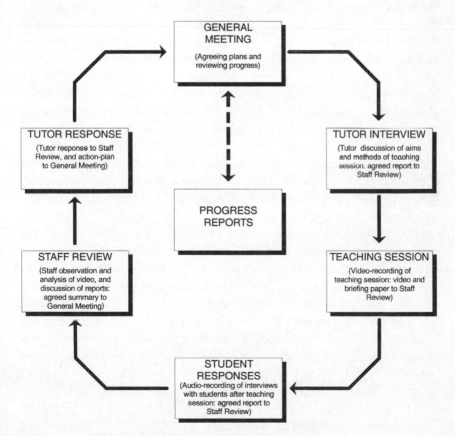

Figure 8.4   Model of teaching sessions review

and secretarial support, as well as the good offices of an independent tutor. But, with a little imagination this model can be easily adapted to suit the particular needs and resources of most departments.[9] And, compared with the investment usually required to produce a single historical article, the time and costs are minimal for all but the facilitator – perhaps a few hours per week. On the other hand, the benefits are considerable. Almost certainly, for tutors who have never previously or only rarely observed themselves as teachers, the experience will be daunting but unforgettable. To be able to see how even apparently trivial aspects of lecturing, such as your own and colleagues' mannerisms and humour, can critically affect the nature of students' attention and understanding, let alone more obvious influences such as the clarity, pace and tone of delivery, the use of audio-visual facilities, and the way that questions are posed and answered, is invariably revealing. To be able to discuss and respond to peer and student criticism with a view to making some immediate changes, and measuring their effects, is equally interesting and rewarding. Moreover, for students the opportunity to explore how and why they react to different kinds of teaching leads naturally to a deeper understanding of their own attitudes to and processes of learning. Nor, in terms of increasing appreciation of one another's needs and problems, should the value of involving students as active and equal partners in research be overlooked. They too can be the subject of video-observation and discussion, and have a vital role to play in offering ideas about what different kinds of teaching might be tried, and how these might best be introduced. Thus against the sensitivity with which many historians over-protect the individuality and privacy of their teaching practices, a more public and informed debate about the effectiveness of teaching and learning can be engaged.

From the point of view of the historians as a whole, one of the advantages of undertaking this kind of work must lie in the opportunity that it affords to provide a process of staff induction and development that is based upon the actual teaching practices of the department, rather than on systems of administration and regulation or quality assurance that appear to have a natural propensity to amass evidence of individual and departmental competence in teaching, without ever setting foot inside a classroom. The new tutor, often still appointed with little or no teaching experience or qualifications, can study the recorded teaching sessions, student responses and debates, and use these to develop his or her own styles and methods before being similarly helped. Moreover, where there are suspected weaknesses (or strengths) in the teaching performances of experienced staff, the opportunity to measure and address these democratically with staff and students, rather than through the fear and favour of some other 'authority', must be welcomed. Thus the critical core of most induction, development and quality assurance in teaching can be reclaimed, managed and where necessary documented by and in the interests of tutors and their students, helping to arrest the growing tendency to be seduced into a culture of dependence upon what are often perceived to be extraneous and labyrinthine, even if benign, institutional procedures.

What is the Role of the Department?

Although collaborative research and analysis may lead to shared but local agreements about changes that can be introduced to improve the effectiveness of teaching, such as the assessment of student seminars or the creation of course handbooks, there is no reason why differences of opinion among staff and students should not prove equally rewarding. Much may depend upon the context of leadership and management in which differences are normally debated, but as heads of department are unlikely to have earned promotion on the basis of their outstanding contribution to good teaching, so they may be disinclined to dominate discussion on this subject. One of the greatest obstacles to research and innovation is the fear that it must either be ignored or marginalized, or lead to the wholesale abandonment of traditional practices. In a department where differences are respected, these fears can be surmounted, and it should be possible to introduce forms of teaching and assessment that are designed specifically to meet individual needs and the particular objectives of the courses offered. Uncritical conformity to the standard system of lectures, seminars, essays and examinations may thus give way to more genuine diversity of choice for staff and students; encouraging both to teach and learn more according to their own talents than to pre-conceived notions about what constitute the proper methods.

As there is no single way to teach or learn that is always 'right' or 'best' for all staff and students – almost any kind of teaching having some disadvantages as well as benefits for both parties on any real occasion – the role of academic leaders and managers should not be conceived as providing answers to the multitude of questions that can be asked about how to make improvements, but to create a context in which research, analysis and innovation will be undertaken and sustained by everyone.

Initially, this may involve the questioning of unhelpful notions: that there is a natural hierarchy of all teaching methods, from best to worst, which transcends the need to describe and understand the complexities of teaching and learning in any actual situation; that the 'best' methods of teaching history have been long-established because they are long-practised; that profound knowledge of subject-matter (as measured by historical research and publication) is always the most important ingredient of good teaching; that experienced tutors cannot benefit from (and therefore need not participate in) review programmes, because their teaching skills will have reached an optimum. But even such discouraging opinions can be turned to some constructive use by calling for the submission of evidence to prove them. More difficult to counter will be the more publicly declared and often genuine objections that current work-pressures are so great that there is no time left to invest in fresh activities. Yet, heads of department or their equivalents can address priorities and stress that one activity at least, the weeding-out of what is ineffective, is an important aspect of improvement, and clearly time-saving in the long run. Many historians will be highly motivated by the personal satisfaction and the benefits to students that can be realized through the making of improvements. But others will probably need constant reassurance that it is possible to develop a culture in which the critical investigation of current teaching can be conducted in a spirit of mutual support and tolerance, rather than correction and intimidation.

Whatever improvements individuals and departments choose to make, they will need to be based not only upon activities that are properly designed to test the effectiveness of current practices but also on ones that inform staff and students about the range of alternative methods that could be introduced. Among the latter are many activities that are taken for granted by individuals and departments in their efforts to advance historical research and scholarship, but which are often undervalued with regard to the quest for teaching excellence. Thus, in creating a culture of research and innovation in history education, there is no reason to suppose that the ordinary habits of reading, attending and initiating workshops, seminars and conferences, and working with colleagues from other disciplines and institutions, are not vital elements. They are also low-cost options which are easily supported, and which permit the participation of all historians according to their interests. More expensive methods of promoting and disseminating knowledge, such as the appointment of research assistants, external consultants, and the establishment of teaching research centres, are not difficult to imagine and should be welcomed. But as the effectiveness of teaching cannot be increased without the constant development of tutor and student skills in real conditions, the raising of awareness and understanding cannot be sufficient in itself to produce improvement. Whatever the merits of placing funds for historical research in the hands of highly selected individuals and institutions, the definition and delivery of improvements in teaching and learning must remain part of every tutor's and student's responsibilities.

To ensure continuous engagement in the search for improvements, it should be possible for departments to produce explicit statements of the activities that are normally expected of all tutors, and how these will be monitored. Such statements will need to be agreed within the general review of the department's resources and priorities and take account of individual needs and interests, but, however formulated, all tutors might be expected to consider the following kinds of questions:

- How are you deepening your knowledge about teaching and learning in higher education?
- How are you obtaining and using feedback information about your own teaching?
- How are you developing your teaching abilities?
- How are you measuring the effects of any changes that you have introduced?
- How are you contributing to the development of colleagues' teaching skills and knowledge?

Of course, improving teaching cannot be confined to what happens in the classroom, or to what one or two individual tutors can accomplish. Each department creates a context of learning, in terms of workloads, assessment systems and so forth, that directly affects student perceptions, motivations and approaches to studying. Moreover, it is easy to overlook how physically, academically and personally intimidating some departments may appear to students; how tutors' comments at staff/ student meetings may seem patronizing or dismissive; how little time we now have to help students with their problems. So, many other questions can be asked about how the department as a whole sets about enhancing the contexts of student learning.

Conclusion

This chapter has explored some of the ways in which we can improve both our thinking about teaching and our effectiveness as tutors. In particular it stresses the importance of constantly learning about and working with our students. However varied our education experiences and values, and however traditional or innovative we regard our teaching methods, we can all benefit from the testing and sharing of our opinions and our findings. In this respect, we are still only just beginning.

Notes

1 See, for example, P. Ramsden, 'Student Learning Research: Retrospect and Prospect', *Higher Education Research and Development*, 4 (1985), pp. 51–69.

2 See K. A. Feldman, 'The Superior College Teacher from the Students' View', *Research in Higher Education*, 5 (1976), pp. 243–88; H. W. Marsh, 'Students' Evaluations of University Teaching: Dimensionality, Reliability, Validity, Potential Biases, and Utility', *Journal of Educational Psychology*, 76 (1984), pp. 707–54; H. W. Marsh, 'Students' Evaluations of University Teaching: Research Findings, Methodological Issues, and Directions for Future Research', *International Journal of Educational Research*, 11 (1987), pp. 255–378; T. M. Sherman, et al., 'The Quest for Excellence in University Teaching', *Journal of Higher Education*, 58 (1987), pp. 66–84.

3 See P. Ramsden and N. Entwistle, 'Effects of Academic Departments on Students' Approaches to Studying', *British Journal of Educational Psychology*, 51 (1981), pp. 368–83; J. H. F. Meyer and P. Parsons, 'Approaches to Studying and Course Perceptions using The Lancaster Inventory – a Comparative Study', N. Entwistle, 'Approaches to Studying and Course Perceptions: The Case of the Disappearing Relationship', P. Ramsden, 'Perceptions of Courses and Approaches to Studying: An Encounter with Paradigms', *Studies in Higher Education*, 14 (1989), pp. 137–53, 155–6, 157–8; N. Entwistle and H. Tait, 'Approaches to Learning, Evaluations of Teaching, and Preferences for Contrasting Academic Environments', *Higher Education*, 19 (1990), pp. 169–94; P. Ramsden, 'A Performance Indicator of Teaching Quality in Higher Education: The Course Experience Questionnaire', *Studies in Higher Education*, 16 (1991), pp. 129–49; L. Gow and D. Kember, 'Conceptions of Teaching and their Relationship to Student Learning', *British Journal of Educational Psychology*, 63 (1993), pp. 20–33.

4 See, for example, the comparison of student and tutor perceptions, in K. O. Doyle, *Evaluating Teaching* (Lexington Books, Lexington, Mass., 1983), pp. 27–42.

5 For discussion of feedback and improvement, see A. Rotem and N. S. Glasman, 'On the Effectiveness of Students' Evaluative Feedback to University Instructors', *Review of Educational Research*, 49 (1979), pp. 497–

511; P. A. Cohen, 'Effectiveness of Student-Rating Feedback for Improving College Instruction: A Meta-Analysis of Findings', *Research in Higher Education*, 13 (1980), pp. 321–41; R. C. Wilson, 'Improving Faculty Teaching: Effective Use of Student Evaluations and Consultants', *Journal of Higher Education*, 57 (1986), pp. 196–211.

6 L. A. Braskamp, D. C. Brandenburg and J. C. Ory, *Evaluating Teaching Effectiveness: A Practical Guide* (Sage, Beverly Hills, California, 1984); J. A. Centra, 'Formative and Summative Evaluation: Parody or Paradox?', and D. H. Gil, 'Instructional Evaluation as a Feedback Process', in *Techniques for Evaluating and Improving Instruction*, New Directions for Teaching and Learning, no. 31, ed. L. M. Aleamoni (Jossey-Bass, San Francisco, 1987), pp. 47–55, and 57–64.

7 A great range of activities are outlined in G. Gibbs, S. and T. Habeshaw, *53 Interesting Ways to Appraise Your Teaching* (Technical and Educational Services, Bristol, 1988).

8 See J. Levinson-Rose and R. J. Menges, 'Improving College Teaching: A Critical Review of Research', *Review of Educational Research*, 51 (1981), pp. 403–34.

9 See F. F. Fuller and B. A. Manning, 'Self-Confrontation Reviewed: A Conceptualization for Video Playback in Teacher Education', *Review of Educational Research*, 43 (1973), pp. 469–528; D. P. Hoyt and G. S. Howard, 'The Evaluation of Faculty Development Programs', *Research in Higher Education*, 8 (1978), pp. 25–38; J. Bergman 'Peer Evaluation of University Faculty', *College Student Journal*, 14 (1980), pp. 1–21; P. A. Cohen and W. J. McKeachie, 'The Role of Colleagues in the Evaluation of College Teaching', *Improving College and University Teaching*, 28 (1980), pp. 147–54; G. Skoog, 'Improving College Teaching Through Peer Observation', *Journal of Teacher Education*, 31 (1980), pp. 23–5; B. B. Helling, 'Looking for Good Teaching: A Guide to Peer Observation', *Journal of Staff, Program, and Organizational Development*, 6 (1988), pp. 147–58.

Further Reading

Of many books to choose from, few are likely to be as stimulating or as challenging to new and experienced historians as P. Ramsden's *Learning to Teach in Higher Education* (Routledge, London, 1992). Drawing widely upon educational theory and academic practices across many disciplines and countries, Ramsden argues that we need to change our thinking about teaching. For tutors who are looking for clear and practical guidance about how to improve the effectiveness of their teaching, two books are particularly useful: R. M. Beard and J. Hartley, *Teaching and Learning in Higher Education* (Harper and Row, London, 1984 edn); and G. Brown and M. Atkins, *Effective Teaching in Higher Education* (Methuen, London, 1988). S. C. Ericksen offers a more relaxed text, which takes the role of tutor as motivator of student learning as a central theme: *The Essence of Good Teaching* (Jossey-Bass, San Francisco, 1984).

In thinking about how evaluation can be used to improve teaching, K. O. Doyle's *Evaluating Teaching* (Lexington Books, Lexington, 1983) is useful for its analysis of many methodological issues and problems. L. A. Braskamp, D. C. Brandenburg and J. C. Ory's *Evaluating Teaching Effectiveness* (Sage, Beverly Hills, 1984) provides a step-by-step guide to the merits of various sources and approaches, constantly distinguishing between evaluations that are conducted for the purposes of making personnel decisions and those for making faculty improvements. A lengthy Appendix includes copies of a wide range of materials used in American universities. Less technical but no less interesting is *Techniques for Evaluating and Improving Instruction*, New Directions for Teaching and Learning, no. 31, ed. L. M. Aleamoni (Jossey-Bass, San Francisco, 1987). This contains eleven articles discussing issues such as faculty concerns about student ratings, differences between formative and summative practices, and how departments can develop comprehensive evaluation systems. L. Elton's *Teaching in Higher Education: Appraisal and Training* (Kogan Page, London, 1987) is a cut-and-paste collection, but with many incisive sections. Maryellen Weimer's *Improving College Teaching* (Jossey-Bass, San Francisco, 1990) is very readable and especially useful for its discussion of the importance of departmental and institutional initiatives to promote improvement.

PART III

Teaching with Multi-media

9

Computer-assisted Teaching and Learning

Donald A. Spaeth

Many historians view computers with considerable suspicion and question their relevance to history.[1] Computer-based research often retains its identification with quantitative history. Although cliometrics has established a firm place within the 'new' social and political history, it has been less successful elsewhere in the profession where there is perceived to be little need to crunch numbers. Computer-assisted teaching also finds it difficult to shake off its early history as programmed learning, in which students answered a succession of factual multiple-choice questions. These views reflect historical computing as it was fifteen years ago, before the advent of the microcomputer placed a rich selection of research and teaching tools at the disposal of historians. This chapter will introduce ways in which computers can be used to enhance the teaching of history and will offer suggestions on the design and delivery of computer-assisted materials. The focus will be on teaching history with the computer rather than computing as a subject in its own right.

Broadly speaking, computers may be used to support computer-assisted teaching and learning in two ways.[2] In the 'workshop' approach students learn to use general-purpose programs to explore and analyse historical data derived from primary sources. The increased opportunity they gain to study documentary evidence is a central justification for this form of instruction. Because of its emphasis on student use of computers as tools to explore sources, the approach may also be termed 'tools-based' or 'source-based'. A second approach is to use the computer as an instructional medium, supplementing or replacing other forms of instruction such as reading, lectures and even seminars. Various materials are available, including not only programmed learning but also simulations, electronic books, and hypermedia, a new form of instructional software which is likely to become increasingly important. By providing both sources and instruction, hypermedia projects such as *Who Built America?* and the UK-based History Courseware Consortium are breaking down the barriers between these approaches to teaching with computers.[3]

The history lecturer may also use computers to support teaching in other ways: to prepare reading lists and handouts, to record and analyse marks or grades, and to generate graphs, maps and textual information for display on an overhead projector during the lecture, using transparencies or a computer screen. These methods will not be discussed further in this chapter.[4]

The Computer as Tool

Many readers will have benefited from the technological revolution of the 1980s, in the form of a microcomputer with word-processing software on their desk. The development of a range of data management and analysis software which runs on the same microcomputer has been equally significant. Most of these 'applications packages' were developed with businessmen in mind, not historians,[5] but they are suitable for handling large amounts of information of all types and much easier to use than the statistical packages of the 1970s. The nature of research requires most historians to read, transcribe, organize and evaluate large quantities of data. Traditionally they have performed these tasks on cards and paper, developing intricate personal indexing and filing systems to help them to organize and locate notes on particular people, places and subjects.[6] Data-handling software running on microcomputers can help with many of these tasks. Historians are likely to find three types of software particularly helpful, both in teaching and research: the database management system, the spreadsheet and the text handler. Limitations of space make it impossible to do more than introduce these applications here.[7]

The *database management system*, or database for short, is suited to handling sources which can be represented as lists of items with a regular structure.[8] The best-known example is the census enumerator's book, but there are many others: poll books, criminal indictments, workhouse admissions, militia records and the Domesday Book, to name only a few. Historians may use a database to record transcripts in a structured format, sort them (e.g. by name and place), search for particular names and subjects, bring together records which share characteristics, and even calculate simple statistics. It is now common practice to transcribe information as it appears in the original source, preserving the uniqueness of individual examples, rather than replacing values with numerical codes; relational databases can provide a useful tool if later one wishes to group values together into categories to facilitate analysis. In short, the database can be regarded as an electronic card–file index which can support teaching and research in many ways. In the UK, it is the software most widely used in history teaching (see figure 9.1).[9]

Name	Occupation	Total estate
ADAM, DOCTOR CHARLES	DOCTOR OF MEDICINE	822
ADAM, JAMES	INNKEEPER	243
ADAM, JAMES	GROCER	285
ADAM, ROBERT	SPIRIT MERCHANT	94
ADDISON, ALEXANDER	STATIONER	218
AIKMAN, ANN OR NICOL	WIDOW	574
AIRD, JOHN	UNSPECIFIED	954
AITKEN, HUGH	DYER AND CALICO PRINTER	
AITKEN, JAMES	UNSPECIFIED	15033
AITKEN, MARGARET OR HUTTON	UNSPECIFIED	3143

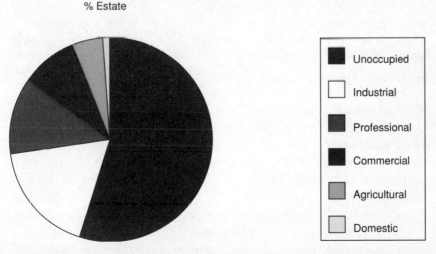

% Estate

Unoccupied
Industrial
Professional
Commercial
Agricultural
Domestic

Figure 9.1 A table and chart from the database of Scottish Confirmations in 1881, used to explore patterns of wealth-holding. The table shows a portion of records for ten people from Glasgow. The pie chart displays the distribution by economic sector of the total estates of the deceased, revealing that those in the 'Unoccupied' sector accounted for the largest share

The *spreadsheet* is an electronic ledger sheet which performs calculations on numerical data.[10] Data and formulae can be entered and form the basis of graphs, charts and (in most mainstream spreadsheets) regression analysis. Calculations are automatically recalculated if any data values are changed. In short, the spreadsheet is a flexible means of exploring numerical data and models, as well as a simple tool for statistical analysis. Numerical data may come from the structured sources already mentioned, as well as from economic statistics, business records and similar sources. Some economic history lecturers use the spreadsheet in teaching as a simpler alternative to the statistics packages (such as SPSS-X).[11] Microcomputer versions of statistics packages are now also available and are generally easier to use than their mainframe ancestors.

The *text handling* package provides tools for studying descriptive textual material, the primary sources most commonly used by historians. Typical sources include letters, depositions, debates, charters and treatises. Literary and linguistic scholars have been using computers to analyse texts for over thirty years.[12] For example, a concordancing package will retrieve and display all passages in which a particular word or words is used.[13] Some packages offer specialized features such as collocation analysis, which involves systematic study of the contexts in which words are used and therefore of their meaning and importance. Text handling packages have so far been used in teaching by only a few historians, but they have considerable potential, particularly for cultural and intellectual history.[14] Hybrid databases which can handle large amounts of text are also appearing, although these generally offer fewer analytical features than standard database packages (see figure 9.2).

These three types of software do not exhaust the potential applications of the computer for historians. Mapping software seems likely to join them in the near future, as easy-to-use and inexpensive packages become available.[15] Scholars have also written specialized software to construct social networks, perform qualitative data analysis and assist nominal record linkage, among other tasks.[16] Online bibliographies such as the *Humanities Citation Index*, library catalogues, the *Eighteenth-century Short Title Catalogue* and many other databases can be accessed via academic and commercial communications networks or CD-ROM. The Internet network also provides worldwide access to 'information servers', a new medium for publishing sources, documents and articles, and to communication via electronic mail. Any of these applications could be incorporated into teaching.

RAINSBOROUGH: For my part, I think we cannot engage one way or other in the Army if we do not think of the people's **liberties**; if we can agree where the liberty and freedom of the people lies, that will do all.

PETTY: There should be an equal share in both. I understood your engagement was, that you would use all your endeavours for the **liberties** of the people, that they should be secured. If there is a constitution, that the people are not free, that should be annulled.

WILDMAN: To their charge that they are dividers. And though it be declared, that the malice of the enemies would have bereaved you of your **liberties** as Englishmen, therefore as Englishmen they are deeply concerned to regard the due observation of their rights, as I, . . .

IRETON: To, nor doth not choose any; and I will make it clear. If a foreigner come within this kingdom, if that stranger will have **liberty** who hath no local interest here, he is a man, it's true, hath air that by nature we must not expel our coasts, give him no being amongst us, nor kill him because he comes . . .

Figure 9.2   A concordance of the Putney debates of 1646, showing uses of the words 'liberty' and 'liberties' by four speakers.

Goals and Objectives

Courses which adopt the workshop approach to computer-assisted history teaching usually have one or all of the following goals:

1   *To introduce students to the application of computer-based tools to historical problems.* Some courses seek simply to provide students with transferable skills which will be useful in the job market (and to attract students who value such skills). Others are intended to teach students specialized techniques relevant to historians, such as quantitative methods and database management. These methods courses will help the next generation of historians to make the best use of computers in their own teaching and research. Advanced courses may also teach students the programming skills they will need to develop specialized computer-based tools for historians.

2   *To enhance students' understanding of how historians work*, by enabling them to explore and form their own interpretations of computer-based versions of historical source material. A few courses seek to teach students the research skills they need to embark on an independent project, such as an undergraduate dissertation. Most are less ambitious, however, and aim to help students appreciate

that history is a dynamic subject based on the interpretation of often conflicting and ambiguous information, not on the memorization of a set of known facts, and to develop their own interpretations. Students are also led to think about the limitations of sources and about how to represent the complexity of their contents on a computer.[17]

3   *To enhance students' understanding of a particular historical topic*, through exploration of primary source material, supplementing lectures and reading. For example, browsing through datasets of bankruptcies and marriages may cast new light on the formation and self-awareness of the Victorian middle class. Students can use the computer to study sources which otherwise would be inaccessible, for example those which provide information about the lives of thousands of individuals.

It is worth stressing that the primary emphasis of most courses is on teaching history, not computing, computer science or programming. Even if it is thought to be a 'good thing' for students to make use of computers during their studies, there seems to be general consensus that this must have an academic purpose. Computer-assisted history teaching is far more than computer literacy, which teaches computing without reference to any subject. Courses will be most successful when computing is integrated fully into history. One of the attractions of the workshop approach is that it is intrinsically open-ended, not pre-packaged; it therefore is consistent with the aim of helping students learn that history is an interpretive subject.

Current Practice

Computer-assisted teaching can now be found in many UK departments of history, but it has had only limited impact on the curriculum. Since the early 1980s, the number of history courses using computers has grown significantly. Research carried out in the UK in 1989–90 by the Computers in Teaching Initiative Centre for History (CTICH), and by Roger Middleton and Peter Wardley, found many history departments using computers in their teaching.[18] CTICH located over one hundred lecturers using computers and were able to collect details on more than fifty history courses. Middleton and Wardley identified forty-three courses using computers to teach economic and social history.[19] It is likely that most departments of history in British universities and colleges of higher education offer at least one course in which students are expected to use computers. Yet few use computers in more than a single course and most of these focus on computer-based methods.

Although no systematic survey has been made of similar courses in the United States, it appears that computers are used less widely there. Courses also tend to differ in focusing more on research skills and quantitative methods. The statistical package SPSS is still widely used, although this is often also because departments must rely on central provision from the institution's 'mainframe' computer. In Europe, the extent of computer-assisted undergraduate instruction varies between countries. In the Netherlands, historical computing is a subject in its own right taught by distinct departments of humanities computing. Graduates of such courses are essentially learning historical information science and will be able to produce the tools which the next generation of historians will use. In Italy and Germany computers are little used in undergraduate teaching, but postgraduates are able to receive training in computer-based research methods.[20]

In Britain computer-assisted history courses differ widely in length and character, but can be broken into three categories: courses on computer-based methods, those which address historical topics but include a distinct unit or module on computer-based methods, and courses on historical topics which integrate computer-based materials throughout.

Computer-based historical methods

The most common type of course concentrates on computer-based methods in history, with a title such as 'History and Computing'. A typical course introduces students to several types of software, most often database management, but also spreadsheets, statistical packages, word processing and, less often, text handling or electronic mail. Students learn that different sources call for different software, so that they will be able to choose the appropriate tool when working independently.

For example, honours students at the University of Glasgow may take the 'Historical Computing' course in their third or fourth year as part of their degree. They learn to use four main types of software: a database, spreadsheet, statistics package and textual analysis package. In the first term, they concentrate on one major source, printed Scottish *Calendars of Confirmations of Estates* (or inventories at death) from 1881. This source was chosen because most students will have a background in either modern, Scottish or economic history. Students also examine related sources and create their own database from university matriculation records. Several political works, including Sieyes's *What is the Third Estate?* and the *Federalist Papers*, are explored for half of the second term, which focuses on textual analysis. The course is assessed by an independent research project, in which students apply the skills they have learned to a problem of their own choice, and by a traditional written examination paper.[21] It is taught by a team of history lecturers with varying degrees of experience with computers, and not by computer specialists. The Glasgow course is typical of many others, in that it is taught by historians, provides instruction in several types of microcomputer software and uses projects to assess student work.[22]

Methods courses are best at equipping students with historical research and computing skills. They are less effective in teaching historical topics, because there is a danger that the techniques students learn will be divorced from their historical contexts. The shortage of suitable datasets and the differing backgrounds of students may mean that they know little of the contexts of particular sources. The use of lectures and reading to provide background information, and of seminars, away from the computer, to discuss the sources and historical literature, can address this problem. Students must also invest a considerable amount of time in learning to use each program, leaving less time to study historical questions. For this reason, some courses are turning to software running on the Apple Macintosh or under Microsoft Windows, since all packages are similar in their graphical appearance and method of use, reducing learning time.

Topical courses

Computing may be more fully integrated into the teaching of historical topics by being introduced to a course covering a historical period or theme, either within a distinct unit or throughout the course. A unit may comprise one or more sessions in which students learn enough about computers to explore a particular set of sources relating to the content of the courses. The remainder of the course therefore provides the historical context within which the source is studied. Since the topic rather than methods is the priority, such courses usually introduce only one type of software. For example, an outline course in American history which was taught at the University of Edinburgh incorporated a six-session unit on immigration, in which six of the ninety students on the course explored a census dataset and created their own from a register of ship passengers.[23] Courses incorporating such units are almost as common as distinct computer-based methods courses. They add a new dimension to courses which otherwise would rely largely on lecturing and secondary reading.

A small number of courses integrate computing fully into a course on a historical topic. This is often most successful when students explore both computer-based evidence and other documentary sources, for example in an undergraduate seminar or 'special subject'. A key aspect of the Lower Manhattan Project is that students are asked to use three kinds of evidence about immigrants living in New York's Lower East Side: a novel, an anthology of documents on social welfare, and a dataset derived from the 1900 manuscript census enumerators' returns which is analysed statistically using the student version of SPSS/PC. They consider such themes as community and neighbourhood, the family, political movements, immigration, urbanization and industrialization. In a course at Tulane University students study the Salem witchcraft trials using documentary evidence such as court testimony, genealogy and probate records. Computer-based evidence has been added to this course, enabling them to explore the chronology of accusations, the tax status and residence of participants and the connections with a dispute over the minister.[24] These topics are supported by extensive historical literature. However, both courses introduce these secondary works only after students have been asked to form their own views from the primary source material. A topical course might equally take the opposite approach, asking students to formulate hypotheses based on their secondary reading which they then test on the primary sources. As these examples suggest, topical courses need not address nineteenth-century social history in order to use computers. Many medieval and early modern topics may also be covered, such as Domesday England or eighteenth-century crime.

Teaching a Workshop Course

The preceding section should have provoked some ideas about ways of using computers in teaching. This section is intended to provide a brief step-by-step guide to developing a computer-assisted history course.

Use computers for a personal project

If you are not already using computers to manage research or administration, it may be a good idea to start a computer-based project of your own before introducing computers to a course; for example, to record a source you currently keep on cards, or for bibliography. Although this step is not essential, it will familiarize you with computers and may have the added benefit of creating a dataset you can ask students to explore. You will also learn of any pitfalls which students might themselves meet.

Decide on course type and goals

It is perhaps an obvious point that the type of course you decide to offer will depend upon your goals. A course on computer-based methods may be most appropriate if your main aim is to ensure that students have an opportunity to use computers and learn to apply them to historical problems. On the other hand, if you wish students to study computer-based data in order to illuminate a particular historical issue, it may be better to introduce computers into a topical course. It is advisable to start small by making the course or unit an option, even if you intend to make it a requirement in the long run, since a large class might need to be broken up into several groups so that every student has a chance to use the computer.

Identify hardware, software and data

In theory, the historical issues and sources to be covered should dictate the software and hardware which are chosen, particularly if computers are being introduced into a topical course. In practice, you may have little control over hardware and software, since these may already be in place. The availability of machine-readable data may also limit the issues you can address. Datasets and electronic texts can be obtained from a data archive or colleague, or created especially for the course. Two British surveys undertaken early in the 1990s uncovered hundreds of datasets, including many which are still in personal hands.[25] Although many datasets have been created, you should still allow considerable time to find appropriate materials. Archives will be able to supply codebooks and other documentation describing datasets which look relevant to your course. It may be possible to obtain datasets in personal hands directly from the creator, although these may not be as well documented or as accurate. It is usually possible to convert datasets from other software formats into your own, or the archive may provide this service for you.

When choosing datasets for teaching, look for ones which are as complete and as close to the original source from which they were transcribed as is possible, retaining personal names, occupations and other textual data. Avoid datasets which use extensive numerical coding (although codes can often be converted to textual labels if necessary). The dataset should also record enough types of information to enable students to explore several issues or aspects of an issue. One of the reasons for the popularity of the census as a source is that it contains information touching on so many issues, including immigration, education, occupational stratification and family structure, and relationships between these.

Creating your own dataset need not be time-consuming. A simple dataset of a few hundred records can be built in a few days and has several advantages. It is more likely to meet your teaching objectives, and you have control over the way in which it is entered; for example, whether original or standardized spellings are used. Furthermore, students will be able to see the original source and compare it with the machine-readable transcript, so that they understand that the latter is itself an interpretation of the source. Particularly in methods courses, students should also be asked to create their own small dataset or electronic text, so that they have an opportunity to think about the nature and reliability of sources, as well as to make decisions about how to interpret a source in order to make what is essentially an electronic edition.

Decide what historical questions students will explore

You will need to spend some time exploring the data, looking for fruitful lines of enquiry which you might ask students to follow. These may be derived from historical debates or directly from the source. This stage is particularly important, since it enables you to identify questions which produce meaningful results. Although the computer allows students to explore source materials independently, they will not be able to do so at first. Data exploration involves looking for patterns, and these do not always reveal themselves immediately even to experienced scholars – let alone to students new to computers. A student whose initial queries produce meaningless results may become discouraged and question the value of the exercise. Later, of course, when students have become comfortable with the software and the source they will be able to explore the dataset independently. A good question should produce clear results that cast light on a historical issue; for example, the occupations and educations of immigrants, or party loyalty from election to election. There is no point in getting students to ask how may boys were named 'John', unless naming practices are being studied!

Prepare and deliver the course

Computer-based courses are often similar in structure to traditional courses in providing a mix of lectures, seminars and reading, in addition to workshops in which students use the computers. Prepare handouts or a workbook which students work through at their own pace. The handout will cover both the historical questions under consideration that day, derived from your advance exploration of the data, and any computing techniques students need to learn to explore them. Ideally, it will start by providing precise instructions of what key to press next, but will gradually give fewer details, until finally students are left to figure out how to answer the questions on their own. Quicker students may abandon the handout entirely, preferring to explore their own questions. Use of a handout is far preferable to the alternative, in which the lecturer merely talks the class through the use of the software. Students working from a handout learn to become more independent, rather than waiting to be told what to do next. Since students work at different rates, you can take the time to help those with problems or to discuss new findings with the quicker ones.

Assessment

If the primary goal is increased historical understanding, then student work can be assessed traditionally through essays and a written examination. An essay may be judged according to the student's ability to marshal appropriate evidence and to recognize its limitations, just as it would in a traditional course; however, now computer-based evidence will be included. If it is considered important to assess students' ability to use the computer, then you might ask them to submit their workshop results. A computer-based project and essay can be incorporated into the formal assessment in addition to, or even in place of, a written examination paper.

Potential problems

Although introducing computer workshops may enhance history teaching, it is not an easy option. It is labour intensive, both for academics and for students, and requires significant expenditure on equipment and software. Besides additional preparation time when the course is first taught, the instructor will need to set aside time to assist students who encounter difficulties with new concepts or software. This is another reason for initially restricting the number of students who take a historical computing course or unit. There is also an opportunity cost for students, who will be using computers in some of the time they might otherwise devote to lectures, seminar discussions or reading. To sceptics this is an argument against the introduction of computers. Many academics will feel, however, that the benefits of increased student understanding of the way historians work, the insights derived from exploration of sources and information management skills gained outweigh these costs.[26]

The Computer as Instructor

So far this chapter has concentrated on the use of the computer as an assistant or tool, which helps the lecturer by enabling students to explore primary source material. The computer may also be used as an instructional medium in its own right, to replace or enhance some aspect of the teaching and learning process, such as formal instruction, independent reading, or assessment. It is widely accepted, however, that the computer cannot replace the many roles of the teacher, although particular packages may be able to replace small well-defined aspects of teaching. For example, no computer is able to make the personalized replies which a tutor can give to students.

Instructional software has so far received relatively little use in UK higher education, although it is more widely available in schools.[27] These packages seek to enhance student learning of historical topics in several ways: to motivate students by providing them with another medium; to use the new medium to evoke new insights; to fill gaps in the literature or free academics for other forms of contact with students. A brief summary of the main types of instructional software follows.[28]

Drilling and assessment

Drilling and assessment programs provide students with a series of multiple-choice questions which they must answer. Some American textbooks come with questions on disk, and software is available in which academics can enter their own. Drilling programs may form part of the formal assessment process, or they may be used by students to check their own progress. They may, however, confirm the prejudice that history consists simply of rote memorization of names and dates, discouraging deeper analytical thinking by students. In any case, they are unlikely to find a place in institutions which do not use multiple-choice questions as part of the examination process, including all British higher education institutions.

Simulations

Broadly speaking, simulations enable students to 're-live' some aspect of the past, for example a key event, in order to increase their understanding of the historical context and of the behaviour of groups or individuals. A simulation may be based on a real event or on a hypothetical model. In the former case, the student takes the part of a historical actor. For example, in Carolyn Lougée's *Would-Be Gentleman* the student is a *bourgeois* who seeks to improve his social position in the France of Louis XIII. In order to succeed in such a simulation, the student must understand aspects of the society (or of the author's interpretation of it). The 'would-be gentleman', for example, needs to know how *rentes* operated. The simulation may be intended to motivate the student to research the topic in order to learn enough to succeed. Alternatively, John Semonche's *Simulations in US History* provides the necessary details within each package.

Simulations may also be based on a hypothetical model, although examples are most often taken from other disciplines, such as economics, geography and archaeology. The student sets priorities, allocates a budget or decides when to travel. For example, in *Sand Harvest* the student makes some of the choices available to a nomad, aid worker and government official.[29] Both types of simulation are intended to motivate students and to provide them with new insights. Academics who are concerned that students will accept the inevitably simplified view of a simulation might consider presenting it to students as another interpretation of the topic and asking them to critique its bias and use of evidence.

Electronic books

Electronic books such as *Viewbook* and *Hyperbook* provide students with text which they can read on a computer screen. On the face of it, there may seem to be little point in using expensive technology to replace the book, particularly since text is easier to read from paper than on a screen. The electronic format does provide automatic indexing, since the student can search for words and names, and easy notetaking using 'cut-and-paste'.

Electronic seminars

One of the most ambitious sets of materials now available are produced by the Historical Document Expert System (HiDES) Project of the University of Southampton. HiDES packages have been published on a small number of topics ranging from the First Crusade to the origins of the Second World War, and are intended to encourage close reading of a text in order to make discussion in a seminar more productive. Students are given a source, such as the text of the Hossbach Memorandum, and asked to explore a series of questions, typing their answers into notebooks. After each question, the computer assesses the student answer, responding differently depending upon whether particular keywords are used. For example, if the choice of words suggests misunderstanding of the source, then the computer will encourage the student to take a second look. So far, HiDES packages have not been widely used in UK higher education. Some lecturers have expressed concern about the limitations of computer assessment, and feel that it may restrict students' ability to form their own interpretations; recent publications have been targeted at schools.

Hypermedia

The term 'hypermedia' (and 'hypertext' from which it is drawn) may be new to many readers. A 'hypertext' is a document which can be read in many ways, not just from the beginning to the end as a book would be.[30] It takes advantage of the potential of computers to jump from one document to another and then back again, for example from the text of a primary source to a different account of the same event to an annotation. 'Hypermedia' extends this concept to other media, so that one may also view photographs, moving films, maps and drawings, hear recordings and explore data. As a result, 'hypermedia' publications can be very large and are often distributed on a CD-ROM.

Hypermedia is most easily explained with an example. *Who Built America?* is a CD-ROM covering American social history from 1876 to 1914. The core of the package is the 700-page textbook upon which the package is based.[31] The CD-ROM also includes hundreds of primary sources, including transcripts and radio broadcasts of speeches, films (e.g. of woman suffragists and of Teddy Roosevelt), recordings of oral history witnesses, as well as images and graphs. The reader may jump to these sources from cross-references in the text (known as 'excursions' – see figure 9.3) or by choosing them directly from a list. An instructor might ask students to read *Who Built America?* as a particularly richly illustrated book or to use the resources to explore different aspects of American society, for example as the basis for an essay. The best-known example of a hypermedia package in the humanities is *Perseus*, which

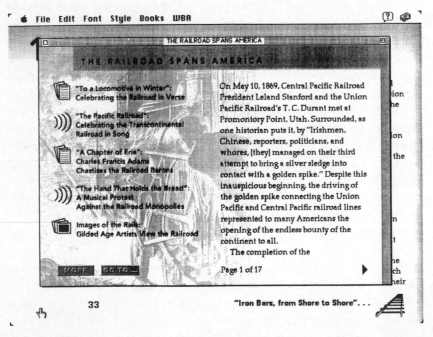

Figure 9.3 An 'excursion' on resources from the *Who Built America* CD-ROM (Voyager, 1993)

provides resources on classical Greece.[32] These include photographs of vases, sculptures and sites, site plans, maps, the complete works of Homer, Thucydides, Sophocles and others, in Greek and English, and a brief overview of the history of fifth-century BC Greece. The HiDES Project is also working on its own hypermedia source collections, including two on India and Yugoslavia in the 1940s.[33]

However, some lecturers have found it difficult to figure out how to make best use of the wealth of resources available on a hypermedia CD-ROM. The History Courseware Consortium is addressing this problem by using the familiar analogy of the lecture as the basis for its hypermedia packages on the Industrial Revolution, the coming of mass politics to modern Europe and other topics. In addition to providing such source material as datasets of members of the French National Convention or of industrial growth, photographs of working and living conditions in industrializing cities and extracts from secondary works, each package will come with an essay which guides a student through these resources. The essay will be similar in style and content to a spoken lecture, supporting the author's observations with evidence drawn from the accompanying sources. The ability of students to interact with sources is being stressed, for example, by allowing them explore datasets rather than merely viewing pre-made graphs. Each package is also intended to be modular, so that lecturers can add new essays and resources in order to meet the needs of their own courses.[34]

Only a few hypermedia publications are available at present, although the number is steadily growing. Specialized 'authoring' software enables lecturers to construct their own packages, and several excellent examples have been developed.[35] In a recent visit to the US, I saw locally produced hypermedia packages on Fort Sumter and the beginnings of the American Civil War, Pompeii, pre-Columbian civilizations, Leonard Bernstein, and the history of western social thought.[36] The construction of one's own hypermedia package is time-consuming and will require the author to acquire technical expertise or to have a local source of technical support. Unless development work is supported by external funding, the investment of time may not produce a commensurate saving of teaching time later on. Yet an increasing number of lecturers find the production of hypermedia materials an enjoyable way of enhancing their teaching.

Hypermedia has great potential to enrich a history course by providing many new resources (such as films), which would otherwise be less readily available, tools to explore them and instructional material in a flexible format which can be adjusted to meet the needs of particular

classes. However, because the medium is new there is as yet little research which tests the impact of hypermedia on student learning.

Using instructional software in teaching

When deciding how to incorporate instructional software into a course,
many of the issues considered when planning workshop courses also
arise. The instructor will need to work through the materials in advance
and to develop possible lines of enquiry for students, so that they get the
maximum out of the resources which are provided. This is particularly
true with large source-based hypermedia publications, for students can
easily lose themselves in a sea of information. It may also be advisable to
suggest appropriate related reading. Although most instructional software is intended to be easy to use, it will be necessary to introduce
students to the computer and software and to relieve any anxieties they
may have. The lecturer may wish to add an instructional package to a
course reading list so that students may refer to it as they would to any
book or article. Alternatively, they may use one or more packages as a
focal point for discussion of a topic or of the author's own interpretation.

Conclusions

At present, when computers are introduced into history teaching the
workshop approach is generally preferred – at least in Britain. This
approach can enhance the teaching of history by facilitating open-ended
exploration of primary sources and stressing the interpretive nature of
the discipline, as well as by equipping students with computing skills. It
is important to be clear about which of these outcomes is paramount, for
example in deciding whether to teach a historical computing methods
course or to introduce a computer element into a topical course.

Although instructional software has left behind its origins in programmed learning, there is still considerable suspicion of the attempt to
pre-package knowledge which it appears to represent. Academics may be
concerned that such software will jeopardize the skills of criticism im-
parted by curricula which emphasise independent reading of books and
articles. Hypermedia is bridging the gap between the workshop and
instructional approaches, enabling students to interact with data and to
explore a variety of primary source material, often much more easily than
with commercial data handling software. The challenge for academics is

to find ways to take advantage of these vast sets of resources in order to enrich their teaching and student learning.

Notes

1 'History' is used as a shorthand for history, economic history and social history. I would like to thank Thomas Munck for his comments on an earlier draft.

2 Computer-assisted learning (CAL) is the most common British phrase to describe the use of computers to support teaching and learning. Alternative phrases include computer-assisted instruction, computer-based learning, computer-managed learning and computer-based training, although the wording of each implies a different teaching philosophy. CAL will be taken in this chapter to apply to student use of computers both as tool and as instructional medium.

3 R. Rosenzweig, S. Brier and J. Brown, *Who Built America?: From the Centennial Celebration of 1876 to the Great War of 1914*, CD-ROM (The Voyager Company, New York, 1993). The History Courseware Consortium involves over forty UK institutions led by the University of Glasgow who seek to develop hypermedia software for teaching history, and is funded by the British Higher Education Funding Councils under the Teaching and Learning Technology Programme. Contact: History Courseware Consortium, University of Glasgow, 1 University Gardens, Glasgow G12 8QQ.

4 J. B. M. Schick, *Teaching History with a Computer: A Complete Guide for College Professors* (Lyceum, Chicago, 1990), ch. 2.

5 A significant exception is Kleio, developed by Manfred Thaller at the Max-Planck-Institut für Geschichte in Göttingen.

6 For a model description of a paper-based system, see A. Macfarlane. *Reconstructing Historical Communities* (Cambridge University Press, Cambridge, 1977). The Earls Colne materials he describes have since been transcribed to machine-readable files.

7 For more details about software for historians see the references in the Further Reading section at the end of this chapter.

8 In 1994 leading database packages on IBM and compatible microcomputers include Borland Paradox, dBaseIV and Microsoft Access, but it is likely that new products will appear in coming years.

9 P. Perkins, D. A. Spaeth and R. H. Trainor, 'Computers and the Teaching of History and Archaeology in Higher Education', *Computers & Education*, 19 (1992), pp. 153–62, esp. p. 155. Cf. R. Middleton and P. Wardley, 'Information Technology in Economic and Social History: The Computer as Philosopher's Stone or Pandora's Box?', *Economic History Review*, 2nd series, 43 (1990), pp. 667–96, esp. pp. 690–3, who find that economic and

social historians continue to make heaviest use of statistics software in their teaching.

10 Industry leaders include Borland Quattro, Microsoft Excel and Lotus 1-2-3.

11 R. Middleton, 'Computer Techniques and Economic Theory in Historical Analysis', *History and Computing*, 1 (1989), pp. 19–37, esp. pp. 29–31.

12 S. Hockey, *A Guide to Computer Applications in the Humanities* (Duckworth, London, 1980).

13 Software products include microOCP, TACT and Wordcruncher.

14 M. Olsen and L. G. Harvey, 'Computers in Intellectual History', *Journal of Interdisciplinary History*, 18 (1988), pp. 449–64.

15 K. E. Foote, 'Mapping the Past: A Survey of Microcomputer Cartography', *Historical Methods*, 25 (1992), pp. 121–31.

16 M. C. Alexander and J. A. Danowski, 'Analysis of an Ancient Network: Personal Communication and the Study of Social Structure in a Past Society', *Social Networks*, 12 (1990), pp. 313–35; *Using Computers in Qualitative Research*, ed. N. G. Fielding and R. M. Lee (Sage, London, 1991); J. Atack, F. Bateman and M. Eschelbach Gregson, ' "Matchmaker, Matchmaker, Make Me a Match": A General Personal Computer-based Matching Program for Historical Research', *Historical Methods*, 25 (1992), pp. 53–65.

17 N. J. Morgan and R. H. Trainor, 'Liberator or Libertine?: The Computer in the History Classroom', in *Humanities and the Computer: New Directions*, ed. D. S. Miall (Clarendon Press, Oxford, 1990), pp. 61–70; R. B. Latner, 'Witches, History, and Microcomputers: A Computer-Assisted Course on the Salem Witchcraft Trials', *The History Teacher*, 21 (1988), pp. 173–93.

18 P. Perkins, D. A. Spaeth and R. H. Trainor, 'CTICH Survey of Computer Use in History, Art History and Archaeology', *Craft*, 5 (1992), p. 5 (for updated figures from Perkins, Spaeth and Trainor, 'Computers and the Teaching of History and Archaeology', pp. 155–6).

19 Middleton and Wardley, 'Philosopher's Stone or Pandora's Box?', pp. 677–80. Some of these courses were not included in the CTICH survey.

20 The Computers in Teaching Initiative Centre for History (CTICH) and the Institute of Historical Research have co-hosted a series of workshops under the aegis of the Association for History and Computing to develop guidelines for an international curriculum for history and computing, leading to the publication of discussion papers and course descriptions. References are given in the Further Reading section.

21 Project subjects have included textual analysis of the autobiography of the Chartist William Lovett, and a study of illegitimacy in nineteenth-century Scotland.

22 For a description of a similar course, see S. E. Kruse, 'Computing and

History Courses for Undergraduates: Issues of Course Design', *History and Computing*, 3 (1991), pp. 104–12.

23 J. Flavell, 'Historical Computing at Edinburgh', *Craft*, 4 (1991), pp. 9–12. Each session lasted three hours. This course used the Lower Manhattan Project dataset described below.

24 W. Crozier and C. Gaffield, 'The Lower Manhattan Project: A New Approach to Computer-Assisted Learning in History Classrooms', *Historical Methods*, 23 (1990), pp. 72–7; Latner, 'Witches, History, and Microcomputers'. For a UK example, focusing on British parliamentary politics, see S. Richardson, 'History and Computing at Warwick', *Craft*, 5 (1992), pp. 20–1.

25 These are listed in K. Schürer and S. J. Anderson, *A Guide to Historical Datafiles Held in Machine-Readable Form* (Association for History and Computing, London, 1992), which includes the names and addresses of dataset creators; and 'Data Sets for Teaching', *Craft*, 5 (1992), pp. 8–10. Further details about archives are provided in the Further Reading section.

26 For an assessment of the costs and benefits of computing courses, see Middleton, 'Computer Techniques and Economic Theory in Historical Analysis', pp. 32–6.

27 CTICH found instructional software being used in only six courses in 1990: Perkins, Spaeth and Trainer, 'CTICH Survey', p. 5.

28 All named products are listed in D. A. Spaeth, *A Guide to Software for Historians* (University of Glasgow, Glasgow, 1991), unless otherwise indicated. See the Further Reading section for other sources of information.

29 *Sand Harvest* v. 3, computer-based simulation (CWDE Software, London, 1990).

30 G. Russell, 'Hypertext', *History and Computing*, 3 (1991), pp. 183–5; M. Deegan, N. Timbrell and L. Warren, *Hypermedia in the Humanities* (CVCP, Sheffield, 1992); G. P. Landow, 'Hypertext in Literary Education, Criticism, and Scholarship', *Computers and the Humanities*, 23 (1989), pp. 173–98.

31 Bruce Levine, et al., *Who Built America?: Working People and the Nation's Economy, Politics, Culture and Society* (2 vols, Pantheon, New York, 1989–92); R. Rosenzweig and S. Brier, 'Historians and Hypertext: Is It More than Hype?', *Perspectives* (March 1994), pp. 3–6.

32 G. Grane, editor-in-chief, *Perseus* v. 1.0, CD-ROM with videodisc (Yale University Press, London and New Haven, 1992).

33 W. Hall and F. Colson, 'Multimedia Teaching with Microcosm-HiDES: Viceroy Mountbatten and the Partition of India', *History and Computing*, 3 (1991), pp. 89–98.

34 D. A. Spaeth, 'Past Masters Head Back to the Source to Mind Riches of Another Age', *Times Higher Education Supplement*, 1023 (13 May 1994), pp. x–xi.

35 Leading authoring packages include HyperCard (for the Mac), Toolbook (for the PC) as well as Guide and Authorware Professional (for either). 'Authoring Systems for Courseware Development', *The CTISS File*, 13 (April 1992).
36 D. A. Spaeth, 'Impressions of Historical Computing in the United States (Part I)', *Craft*, 8 (1993), pp. 25–8.

Further Reading

The Computers in Teaching Initiative Centre for History with Archaeology and Art History advises academics in these subjects about using computers in their teaching: CTICH, University of Glasgow, 1 University Gardens, Glasgow, G12 8QQ, United Kingdom. CTICH publishes a bi-annual newsletter, *Craft*, which prints course descriptions and reviews, and provides announcements of software, books and resources.

Listings of software and discussions of their use in historical teaching and research are provided by D. A. Spaeth, *A Guide to Software for Historians* (University of Glasgow, Glasgow, 1991); J. L. Reiff, *Structuring the Past: The Use of Computers in History* (American Historical Association, Washington, DC, 1991); *The Humanities Computing Yearbook 1989/90*, ed. I. Lancashire and W. McCarty (Clarendon Press, Oxford, 1991). The *Economic History Review* publishes an annual review of developments in information technology for economic and social historians in the May issue, edited by R. Middleton and P. Wardley. Since 1991 these issues have included detailed software reviews: *Economic History Review*, 44 (1991), pp. 343–93 (spreadsheets); *ibid.*, 45 (1992), pp. 378–412 (databases, with J. Colson); *ibid.*, 46 (1993), pp. 379–409 (computer-assisted learning, with D. Dunn). *Ibid.*, 47 (1994), pp. 374–404 (statistical analysis and *ibid.*, 48 (1995), pp. 317–95 text-handling packages). The journal *History and Computing* prints articles on teaching and research with computers, and software reviews. *Perspectives*, the bulletin of the American Historical Association, also publishes regular articles describing the application of computers to history.

A textbook on historical computing, stressing database management, is now available: E. Mawdsley and T. Munck, *Computing for Historians* (Manchester University Press, Manchester, 1993). The Association for History and Computing has published two books describing historical computing courses, primarily in Europe. See D. Spaeth, et al., *Towards an International Curriculum for History and Computing* (St Katharinen, Germany, 1992); V. Davis, et al., *The Teaching of Historical Computing: An International Framework* (St Katharinen, Germany, 1992). For US courses, see J. L. Reiff (ed.), 'Special Issue: History, Microcomputers, and Teaching', *Historical Methods*, 21 (1988); M. P. Gutmann, 'Computer-Based History Teaching in Higher Education: The United States', *History and Computing*, 2 (1990), pp. 24–30.

In the UK, datasets can be obtained from the History Data Unit of the ESRC Data Archive, University of Essex, Wivenhoe Park, Colchester, Essex CO4 3SQ. In the US, contact the Inter-University Consortium for Political and Social Research (ICPSR), University of Michigan, Institute for Social Research, PO Box 1248, Ann Arbor, MI 48106. The Oxford Text Archive, Oxford University Computing Service, 13 Banbury Road, Oxford OX2 6NN, provides electronic texts. Information about electronic texts can also be obtained from the Center for Electronic Texts in the Humanities, 169 College Avenue, New Brunswick, NJ 08903.

10

Structured Distance Teaching

Arthur Marwick

In these philistine and market-oriented times, the notion of structured distance teaching has great appeal for our political masters. Structured distance teaching has indeed been the basis of the success of the Open University, both educationally and with respect to cost-effectiveness, but it is important to stress that the economies of scale inherent in the Open University operation are not necessarily available elsewhere. The Open University's Arts Foundation Course enrols 6,000 students a year, the course running, with only relatively minor alterations, for eight years; the strongly historical, second-level interdisciplinary courses enrol over 2,000; and the 'single discipline' history courses are currently taking 500 or more. Distance-teaching packages to OU standards are in themselves expensive to produce. Obviously, in the age of desktop publishing, there are possibilities of economic production for relatively small numbers of students; but not even the miracles of electronics can overcome the fundamental fact that the creation of good teaching material requires careful planning, is labour-intensive, time-consuming and intellectually taxing. It is fairly easy to produce a simulacrum of structured distance teaching, apparently trapped-out with all the mechanisms of Aims and Objectives, Self-Assessment Exercises, Overall Assessment Strategy, and so on, then find that it simply doesn't work; distance teaching material that requires constant face-to-face explanation or qualification has simply failed in its essential purpose. Badly thought-out distance teaching employed in a genuine distance teaching situation can be disastrous.

Distance teaching, in essence, is aimed at the solitary, independent learner. Even so, it operates best in conjunction with certain enhancements, at least one of which could be described as essential. This is the production by students of essays and other written work for formative, rather than merely assessment, purposes; that is to say, there must be a corps of correspondence tutors who do not simply mark essays, but who comment on them copiously and offer the maximum of constructive advice. These tutors, of course, have to be integrated into an overall system ensuring that all are working to the same standards, and, even more critically, to the same course aims. The other major enhancement is the systematic use of television, video, and audio cassettes (the last usually in conjunction with print or visual material – maps, paintings, etc.). Used to its full potential, structured distance teaching offers almost limitless possibilities; used merely as a cut-price substitute for face-to-face teaching it becomes a travesty of education. Perhaps there is an ideal mix of high-quality structured distance material (which can be used to release teachers from the unsatisfactory, and often unduly authoritarian, mass lecture), and intensive face-to-face tuition. Let me, therefore, pin down the fundamental character of structured distance teaching; identify the essential requisites; and summarize the main logistic constraints. Throughout, I shall be drawing examples from the experiences of the Open University History Department. There are a number of admirable guides to the writing of distance teaching, but all are rather general and do not address the particular problems of historical study.

The Character of Structured Distance Teaching

Distance teaching is designed for students who, for whatever reason, do not have access to the lectures, seminars and tutorials of traditional educational institutions. All good teaching must, in some sense, be 'structured', but while the traditional environment allows much scope for the constructive deployment of flair and improvization, distance teaching, which has to be completely set in print in advance, with no scope for qualification or second thoughts, must be rigorously structured throughout. The challenge is to meet this imperative, while maintaining the elements of excitement and participation which are central to all effective teaching. Student participation is largely ensured through 'Self-Assessment Exercises' (a term whose reductionism I deplore, but which can serve as useful shorthand), which are themselves extremely difficult to design. Structured distance teaching, manifestly, is very different from the traditional diet of lectures and tutorials; but in no way is it analogous to the traditional textbook. This is one of several points made on the opening page of one of the Open University's history courses.

The Course Title Explained

This is the first book in the Open University course A318 *War, Peace and Social Change: Europe 1900–1955*. The first part of the course title brings out that, while, as indicated, there will be a discussion of developments taking place in time of peace, particular emphasis will be placed upon the contrasts between 'war' and 'peace', with questions being raised about the significance of war in twentieth-century European history; the first part of the title also indicates that we shall have a special concern with 'social change'. The second part of the title indicates that it is a course in twentieth-century European history up to about 1955. It would have been possible to construct a course which was more simply a general history of Europe between around 1900 and around 1955, much as the textbook by J.M. Roberts, *Europe 1880–1945* (the set book for this course) is a general history of Europe between the two dates contained in its title. Roberts's aim is, within the space at his disposal, to cover anything that is of importance in understanding the development of Europe in the period he is concerned with. Inevitably he emphasizes certain topics at the expense of others, but he has chosen his topics in order, firstly, to give as fair and comprehensive a coverage as possible and, secondly, because he believes the topics he has chosen to be the most important in explaining the development of modern Europe. Naturally he discusses the two major wars ('total' wars we shall be calling them in this course), but he does not give any special emphasis to them. Our course (while making great use of Roberts's excellent book as a basic secondary source) does give a special emphasis to the two total wars. This is partly because we believe a history course is more likely to arouse and maintain your interest, and is more likely to be effective as teaching material, if it sets up some central questions and issues to be discussed, and partly because there actually is quite a good case (perhaps greater than Roberts allows) that it is impossible to understand twentieth-century European history without being fully aware of the various implications of the two total wars. You do not have to agree with this proposition: the course encourages debate and argument over it. Indeed, you could say that there is a third reason for designing the course in this way, which is that among historians and students of twentieth-century history everywhere this debate is considered a most important one, as shown, for instance, by the fact that 'war and society' courses now exist in a number of other universities.

As a teaching course, *War, Peace and Social Change* differs in other ways as well from a general textbook such as that by Roberts. In a very skilful way, and at a quite advanced level, Roberts presents his readers with information, ideas, interrelationships, causes, consequences, comparisons and contrasts: he presents a balanced, carefully structured account, involving narrative, analysis and description. But our course encourages you (the student and reader) to be active. It seeks to help you to develop and practise some of the skills of history. It seeks to show you how to discuss important historical issues relevant to the course, how to develop these arguments in properly written essays. It seeks to develop your understanding of the nature of the primary source materials upon which all historical writing is based, and of how to analyse and use such sources. It seeks to help you to master many of the problems involved in historical study and to help you to understand the significance of the different approaches which have been taken in that study (Marxist and non-Marxist approaches, for instance) . . .

The Essentials of a Structured Distance Teaching Course

A *It must be thoroughly thought through in advance, with the issues, controversies, differing approaches, and exact roles of the individual contributors fully explicated.*

Traditionally, Open University courses have been produced by course teams. There is no organic reason why a course should not be created by one individual; course teams can be at least as ideologically monolithic as individuals. But since there is an irreducibly authoritarian element in print material directed at the solitary learner, plurality of input is always desirable. Explicit recognition of the existence of differences of approach is essential. There is little more disturbing for the independent learner than to find what is said in one unit apparently contradicted or criticized in a later unit, without there being any upfront recognition that this is what is actually happening. (I am taking it that the most productive and economical strategy is for individual units to be the responsibility of individual authors). The spirit should be of openly conducted, friendly debate, with evidence adduced so that students are encouraged to develop whichever lines seem to them most persuasive. Sometimes it may have to be explicitly recognized that students will not be in a position to make a fully informed choice, in which case they should simply be guided towards a full awareness of the existence of different viewpoints.

B   *There must be a set of Aims, covering the course as a whole, and, usually (though this is not always essential), several sets of Objectives, relating to individual sections, or units, of the course.*

The notion of identifying Aims and Objectives (the two terms often being run together, though properly conceived they have very different functions) has been something of a commonplace for some years. It is vital to successful distance teaching that Aims and Objectives are not merely bogus top-dressing but are: (a) exhaustive; (b) achievable; (c) integrally related to what is actually contained in the course. A common reaction of traditionalists, of course, is that the really important things, the subtle and complex things, cannot be pinned down in Aims or Objectives. It may be that defining clearly and explicitly what it is that some traditionalists are trying to do (supposing they know themselves) is beyond their talents; the task is certainly a taxing one. But, with careful thought and thorough self-analysis, it can be accomplished. Aims should express what the designers of the course have set out to achieve. The ultimate tests of the relevance and precision of Aims are: (a) that students do not in practice spend time on activities not clearly included within the Aims; (b) that by the end of the course all but the most hopelessly incompetent of students can answer questions, write essays, and carry out activities which demonstrate that they have indeed learned what the Aims of the course say they are expected to learn. Objectives should be expressed in terms of what students should be able to do at the end of each section or unit of the course. A section or unit can often usefully be concluded by asking students to check through the Objectives to see if they can now do what they are supposed to be able to do. If not, they should work through the appropriate parts again. Or, of course, the Objectives may have been sloppily designed in the first place. In the well-worn platitude, Aims are strategic, Objectives tactical. More critically, the subject in expressing Aims is the course team; the subject in expressing Objectives is the student. Before citing the Aims which immediately follow the introductory paragraphs to *War, Peace and Social Change* quoted above, I should remark that, because the themes of that course are so closely woven together, making the learning process cumulative as much as sequential, Objectives are not usually spelled out for individual sections or units (sometimes specific Aims relating to an individual section are given; and sometimes Objectives). Perhaps the course team should have striven for greater consistency: certainly my advice would be that it is best to adopt the consistent specification of Objectives, unless considered and convincing reasons can be given to the contrary.

The Aims of '*War, Peace and Social Change*':

1   To enable students to argue in an informed way about the nature, extent and causes of social change within and across the main European countries *c*.1900–55, which are defined for the purposes of this course as Russia, Austria-Hungary (up to the aftermath of the First World War only), France, Germany, Italy and the United Kingdom; Turkey and the Balkans, and Central European Countries will be discussed as relevant. (There will also be references to Scandinavian and other European countries.)

2   To help students to understand the nature of total war and the differences between different kinds of war, including internal and civil war, and to help them to discuss in an informed way the relationship between war and revolution in the twentieth century.

3   To enable students to discuss the causes of the two total wars, evaluating 'structural' (that is to say 'concerning economic and industrial imperatives') forces against other forces such as those of geopolitics, ideology, nationalism and contingency.

4   To enable students to argue in an informed way about the causes of twentieth-century social change, and in particular to evaluate the significance of the two total wars with respect to this change relative to 'structural' (see Aim 3), political and ideological forces, and to enable them also to discuss the relationship of the wars to the major geopolitical changes.

5   To assist Open University students to develop skills learned at Foundation and Second Level in:

(a)   the critical analysis and interpretation of primary source materials, including written documents, as well as literary and artistic materials, film, radio, and manifestations of popular culture;

(b)   understanding some of the different approaches to historical study, in particular Marxist/sociological/linguistic approaches on the one side, and 'liberal humanist' ones on the other, and also quantitative and qualitative approaches;

(c)   dealing with such problems as periodization and historical semantics;
and

(d)   writing history essays of BA (Honours) standard.

6   To take further students' understanding of the nature of historiographical controversy (a matter first raised in the Foundation course, dealt with further at Second Level), and to enable them to

arrive at informed judgements on the issues and debates presented within the framework of the course.

These Aims were only finalized once the course had been completed, and differed considerably from those originally sketched out when the course was first being planned. In response to a thorough review of the course, involving student and tutor feedback and further external assessment, three of the Aims were further refined. Entering into the spirit of structured teaching, readers might care to pause here to decide for themselves which aims need refining.

In fact, we felt that the countries to be studied (Aim 1) could be specified more clearly, that Aim 4 (at least till elaborated in the immediately following section, 'The Six Aims of the Course Explained') seemed too like Aim 1, and that Aim 5(b) was overly condensed and not altogether clear. Aim 1 now ends: 'as relevant, and, as appropriate, there will be references to the Scandinavian and other European countries.' Aim 4 now reads:

> To enable you to argue in an informed way about the role of war with respect to social change, and in particular to evaluate the significance of the two total wars relative to 'structural' (see Aim 3) political and ideological forces, and to enable you to discuss the relationship of the wars to major geopolitical changes.

With regard to Aim 5(b) it was also necessary to rewrite the explication of this Aim in simpler terms, and to create a new audio cassette to be switched on at specific stages in the course where the contrast between different approaches is particularly relevant. Aim 5(b) now specifies:

> understanding some of the different approaches to historical study, ranging from the highly theoretical (as for example in some forms of Marxism) to the thoroughly empirical (as for example in the approach to history introduced in the Arts Foundation Course); and also quantitative and qualitative approaches.

Here are the Objectives for Unit 13, 'Challenges to Central Government, 1660s to 1714' from the course, *Princes and Peoples: the British Isles and France c.1630–1714*:

1   You should be able to expound the contrast between the turbulent political history of the British Isles and the events preceding, including and succeeding 'The Glorious Revolution', and the relatively stable progress of centralised monarchy in France.
2   You should be in a position to analyse and compare the nature and extent of the political challenges to central government in the different

countries and how they were dealt with, being able, in particular, to discuss knowledgeably the notion that in this period the French monarchy won its struggle with the nobility and the English monarchy lost.

3 You should be able to assess the character and significance of the different kinds of religious opposition manifested in the different countries.

4 You should be able to itemise the main outbreaks of popular protest in the various countries, analysing their causes and significance, and identifying the main differences between events in France and events in the British Isles.

5 You should be able to demonstrate an understanding of the way in which political, religious and popular protest were often intertwined.

6 You should have further advanced your skills in historical methodology and comparative historical study.

C   *All the other materials required by students, apart from the basic course units (textbooks, documents, articles, map books, videos, etc.) must be clearly specified at the outset, and fully integrated with the teaching units.*

History is a reading subject, and students need to be familiar with the leading authorities on whatever period or theme is the subject of the course. However, there is no point listing reams of books that students will have no possibility of reading. It is vital that the teaching units, which should at particular points instruct students to do certain additional reading, are written in the precise knowledge of what additional resources are available to students. It is fairly standard practice at the Open University to compile a special collection of primary documents, sent to students with the course units, to edit a Reader of key articles which students are required to buy, together with one or two standard textbooks.

D   *The teaching material throughout must be structured upon a series of Self-Assessment Exercises which provide a genuine learning progression for the particular topic immediately under study.*

This is the most difficult task of all. Not only must questions be set, but each question must be followed by a 'Specimen Answer and Discussion' (the standard rubric in OU history teaching) which not only gives the 'correct' answer (if there is one) but tries to anticipate all the possible answers students might give, and adjudicate between them. The questions must be written so clearly and unambiguously that students have absolutely no doubt what it is that is being asked of them. They must be such that students have sufficient knowledge to be able to make a genuine attempt at them, either from previous course material, or from special reading of Documents, Textbook, or Reader.

In Units 8–10 of *War, Peace and Social Change*, discussing 'The Debate over the Impact and Consequences of World War I', students are given a chart simply listing the main pieces of social legislation enacted in the various European countries before, during, and after, the First World War (Table 8–10.2). Here are two exercises from these units:

Exercise:

1 Look at the information contained in Table 8–10.2 below. What point could be made in support of the argument that a change of regime was certainly not a necessary reason for social reform in the post-war period?

2 On the basis of discoveries we have made so far in this section, what argument could be advanced to link post-war social change with the war?

3 Can you think of any other general arguments linking post-war social change to the war?

Specimen Answers and Discussion:

1 Social reform also took place in countries, such as Britain, France and Italy, where there was no (immediate) change in regime.

2 Social reform, albeit often of a very limited and sometimes rather hollow character, was already taking place during the war. It could be argued that the post-war reforms were simply a culmination of this trend, coming to fruition once the negative circumstance of war had been removed.

3 There are the points already made about the desire to reward those who had supported the nation in its hour of need, and the arguments about labour being in a strong position to exact rewards. There is also the even more general argument that there was a feeling that this horrific war must result in a better world, and that social reforms were a concrete expression of that feeling. With regard to the reforms associated with a change of regime, it is of course legitimate to link these very changes in regime to the circumstances of war.

Exercise:

1 What arguments would you put forward if you wanted to argue that these social reforms were not primarily associated with the war?

Specimen Answer and Discussion:

1 It could be pointed out that social reforms were already taking place before the war. It could be argued that they were due to the politicians and parties which came into power in the post-war years, and that

election results and the detailed developments of politics had little or nothing to do with the war. It could be argued that the reforms were primarily aimed at new developments taking place in the post-war years, rather than anything to do with the war – for example depression and unemployment. It could be argued that limited social reforms are a characteristic of a certain phase in the development of modern society which was coming about whether or not there was a war. On a totally different track, it could be argued that in fact the social reforms were of a very limited character and that therefore, even if they are in some way related to the war, they are so trivial as not to count in any general argument about the war being related to significant social change.

One of the most potent developments in distance teaching is the development of interactive audio and video. Here the printed unit directs students to play a particular section of, say, video (containing newsreel, documentary or feature film, or, for earlier centuries, specially shot film of particular environments), while posing questions based on that section of video for students to answer. I now reproduce most of page 127 of Book IV, 'World War II and Its Consequences', from *War, Peace and Social Change* (readers who are agog for the answers could consult pp. 127–8 for themselves):

Exercise on four French newsreels
These newsreels, items 7–10 on video-cassette 2, are dated respectively May 1940, April 1944, May 1944 and June 1944. We discovered the first one by accident, having actually asked the Imperial War Museum for another issue from 1944. It occurred to me immediately that looking at the four items together gives a very good sense of the beginning and ending of the war for France, and of some of the particular ways in which the war impacted on French society. I shall talk you through each item separately (because of shortage of space we have made cuts in all of these; item 9, which is in the condition in which we found it, starts rather abruptly), but you should try to find time (perhaps when revising for the exam) to play the four items together to get a general overview of certain important developments in France. The aims of this exercise, then, extend beyond the single topic of political institutions and values:

1 Film material can make vivid to you (as it made vivid to audiences at the time) events and developments (which you already know about from your *written* course material; you, of course, are in a position to make a detached historical analysis, knowing how events unfolded – a position not open to film audiences at the time).

2   You can see the *uses* that were made of this particular form of mass communication, a subject to which Tony Aldgate will return shortly.

3   You can see (and hear) some of the political, social and ideological responses to invasion (two rather different ones) and occupation.

4   You can see directly and physically something of the impact of the war on civilian life.

Exercise

Play item 7 on videocassette 2, noting down answers to the following questions:

1   What military stage of the war is being reported here?

2   Against whom is the commentary directed, and for what in particular?

3   The film shows two of the most characteristic tragedies inflicted on civilians by twentieth-century war: what are they?

4   What device is used by the film-makers to heighten the sense of tragedy?

5   Do any scenes strike you as obvious clichés, possibly deliberately set up, presumably to impress French audiences? (I have in mind a scene near the beginning of the extract.)

6   Had you been a French person of the time would you, overall, have found this film reassuring? Give reasons.

E   *There must be an assessment policy totally integrated with the Aims, Objectives and Content of the course.*

Students on *War, Peace and Social Change* have seven assignments to do throughout the year, and one three-hour exam. The assignments are of four types: conventional essays, designed to be written without recourse to any reading outside the complete assemblage of course materials (but making the fullest use of these materials); exercises on documents; one 'thematic' essay, to be written as far as possible under exam conditions, and intended to test mastery of the general themes of the course; and a 'double' essay for the preparation of which students use the resources of the library of York University, where the summer school is held. The significance of Summer School is explained to students in the Course Guide:

> Your week at summer school forms an essential and integrated part of your studies for A318. It will provide the opportunity for you to develop your skills of discussion and analysis, of writing essays and of evaluating and interpreting primary sources. It will also give you time to consider the effects of war on music, art, and literature, and provide you with the chance to view and discuss films in their entirety. You will see from the assessment strategy of A318 that you have the opportunity to submit an

extended essay (TMA 06/07), and the summer school programme is designed to give you time to research, plan and discuss with your summer school tutor your proposed outline for this TMA before submission.

Part I of the exam calls for the analysis of fairly extended extracts from primary documents; Part II contains 'conventional' (relatively limited) essay questions; Part III is dedicated to thematic questions. Performance overall is see as vindicating, or otherwise, the course Aims and their integral relationship to the course and the course assessment.

F   *There must be some form of personal back-up, if only in the form of correspondence tuition (marking of, and commenting on, student assignments), and it is vital that this back-up be carefully monitored by those responsible for the course and its aims.*

In fact the Open University provides a good deal more than this, through its highly dedicated part-time tutors and through its summer schools (only one, attached to *War, Peace and Social Change*, for all history courses). The marking of assignments is carefully monitored, there are visits to tutorials, with, as necessary, follow-up letters. In sum, tutors are kept in very close contact with the central designers of the courses.

Logistics

Even in small-scale distance teaching projects inspired by, or conceived outside, the mass Open University system, it will be necessary to pay heed to the following considerations.

1   Carrying through all the essential operations listed above calls for the development, well in advance, of sophisticated production schedules.
2   Clearance of copyright for quotations, tables, maps, illustrations within units, and for documents and Reader articles, can be a time-consuming and expensive business.
3   Ideally, material should be subject to some kind of external assessment (this is obligatory at the OU), and if possible, subject to advance testing on sample students (practice varies at the OU); it requires the highest standards of proofreading, and, ideally, of editing. The Open University has an entire infrastructure of course managers, editors, designers and cartographers.

Conclusion

In that it is highly self-conscious, thoroughly planned, and very explicit about what it is seeking to do, and how it is doing it, properly prepared structured distance teaching is extremely effective. But, it is not a short cut to economy. In institutions other than the Open Unviersity it could probably be best deployed in a mix of teaching modes, in which teachers would be released from the need to give formal lectures to large student audiences in order to be free to provide more seminars and tutorials.

Further Reading

Distance, open and resource-based teaching and learning methods have experienced a surge of popularity in recent years, and consequently have given rise to a growing body of literature. A reliable guide is D. Rowntree, *Exploring Open and Distance Learning* (Kogan Page, London, 1992), as is his practical *Preparing Materials for Open, Distance and Flexible Learning: An Action Guide for Teachers and Trainers* (Kogan Page, London, 1993). *Beyond Distance Learning towards Open Learning*, ed. V. Hodson, S. Mann and R. Snell (Open University Press, Buckingham, 1994) also provides a stimulating guide to recent developments in this area.

For an intelligent survey of the whole field of media-based learning, with clear and thoughtful advice about designing learning materials, see D. Laurillard, *Rethinking University Teaching: A Framework for the Effective Use of Educational Technology* (Routledge, London, 1993). Practical tips are to the fore in P. Race, *53 Interesting Ways to Write Open Learning Materials* (Technical and Educational Services, Bristol, 1992), whilst *Course Design for Resource Based Learning: Humanities*, ed. J. Wisdom and G. Gibbs (Oxford Centre for Staff Development, Oxford, 1994) presents a number of proven case-studies, including some in history, in the general area of open-learning materials and a useful bibliography. Module 2 of P. Cryer and L. Elton's *Learning Actively on One's Own* (CVCP, Sheffield, 1992), deals with preparing self-instructional material and includes examples of materials from the Open University and the Open Learning Foundation. The journal *Open Learning* (formerly *Teaching at a Distance*, 1974–85) provides a regular stream of scholarly articles on the subject.

11

Teaching and Learning through the Visual Media

John Ramsden

The Historian and the Visual Source

The use of visual sources in history teaching is now so widespread as to be a core part of many degree courses and the entire justification for others. In some sense this approach is highly traditional, for historians' attachment to documents as the basis of their work has always included a wider definition of what constitutes a 'document' than was perhaps generally appreciated when the bulk of the profession worked mainly on such written sources as charters, diaries, state papers and the press.

Historians of the medieval period have always relied on the evidence of stained glass, funeral monuments and illuminated manuscripts as well as on charters and missals. But this reliance on visual sources has been different from the way in which an archaeologist uses the artefact itself as evidence. Historians working on the development of art and architecture, whether for its own sake as the analysis of aesthetic form or in relation to the wider role of the castle or the farm building in social history, have necessarily used both available physical evidence and contemporary visual records in their teaching and research. Early modernists have long been aware that from the Renaissance onwards – and in some ways from a much earlier time, as the size and scale of Norman cathedrals indicates – art and architecture were at the service of political and social forces, and were an arresting form of visual propaganda. Elizabethan houses celebrated their monarch not only in the pomp and splendour of their design and the heraldic decoration that adorned their principal frontages, but were also frequently built to a ground plan in an 'E' shape, a concept that neatly married loyalty and practicality. And the extensive circulation, copying and imitation of authorized, stylized, portraits of both Elizabeth I and Charles I indicate an awareness of the impact of visual influences on elite opinion that seems to belong more to the age of Leni Riefenstahl than of Van Dyck. Similarly, in sixteenth-century France a cult of Hercules was deliberately fostered in painting and sculpture, with the aim of associating Francis I with a classical hero. The decision to move to classical styles of building and ornamentation in the early modern period and the decision to revert to a gothic tradition in the nineteenth century were cultural movements that encompassed the whole range of social, political, economic and aesthetic considerations; the planning and decoration of the new Palace of Westminster, completed in the 1850s, was therefore an important statement of Victorian attitudes and policy in all of these spheres. None of these or equivalent issues can be discussed with any great sensitivity unless students are presented with the visual record as well as encouraged to read analyses of that record. Visual evidence then has long been used by teachers as an essential means of recreating the past.

In one important way, however, the advance of the present century has necessitated a new awareness of visual sources. Photo-journalism in mass-selling newspapers is now a century old; the existence of magazines devoted almost exclusively to quality pictures, of easily accessible talking and moving pictures, and of television in the home are all half a century distant. That revolution was remarkable enough; in popular culture it transformed patterns of marketing and mass-consumption; in both popular and high art it effectively removed frontiers that were more than a millennium old in favour of the global village that we now inhabit. In political life, it introduced the type of response epitomized by Joseph Goebbels and by George Orwell's *1984*, but it also ensured that a low-key, lowbrow political operator like Stanley Baldwin in Britain was able to become by 1935 the most familiar British politician to date; in one newsreel broadcast of 1930 he was seen and heard in five minutes by more voters, and by a larger proportion of the electorate of the time, than ever heard Gladstone speak in a political career that lasted for much of the last century. The nature of the very different appeals of Adolf Hitler and of Stanley Baldwin *can* be described in prose, but it makes very little sense to do so, for in each case the ephemeral nature of their skills can easily be missed – the message was largely in the 'way they told 'em'. Fortunately, in both of these examples and in most equivalent cases from the 1930s onwards, the archives provide sufficient material for students of modern history to re-live at least part of the visual experience that contemporaries underwent; students can be invited to see and hear Hitler as well as to read about his style of public speaking. Styles in Nazi posters and popular heraldic art can be contrasted with the more matter-of-fact material of Nazi newsreels, or with the subtly effective presentation of the Führer in *Triumph of the Will*.

The revolution goes on. Eighteen-year-olds entering higher education in the last decade of the twentieth century can only remember times when television was in colour, when live reports from anywhere in the world were instantly on call, and when video recorders were almost universally available for instant replay and library use. Given the advances of the camcorder market, it will not be long before there are few students who are unused to making moving pictures for themselves and to exercising editorial judgements as well in putting together a 'film'. Since history teaching in higher education has long concentrated its pedagogical objective on inculcating life skills in the assessment and judgement of evidence, the increasingly visual domination of mass communication now practised in the world makes it both natural and essential for teachers to incorporate the evaluation of visual sources into their programmes of study.

Problems of Visual History

There are obvious practical problems. A photocopier enables extracts from a medieval document to be put in front of a class of students quickly and cheaply; Hogarthian engravings and *Punch* cartoons can be incorporated into teaching with equal ease. But other visual sources can be evaluated only in teaching-space designed or adapted for that special purpose. Art history requires high-quality dual-slide projection in darkened rooms; building up a library of slides involves a considerable investment of time and money; the taking of pictures of buildings involves the use of special lenses to avoid the lop-sided effect of photographing a large, towering entity from ground-level with an ordinary camera; the showing of moving pictures requires even more expensive equipment, and the showing and discussion of a feature film involves a lengthy slot in a timetable that is usually constructed in hour-long chunks. Given the commitment to visual history in the first place, these practical issues can be overcome over time, but the commitment must be long-term.

Booking a suitable room and securing the investment is not perhaps too difficult when a whole course revolves around visual sources – as, say, a course in architectural history must do. Even so, universities are not so good at finding suitable space (or money) when an early modernist teaching a conventional course wishes to devote a couple of weeks to the evaluation of the visual evidence of baroque splendour in the Counter Reformation or at Louis XIV's court. But these administrative difficulties may well become less pressing as the time arrives when all historians are using visual material.

A more serious problem is what Nicholas Pronay, describing British newsreels, called 'the illusion of reality'. This applies as much to the past as to the present. One of the main pitfalls in the use of visual evidence is to reinforce existing stereotypes, instead of gaining new insights. For instance, Dutch landscapes of the seventeenth century presented the countryside as the picture-purchasing public wished to see it – idealized, unspoilt and with no reference to the commercial crops that occupied so much of the actual space. The same can be said of many portraits, whether the 'auto-icons' of commissioned portraits of rulers and generals, or representations of the contented poor which may have been as much intended to assuage the Calvinist consciences of patrons as to demonstrate the actual social conditions in which ordinary people lived. The social truth of most paintings and prints, even of many photographs, has to be sought beyond as well as within the intentions of their originators.

Few students used to the special effects in contemporary feature films would be as likely as a 1930s cinema audience to think that 'seeing is believing', but until more of them (and their teachers) have practical shooting and editing experience there remains the danger of underestimating the impact of technical influences. The speed of editing of a moving film, the use of musical backing, and the camera angle from which a sequence has been shot are all skills with which students need to be made familiar, and most history departments will need to draw on colleagues in Media Studies for this type of instruction. A good handbook such as James Monaco's *How To Read A Film* would be the bare minimum. But these skills are in any case valuable assets for students' subsequent evaluation of the political messages that will be fed to them on television news and current affairs programmes for the rest of their lives, and of the advertising to which they will be subjected. Lawrence Rees's book *Selling Politics* shows just how the experiencing of Nazi propaganda, which can be deconstructed in calm analysis, can be useful in fostering an understanding of the contemporary political broadcast. Relatively cheap and extraordinarily user-friendly editing suites are now available, as for example in the Sony range. There is no real substitute for that hands-on experience. History students working on modern topics for which visual evidence is plentiful can now be given the opportunity to undertake projects on video, and acquire the necessary technical skills remarkably quickly. Indeed, the university auditors' reported interest in the encouragement of wider varieties of assessment methods may well be a powerful stimulus in that direction in the near future. History of Art courses frequently use slide tests as part of their examination; other courses taught mainly by visual means will also lend themselves naturally to non-traditional methods of assessment.

The key in all of this is the recognition that visual material is a document like any other, but that like all other types of document it also has its own special characteristics. Slides taken personally by the tutor to illustrate a range of church-building styles are in effect no more than a cheaper and more practical substitute for getting students to go and see those same buildings for themselves – the building rather than the slide is the real document. The same goes for a photograph of any artefact that might otherwise be found in a museum: the photograph is merely the record of the evidence, not the evidence itself, as is a typed or printed version of Magna Carta.

Written sources can be genuinely thought of as raw material in no way connected with the writing of history until the historian stumbles on them: a diary or a letter may have been written with no wider audience intended than the writer and his/her correspondent. However, in most cases, visual material has to be viewed as something manufactured, not as raw material but as artefacts constructed for a wider audience, precisely to influence contemporaries and posterity. But then much the same can be said of books and newspapers. The evaluation of such evidence requires careful analysis, not only of what the finished product shows but also of the motivations of the author/editor/reader and the social and economic forces that lay behind its production and consumption. With the emergence of a more open attitude towards the news industry, it is possible, for instance, to compare 'flash' material, sent to the television studios via satellite, with the content of the eventual bulletin. Here the visual source needs to be integrated with other traditional skills of the historian. But, just as the analysis of a seventeenth-century Leveller tract requires familiarity with the vocabulary and nuances of the 1640s to appreciate its contemporary impact, so students of films in the 1930s need to immerse themselves in the visual as well as the verbal clichés of the time if they are to understand the contemporary audience's responses to those films. This too needs to be taught: there is a natural tendency to assume that no special mindset is required for the evaluation of an entertainment medium of the relatively recent past, where the methods and the medium are in some ways very familiar to viewers of contemporary products in the same medium. Students who are used to daily exposure to their national leaders as living, breathing personalities may find it hard to understand how great an impact that familiarity could have on the first generation who experienced it. As in any popular medium, the tendency to repetition of form has dulled the critical senses. A director who invented a particular filmic cliché in, say, 1935 may easily be underestimated by audiences who have been saturated with parodies and derivatives over the following fifty years.

For example many historians teaching American history would now consider it necessary to use films in their evaluation of public opinion and popular attitudes from the 1930s onwards. In considering the Warner Brothers film *Forty-Second Street*, which made such a big impact on American opinion when it came out in 1933 at a key point of the Depression and New Deal period, it is certainly essential to see and discuss the film. But it is also necessary to get behind the finished product to its origins in studio planning and to its reception by the public. This can be done through the literature derived from the deposited archives of the film company, by reviewing the opinions of 1933 film critics, and by relating its marketing to the political vocabulary and agenda of Roosevelt's first few months in office. Viewed in this way, with the students' personal and perhaps subjective reactions to the film moderated by their readings of what contemporaries thought of it, and with some scepticism injected into the argument through their consideration of the disciplines of the 1933 box office, the film itself becomes an invaluable two-way mirror for the analysis of New Deal America. Along with other films of the time, it enables us to see both what appealed to popular taste, and also the way in which some subtle (and some not-so-subtle) messages of hope and patriotic discipline could be inserted into 'mere vehicles of entertainment'. Such a way of approaching popular culture relies on the demonstrable fact that, by the 1930s, cinema had such a central place in the lives of millions of Americans that it provided such a two-way mirror.

Sources and their Problems

The visual historian has, in principle, the same problem as the historian working with other documents, but with an added twist. What can be used for research and teaching is only that which happens to have survived. In part this is not a major difficulty: even where buildings or artworks have not survived in their original form, there are often secondary visual records that can be of great value; theatre historians have pressed into service all sorts of visual records, originally produced for quite different purposes, to underpin a reconstruction of Shakespeare's Globe Theatre. Maps, plans, and panoramas, in none of which were the theatres especially prominent, have provided a remarkable cache of design material. There are good drawings and paintings of many buildings no longer extant, and these can be used to demonstrate changing patterns of building over time. Inevitably, the visual record for earlier periods is more patchy, and it is easier to reconstruct the buildings and lifestyles of the rich and famous from visual sources than to enter into the lives of ordinary people – but written sources tend to produce exactly the same difficulty here. None the less, 'history form below' is not entirely bereft of material. Thousands of contemporary woodcuts of the German Lutheran Reformation appear close to grass-roots opinions, offering genuine manifestations of popular attitudes, as when an outraged peasant wipes his behind with a papal bull. Likewise, the cheap Épinal prints of nineteenth-century France are a rich source for the study of popular opinions, not least in showing the widespread support for the Napoleonic legend, a potent ingredient in the politics of the time. Future generations will be better placed: not only is the National Trust attempting to retain some 'ordinary buildings of this century, as at 'Mr Straw's House' in Worksop, Nottinghamshire, but the existence of town and country planning legislation from the 1940s means that local authorities have and must keep rich archives relating to all applications for land and building development – plans, drawings and photographs that in some areas already go back a century or more.

With moving pictures, the problems are somewhat different. Much that is very recent has not survived, or may only have survived in an inaccessible form. The thriving video market means that popular films have relatively good accessibility; many older films are regularly recycled through television, and an off-air recording licence allows an educational institution to build up a good stock of material (for its own educational use) remarkably quickly. Students working on British or American feature films can get access to a lot of material, relatively easily; material in other languages is broadcast much less frequently and can be a serious problem, though the advent of satellites now provides a way out of this dilemma, and D-2MAC promises instantaneous subtitled translations. Topics relating to warfare in this century can derive enormous benefit from the large stock of films available for hire to educational institutions from the Imperial War Museum; their archive contains much German material captured in 1945, as well as British and American films, and the range of material is highlighted in the annual *Imperial War Museum Review*. The peaceful arts practised by social historians are, by and large, less easily underpinned from filmic sources; many are in private hands, as for example those of the Port of London Authority or the Shell Corporation, but in other cases local record offices have tracked down invaluable material; the University of East Anglia has rescued a remarkable collection of film resources relating to East Anglia throughout the century. Other regional archives are paying similar dividends, notably in the Yorkshire and North Western Film Archives.

The next stage, whereby for a specialised project it is necessary to see a particular, and relatively obscure, piece of film, can be far more difficult. Even if a viewing copy exists in the National Film and Television Archive (NFTVA from 1993, previously the NFA), it tends to be expensive to get to see it, and copyright generally prevents such films from being seen elsewhere. If there is no NFA viewing copy, even if the film is in stock, it is *very* expensive to have a viewing copy made. For films of 'fact' rather than films of 'fiction', the position is slightly worse; documentaries were frequently made for private companies, and their survival rate has not been good; newsreels have for the most part survived, and in some cases the archives also contain interesting material that was not issued, but access is not easy and the cost of viewing can be prohibitive since these archives now exist mainly to service television researchers with large budgets. For researchers, the newsreels can produce a rich harvest, and they provide the further benefit of content description in weekly issue-sheets, widely available on microfiche. There is also much valuable material about the structure of the industry, the provenance of individual items and general backround in the BUFVC's three-volume *Researcher's Guide to British Newsreels*. But for classroom use, the history tutor probably needs to rely on published compilations of various sorts: there has been useful material from time to time on the BBC, a seemingly

endless re-showing of Gaumont British News by ITV, excellent programmes using newsreels from the Open University (all of these needing
recording licences); there are also two series of newsreel-based compilations by the InterUniversity History Film Consortium.

Film History in British Universities

Historians like Nicholas Pronay at Leeds and Ken Ward at Coleraine
were, in the 1970s, among the first to offer specific courses in film and
cinema history. The same period witnessed the advent of the Open
University, which naturally gave a high priority to all aspects of visual
sources in establishing its identity as a broadcasting institution of higher
education. Since that time, there has been a growing appreciation that
the study of film – and more recently of television – must not be left to
the Cultural Studies departments. The Universities of Lancaster, East
Anglia, Sussex and Warwick, and Queen Mary and Westfield College in
London, have all given film history a high profile in their work. Their
common belief is that the visual text is not just an artefact to be
deconstructed but a product that needs to be set in its social, economic,
political and cultural context. This requires an approach encapsulated by
the Institute of Communications Studies at Leeds, founded by two film
historians, Nicholas Pronay and Philip Taylor: a multidisciplinary programme, crossing the Arts/Technology divide. Communications as a
process is rooted in technology which requires creative applications, and
if the historical function of universities is to help citizens to understand
the world in which they live, then this broad approach to understanding
'the information age' is likely to provide the future pathway for the
subject. Historical understanding of communication principles and practice, locked into empirical approaches to evidence, can enhance the
appreciation not just of the past but of the present.

The universities named above have many years' experience in this
field. The following example is given to indicate just one way in which
this type of activity has been successfully pursued over a period of years.
Queen Mary College in the University of London introduced a film
course entitled 'Cinema and Society: Britain in the 1930s' in 1980;
Queen Mary and Westfield College in 1994 has four such courses. The
aim of the original course is both to provide, through a specific case
study, a detailed exemplification of the way in which cinemas, films and
the habit of cinema-going played their part in social history and to

examine the way in which visual methods of communication took part in the influencing of popular attitudes. Students receive lectures on cinema architecture; the varied social world of the cinemas from community singing to fan magazines; the nature of and constraints on the newsreels; the documentary film movement; the use of film by the Conservative Party and the left; modes of production and the place of the British film industry in the international film world; censorship; recurring themes in feature films, such as the role of monarchy and the nature of the Empire; the portrayal of social problems; and the claim that British films were becoming more realistic at the end of the 1930s. Each lecture introduces either a full-length feature film, or a group of shorts in weeks where documentaries or newsreels are being considered, and lectures are often illustrated with extracts from other films of the same type. Students are required to attend discussion classes later in the same week, in which the topic of the week and the film(s) shown can be further analysed; there is therefore a contact time of four hours a week, which is in part compensated for by the fact that less time need be spent in libraries than on most other courses. For coursework, students need to see more films in their chosen field, and personal video presenters with headphones are available to allow the playing of such background material; this type of research also allows for the repeated re-playing of key scenes as notes are taken; a number of students go on to undertake final year dissertations on film history using the same technicques. To facilitate understanding of film technique as such, students have in the past been offered informal instruction, but all students taking such film history courses are now normally required, first, to take a Faculty 'Introduction to Film Studies' course which gives a proper grounding in film theory; without an understanding of the concept of 'genre' or of the origins and functioning of the star system, the traditional case study courses are less effective. These courses are examined partly by traditional examination and partly by a film test in which candidates are asked to write about the technical and visual implications of a short sequence, usually extracted from a full-length film that they have already seem. The accumulation of courses of this type has meant that the transferable skills achieved in one course can now be applied with greater sophistication in later years.

Sources of Help and Advice

Without doubt the key contact for anyone working in higher education and seeking to use visual sources is the British Universities Film and

Video council (55, Dean Street, London W1V 5LR). Most universities are members of the BUFVC and all are eligible for membership; it is run by its members, has an annual conference, and publishes a periodical newsletter, *Viewfinder*, that brings members up to date with publications, events and handbooks. It publishes its own directories of visual sources available as teaching aids, and is willing to help and advise staff of member institutions. For historians seeking a more active role, universities can join the InterUniversity History Film Consortium which currently contains about a dozen member universities. Members receive copies of all films made by the Consortium and take it in turns to make films at the Consortium's expense. These films are of two types. The first is the Historical Studies in Film series, similar in character to television documentaries in that they use stills, animations and voice commentary as well as edited newsreel footage; the series is being made entirely under the direction of working historians. It has covered a number of key events in modern European history, relating the visual evidence to the historiography of the topic. A recent film showed how the Soviet Union was presented to the British people through British newsreels during the Second World War. The second, the Archive series, provides a deliberately *un*edited sequence of pieces of film, the provenance and background of which are described and analysed in an accompanying booklet. This enables a teacher using, say, the film *Neville Chamberlain* to show the uncut version of a newsreel describing the Munich Crisis, exactly as the British public saw it in cinemas in 1938, but also provides the background material for discussion of the item in class. The IUHFC has made films on Russia and on International Relations, but has relied heavily on British sources to analyse British subjects.

For those seeking a wider perspective there is the International Association of Media Historians (IAMHIST) whose annual conference is the major event in the field. There is also the *Historical Journal of Film, Radio and Television*, whose very existence since 1981 has been a demonstration of the new prominence of film and visual history in British Universities. In London, the Museum of the Moving Image provides a regularly renewed resource of display material and the National Film Theatre offers a valuable opportunity to see historic film material as it was meant to be seen – in cinemas. Perhaps the most insidious trap of all is the illusion that films can be adequately studied in video format, on small screens, and in lighted rooms. Such video showings have their research value, but they do not recreate much of the circumstances in which films were meant to be seen.

Conclusion

Teaching and learning through the visual media poses many of the challenges that accompany interdisciplinary studies. Scholars in neighbouring fields can be rivals as well as allies. The art historians seceded from the main body of historians barely a generation ago. It is hardly surprising therefore that art historians are jealous of their independence and suspicious of historians who place art in its social context; something similar occurs on the borderline of history and literature. In his/her own field, the historian must supplement the aesthetic judgement of art historians with the input of sociologists and economists, particularly, but not only, when working in the present century. The example of France is instructive here: during the *ancien régime* the objectives of royal patronage were clear – as was shown by the rehabilitation of Louis XVI, using artworks that associated him visually with France's glorious military past; the revolutionaries of the 1790s, on the other hand, wanted to see their democratic aspirations expressed in art, and Napoleon sought personal glorification in this as in other ways; later in the nineteenth century, art patronage was influenced more by wider market forces than by governments, and without an understanding of sociological impulses within the bourgeoisie their artistic decisions can be hard to fathom. In each phase, the visual must be married with more traditional sources to achieve a fully rounded pictiure. In the present, when moving images in films and on television exert such influence, the task of providing students with the means to decipher and decode them becomes both more difficult and more necessary. In the postmodern world, the public is still manipulated, without being aware of the fact, by covert influences that scholars are only now beginning to desconstruct. In this lies the challenge of teaching and learning in the visual media.

Note

I am grateful to many colleagues for advice with this chapter, but especially to Jim Ballantyne, John Mackrell and Philip Taylor.

Further Reading

This chapter has suggested some professional sources of help to which those wishing to incorporate visual sources in their courses might turn. There is in addition a huge literature on film, in which it is not easy to draw a sharp distinction beween the history of films, film as a historical source and film in the teaching of history. For an annotated guide to the wide range of sources available, see the British Universities Film and Video Council's *Researcher's Guide to British Film and Television Collections* (BUFVC, London, 1985 edn).

Introducing the issue of the significance and value of film as history is a useful way of encouraging students to think about visual sources. Here the following are particularly helpful: P. Sorlin, *Film and History: Restaging the Past* (Blackwell, Oxford, 1980); K. R. Short (ed.), *Feature Films as History* (Croom Helm, London, 1981); N. Pronay and D. W. Spring (eds), *Propaganda, Politics and Film 1918–1945* (Macmillan, Basingstoke, 1982); L. Rees, *Selling Politics* (BBC, London, 1992). For those requiring a comprehensive basic guide to the whole process of film which would be of use to history students, J. Monaco, *How to Read a Film: The Art, Technology, Language, History and Theory of Film and Media* (Oxford University Press, Oxford, rev. edn, 1990) fits the bill very well.

Practical advice on teaching history through film is contained especially in P. Smith (ed.), *The Historian and Film* (Cambridge University Press, Cambridge, 1976); K. Fledelius (ed.), *History and the Audio-visual Media* (Eventus, Copenhagen, 1979); M. J. Clark (ed.), *Politics and the Media: Film and Television for the Political Scientist and Historian* (Pergamon, Oxford, 1979); J. E. O'Connor, *Teaching History with Film and Television* (American Historical Association, Washington, 1987). More generally relevant to the use of audiovisual methods in higher education are O. Zuber-Skerritt (ed.), *Video in Higher Education* (Kogan Page, London, 1984), and D. Laurillard, *Rethinking University Teaching: A Framework for the Use of Educational Technology* (Routledge, London, 1993) which puts the use of film and video in the wider context of approaching teaching through multi-media approaches.

PART IV

Linking History with Society

12

History and the Community

Michael Winstanley

This chapter discusses reasons why students *in* university ought to be more aware of the resources for, and the significance of, their subject *outside* the academic environment, and suggests how teaching programmes could be amended or devised to promote this.

There is enormous potential to benefit from and contribute towards history in the community. Unlike most university subjects, history is doubly fortunate in that there is not only a large public appetite for historical material at a variety of levels, but that many sources for its study are widely and freely available. An appreciation of the ways in which history is, or could be presented to different audiences can raise students' awareness of a wide range of historiographical, methodological and presentational issues, many of which have relevance beyond the confines of the discipline itself. Making use of community-based resources can be used not just to supplement university-based teaching materials but to encourage new modes of task-oriented learning and collaborative work. 'Non-academic' organizations and individuals responsible for, or interested in, the preservation and promotion of the past have much to offer staff and students alike, both in terms of expertise and resources. Forging links with them can also help to breach the 'Chinese Wall' which often seems to separate academic and popular history, by providing opportunities for staff and students to contribute constructively to a broader dissemination of the results of original research.

The Rationale: Academic History and
the Community

Academic historians usually relate to the wider community in one or
both of two basic ways. They can, and increasingly do, exploit community resources and institutions to supplement academic provision;
they can also contribute to the enhancement of what might be called
'popular' history. This section argues that establishing and sustaining
reciprocal relationships is both possible and desirable.

The potential of community resources

Students traditionally 'read' History 'at' university. The words still con-
jure up images of institutionalized, solitary book-learning which takes
place in an exclusively academic environment. In many cases this remains a fair reflection of the approach to study which underpins most
teaching methods, whether they are based on lectures or small group
discussions, and whether they rely on textbooks or encourage students to
select from extensive bibliographies. In many institutions access to a
wide range of published material is increasingly problematic as the size of
the student body expands without any commensurate increase in funding. Yet staff in their own work restrict themselves neither to reading,
nor to studying exclusively at university. They 'do' research and they tap
sources which are housed in public libraries and record offices, are visible
in the surrounding environment, or, in the case of oral evidence, are
lodged in people's memories. Without access to the community's extensive resources much of what we conceive of as 'academic' history would
not be possible. Since the preservation of many documents is the responsibility of local and national government most are freely available for
public consultation. In Britain, for example, as well as recognized international and national archives, every county council supports a local
record office to house printed and manuscript sources relating to public,
commercial, voluntary and individual activities within its administrative
area. Library and museum services supported by county and district
authorities also regularly keep primary material related to their localities.
But is not necessary to rely exclusively on institutional depositories;
fieldwork can yield much about urban topography or the rural landscape,
while human resources, in the form of oral recollections, are available
everywhere.

Unlike schools, which already view these resources as valuable teaching aids for delivering the curriculum, staff in the university sector still generally regard local archives as the raw material for professional research; they are rarely systematically used for teaching purposes except for individual students' dissertations or in 'Local History' classes. There are various practical reasons for this neglect, including the obvious ones that not all subject matter lends itself to the exploitation of local sources and that logistical difficulties associated with time management and physical distance may restrict access by students. Some original documents are also clearly too fragile to tolerate anything other than infrequent handling. But, when such resources are available, especially those on microfilm or microfiche, there is no reason why the community's resources should not be more profitably and systematically deployed.

Contributing to history for the community

History written by both staff and students at university usually has a limited academic audience in mind. In the case of staff this is usually professional practitioners. We would be failing in our professional responsibility if this were not the case, and the criteria currently used to assess academic research performance consequently take most regard of monographs and articles. Unfortunately, however, this means that there is little incentive to write for, or even consider, the popular market. Consequently, many academic historians are neither accustomed nor trained to present their findings in any other form or for different audiences. The written, as opposed to the verbal and the visual, remains their primary mode of communication, and they often employ language which can be intimidating or inaccessible to non-specialists. Most students are also expected and trained to write for an academic readership – their tutors and examiners – with their degree schemes offering little or no opportunity to develop other ways of communicating their ideas or of considering how history is currently presented, or could be presented, to a non-academic audience.

It is not that history is short of a market. The public has an apparently insatiable appetite for all things historical. This is evident in the documentary and 'factional' drama and output of television, film, and historical fiction; in the plethora of biographies which litter publishers' catalogues, and the review columns of the quality press; in the fascination with collecting antiques, the popularity of genealogical studies, and the flourishing state of many local history societies; in the enduring popularity of organizations like the National Trust and the burgeoning commercialization of 'heritage' attractions in the 1980s; and in the fascination with stately home visiting and archaeology. This popular interest raises a number of issues of profound significance. Interpretations of the past are frequently paraded to justify current ideological stances across the political spectrum, with 'traditions' being 'invented' to sustain or promote national or cultural stereotypes, identities and government policies. Economic redevelopment constantly modifies or destroys the legacy of both the urban and rural past, generating debate about the value systems which underpin attempts to preserve or conserve specific environments, buildings, artefacts and documents, and raising questions about who defines what is considered to be 'historically important'. The exploitation of the past for commercial profit also raises a number of disparate issues relating to intellectual rights of ownership, custodianship and interpretation, and to the potential commodification of the past.

Historians have contributed at an intellectual level to many of these debates, usually to explain why and how such developments occur or to criticize what they regard as vulgar misrepresentations of the past carried out for unacceptable motives. But, significant exceptions apart, their own direct contribution to the popularization and the broader understanding of the past has been less evident, often for a variety of reasons not of their making. Commercial publishers continue to reissue bestselling 'popular' national histories written a generation or more ago which have a proven sales record. The book-club market prefers lavishly illustrated 'coffee table' volumes which few academics are equipped to write. Local history output tends to be dominated by the enthusiastic amateur and can sometimes be antiquarian, devoid of a broader historical context or awareness. The overtly commercial 'Heritage' attractions of the 1980s aimed to entertain rather than instruct.

For a variety of reasons, therefore, too little of what goes on in university reaches a wider audience and the impact which academic history has on popular conceptions, or misconceptions, of the past is often considered to be decidedly limited. This lack of influence is most acutely felt in countries like Scotland and Ireland, where recent revisionist research has challenged virtually every aspect of widely held, nationalist constructions of the past:

One big problem which faces those presently in the engine room of the manufacture of Scottish History is that while much new work has been done, especially in the universities, little of this has percolated through to the wider public. New findings in learned journals, disparate collections of essays, and expensive monographs often go unnoticed and are, in effect, inaccessible. . . . Listening to the speeches of Scottish politicians, reading the columns of respected journalists, and letters to the editors of newspapers, or in conversation, it is clear that there is little recognition that Scottish History is in the process of being remade.[1]

The challenge which faces those in higher education is to prevent 'history at university' being seen as a self-contained, exclusive world, increasingly marginalized, communicating only to the initiated and privileged, which does little to justify its existence to the wider community and which is largely irrelevant in terms of moulding popular conceptions of the past. If history is valued by society, if there is a market for its products and if it is important in determining social identities, then an awareness of how the past is presented in the media, and the facility to develop the skills necessary to present it to a non-specialist audience, ought to be more central to a historical education.

Defining Objectives

There is thus both an opportunity for students to exploit community resources and a need for them to achieve an appreciation of the forces which determine how the past is perceived, pursued and interpreted for a wider audience beyond the confines of academia. A consideration of the community's resources and provisions can also be effectively linked with specific learning objectives, encompassing the acquisition of both generic and subject-specific skills. These could broadly encompass one or more of the following aspects:

- *Acquiring and understanding specific historical knowledge.* This is the most obvious rationale for the deployment of community-based resources in subject-related courses, and it applies to all levels of education, from primary schooling through to postgraduate research. It can be used to support a wide range of subject areas, and can involve the utilization of published material on international and national history held in civic libraries through to the investigation of original sources lodged in local and national archives for specific projects and dissertations.
- *Practical skills.* Original research using resources outside the university not only obliges students to become more aware of the

location, provenance and significance of primary material, it also
provides the opportunity and incentive to acquire specific skills
such as palaeography, to practise oral history interviewing techniques, and to apply computerized database and spreadsheet packages for both the analysis and, through the construction of graphs
and charts, the visual presentation of findings.

• *Communication skills*. Presenting material for different audiences
could encompass the acquisition of a variety of practical skills
involving word processing and desktop publishing, photography
and even audio and video technology.

• *Personal and inter-personal skills*. Work in the community can require students to communicate or co-operate with organizations
or individuals responsible for preserving or presenting historical
material. It also offers considerable scope for introducing task-
oriented, student-centred group work, which is not only a powerful vehicle for inculcating the values and practices required for
successful collaboration but also is a pragmatic alternative for the
tutor to time-consuming independent study/supervisions and
individual dissertations.

Strategies

How can such objectives be pursued in practice? There is no need to be
prescriptive here; it is possible to pursue them in a variety of ways, either
through single courses or integrated packages of related units, and to
employ teaching approaches which range from 'traditional' methods
based on lectures and secondary reading through to student-centred
group work. Wherever possible, however, it would appear desirable to
integrate the subject matter of history with the acquisition of understanding and skills, rather than viewing them as separate entities.

Vocational and professional schemes of study

Degrees and diplomas which are exclusively concerned with the organization, management, preservation and possible promotion of historical
archives, artefacts, sites and attractions clearly fulfil many of the objectives outlined above. Included amongst these are courses on archives,
museum studies, industrial archaeology and heritage promotion. But
most of these are viewed as professional training, with an emphasis on

theory and practical applications rather than historical subject matter, and are usually available only at postgraduate level; it is rare to find such specialized, vocational offerings at undergraduate level. Consequently they are available only to a relatively small number of people.

Courses on local and regional history

It is relatively easy to incorporate an introduction to primary sources and some project work based on access to local archives and libraries as a central component of assessed work in undergraduate and sub-degree programmes of study on the history of specific regions, districts or towns. In Britain, such courses are relatively widespread in further and higher education and are supported by a number of specialist journals and societies. These include CORAL (Conference of Regional and Local History) which publishes the *Journal of Regional and Local Studies*, a network of local history societies, and the British Association for Local History which supports *The Local Historian*. Active learning through individual research is further facilitated by the availability of publications detailing the major sources for such work and offering examples of good practice, and by published guides to specific record offices and libraries.

There is only restricted scope for expanding such courses, however. They have limited appeal to those not resident in the area, while it is obvious that staff whose interests cannot be easily translated to the local context, either because of the nature of the subject matter or because of the intractability and inaccessibility of the sources they use, would find the mounting of such courses impossible. It is also difficult to provide students with an appreciation of the broader historical context of their work, which is necessary if they are to understand the significance of their specific local studies. Local history, therefore, is not an easy option; courses need to be both extensive and rigorous in their coverage.

Courses on historical methodology and skills

To avoid undue concentration on specifically local or regional subject matter, courses often emphasize sources and research methods. The purpose of these is to introduce students to a variety of issues and practical skills relating to 'doing' history, including, for example, the development of different schools of history, qualitative and quantitative analysis of primary material, oral history techniques and computer 'literacy'. There is a danger here, however, that such approaches can be viewed by the students as self-contained additions to their 'normal' courses in which they acquire 'skills' in a vacuum, devoid of historical context and with no opportunity or incentive to put them into practice or to relate them to other aspects of their study. Similar criticisms could also be levelled at field trips and work placements which do not have clearly defined objectives. Any teaching of skills and methods which does not integrate the process of acquiring knowledge and understanding is likely to be ineffective.

Varying assignments and assessment objectives

A relatively straightforward way of adapting existing courses to take account of the public issues raised in this chapter is to vary the nature of assignments which students are required to undertake.

> There is evidence from various studies that when a task has an audience or purpose beyond assessment then writing often improves. This finding implies that writing tasks for specific audiences may well be of value. . . . Changing the type of assignment set may well change the level of student thinking exhibited.[2]

One possible approach, therefore, would be to oblige students to present their arguments and evidence to a specified, non-academic audience rather than writing formal academic essays. Such an exercise encourages students to develop practical communication skills, promotes adherence to specified conventions relating to the presentation of their work, confronts them with the need to make explicit their assumptions about the knowledge and background of their intended audience, and forces them to consider how to generalize and to present disagreements which might exist about interpretation. Students must consider their choice of vocabulary, their selection/rejection of material, deciding what to explain and in what detail. They could be introduced to the implications of commercial and public pressures, and to working within specified resource limits and time constraints.

Currently the most widespread alternative to traditional essay/exam assessment in undergraduate study is the dissertation. Dissertations are employed as a means of obtaining evidence on a variety of aspects of a student's performance; including the ability to undertake original research, sustain extended argument, simplify and synthesize, deploy and weigh appropriate detailed evidence, and follow specified presentational conventions. They frequently rely on primary sources held in public archives, but are still primarily written up for an academic audience. There is no insurmountable obstacle to adapting their purpose or format to advance the fulfilment of community-related objectives by suggesting that students consider how they could present their findings to different audiences or in different forms. This could involve them considering the viability of other media for the presentation and dissemination of their work: reports, videos, computer packages and databases; potential designs and guidebooks for heritage attractions or museum displays; educational source books; course or site guidebooks; captions for artefacts or photos; and even pamphlets or articles for publication. Such work could contribute directly to the promotion of history in the wider community if it were deliberately focused on the needs of outside individuals, societies or institutions. But it can be adopted without any such formal links by utilizing role play in which students are asked to imagine that they are performing such assignments.

Presentations can utilize both published and primary sources available locally and in the university library and those which are capable of being accessed through networked information services. As such, this transformation of the traditional academic assignment to take account of resources, audiences and forms of presentation is capable of being incorporated into courses which deal with almost any historical subject matter. Subjects of national and international interest, for example, can be explored and explained through a case-study approach, by incorporating explorations of particular localities, themes or topics as an integral component of broadly based courses in order to help students to test the validity of generalizations and to enhance their understanding of the nature and causes of regional or social differences. The case study can be tailored to take account of specific staff or student interests and designed to accommodate both individual or group work, to incorporate computer applications and audiovisual presentations.

Implementing Change: A Case-study

This case study is offered merely as an example of how a number of staff in one academic establishment have chosen to approach the issues raised by this chapter. It may not suit the needs of learning in differently constructed institutions. But hopefully it will encourage others to consider issues related to the role and perception of their subject matter in the wider community, and ways in which what they currently do can be modified to equip their students to evaluate that role and to develop the skills necessary to communicate ideas and information.

Background and objectives

The strategies described here are drawn from experience at Lancaster University. They were developed initially in 1988 as a response to the British government's 'Enterprise in Higher Education' initiative which encouraged alternative forms of teaching and assessment with a view to promoting student capabilities more explicitly, if possible through association with, or consideration of, the needs of non-academic bodies. The innovations sought, in particular, to develop group work through research projects and to enhance communication skills by obliging students to consider how their results could be presented to outside audiences in a variety of formats. This also allowed for the introduction of basic computer training, initially word processing to present their findings and reports. Increasingly, however, the projects have been designed to incorporate databases or spreadsheets as tools for handling, sorting, analysing or presenting material.

Designing course structures

The changes have involved both adapting an existing course and introducing new modules specifically designed to cater for staff, student or community interests.

The former involved changing the assessed assignments of a third-level, double-weighted, seminar-based course on England, Scotland and France, 1543–60: replacing a traditional examination in which students were required to comment on prescribed primary sources with a group project which required students to relate their knowledge of the period and its sources to a specific task – in this case, the preparation and production of an illustrated historical guide to a fortified site which both described the artefact and explained its significance. This exercise incorporated an existing fieldwork component of the course, but also introduced computer-assisted presentation and analytical skills. Five such publications have now been produced by students on the course.

A new course, 'History and the Community', was also launched which has as its core a research project, usually collaboratively undertaken, based on original material but with the requirement that its findings are presented in a format capable of being appreciated by a non-academic, usually local audience. To date, this has involved original projects each year, the nature of which have been negotiated between students, staff and interested outside organizations. Through these assignments students have been able to explore a wide range of themes and sources, to acquire and practise relevant skills of historical analysis and to consider issues related to the presentation of their findings.

Religious history, for example, has been pursued in collaboration with local churches to produce a computerized bibliography for a Catholic diocesan library; an illustrated booklet on the history of a local Catholic community; a guide and video describing Quaker meeting houses in the region; and an exhibition in the Catholic cathedral. Work on industrial and business history has included blind and sighted students working together to research and write Braille guides related to the history of two regional industries for local museums; a census-based study of a textile community for a local school; and the research and publication of oral and primary source-based histories of retail and manufacturing businesses. Aspects of agricultural history have been explored through the production of a video for a local village outlining how a computerized analysis of early nineteenth-century tithe apportionments was undertaken and what its results were. The implementation of nineteenth-century penal reforms has been studied through exploration of prison and assize records, and a computer-assisted analysis of nineteenth-century census enumerators' books of a local residential/commercial district has been undertaken, the results all being published as short, illustrated booklets by Lancaster City Museum. The same organization also offered space for the display of Soviet revolutionary art posters collected and described by a student. Child labour in nineteenth-century Lancashire has also been explored using spreadsheets to analyse printed census material, supplementing this with official government enquiries, contemporary printed and photographic sources and oral evidence. An illustrated booklet is being published by the County Library Service.

The implications of change

The role of staff Adopting an essentially activity-based approach to learning has had implications for the teaching approaches of the staff involved. New strategies to facilitate learning have had to be adopted which have more in common with postgraduate supervision than with traditional undergraduate class-based teaching. These have involved various combinations of the following:

- making clear, either unilaterally or after consultations with students, the precise aims, objectives, assessment criteria and format of their work;
- exploring the feasibility of any study prior to its introduction by checking that students will be able to obtain access to the relevant sources and equipment;
- advising on writing up reports and projects and making students aware of conventions appropriate to the proposed form of presentation;
- making available any training necessary to undertake the research, for example, in computer analysis or palaeography;
- sustaining enthusiasm and motivation.

Practical considerations   Project work has also demanded prior consideration of a variety of logistical issues. Fostering relationships between universities and outside organizations takes time to function effectively; each side has to build up a shared understanding of aims and responsibilities and agree that there are potential benefits accruing to both parties. Such negotiations are probably best, and consequently have been initiated and conducted by academic staff. Similarly, staff have also had to take into account possible costs associated with travel, equipment provision and production. Unless outside funding has been available, projects have had to be supported from institutional or student resources. In most cases, however, it has been possible to utilize existing equipment on campus – computing and printing facilities, tape recorders, photocopiers and videorecorders – for little or no cost. Relatively unsophisticated, user-friendly and inexpensive generic software packages for word processing, databases and spreadsheets like Microsoft Works for Windows have proved adequate for most computing purposes.

Time management   In considering the feasibility of project work, account also has to be taken of the quantity, and quality, of the time available to the students. This has involved assessments of the proportion of their time which could be allocated to the work. Institutional teaching timetables and course structures clearly determine possible patterns of working, affecting both the possibility of securing extended blocks of time for work away from campus, and the feasibility of effective group work. Generally speaking it has proved easier to implement change for single major students and for those who are taking a limited number of other courses at any one time and when relatively long periods of time are formally allocated in the official timetable for each course. Extensive student choice combined with short teaching sessions restrict students' ability to devise effective time-management strategies or to co-ordinate group activity. Electronic mail and computer conferencing can be used to overcome some of these problems, but this strategy clearly requires extensive information technology provision and training.

Student demand   The problem of matching student demand with available resources has to be addressed. Problems can arise both when too few or too many students opt for, or are required to do, the courses. Given unrestricted free choice, students can often exhibit an understandable conservatism, preferring to stick to subjects, methods and practices with which they are already acquainted because, like their tutors, most of them are attracted to history by its subject matter, not its potential for delivering desired learning outcomes, and because they measure their achievements in terms of grade marks rather than skills and competencies. The topics studied as part of any project, therefore, have to have a popular appeal. If these are sufficiently attractive then they can conquer fear of the unknown and provide an incentive to acquire new skills.

Assessment   Effective and equitable assessment of such work requires taking account of a number of factors. What students bring to each course varies; some already possess specific skills, experience or knowledge; some do not. This poses potential problems of equity if students are obliged to work in groups which are arbitrarily constructed and assessed only with a collective grade. Effective learning can also be achieved even when co-operation within groups manifestly breaks down or when the final product is considered to be deficient in some way, possibly through no fault of the students concerned. Learning by experience involves making mistakes, and procedures and exercises have to be devised which take into account and allow individual students to express what they have learnt, rather than simply being assessed on a specific product. The quality of that learning can be judged either explicitly through exercises designed to test specific skills or knowledge, or implicitly by assessing the success to which students utilize these to achieve a desired outcome.

In practice it is not appropriate to be prescriptive about assessment procedures. A variety of strategies can, and probably should, be devised to test different aspects of student learning and, if group work is adopted, to distinguish between individuals. Formal academic essays, computer assignments, final presentations and project reports can all be successfully employed in this context as long as their objectives, their relative importance and the criteria on which they are assessed are clearly thought out and agreed in advance.

Evaluating the experiment

Assessing the relative effectiveness of different approaches to learning is a contentious issue since it is virtually impossible to measure value-added in any crude quantitative way. When combined with the question of whether different methods are efficient as well as effective, definitive answers become even harder to find. Even if a particular approach is universally accepted as an effective way to learn, it might be possible to find cheaper ways of achieving the same objectives.

Qualitative evidence to date suggests that the project-based approach does provide an effective learning medium and that it might also be more efficient than might first be thought. Students' feedback suggests that the acquisition of skills and techniques is fostered because they view the process as an integral means to an end and not an end in itself. Among the specific abilities they identify are an enhanced appreciation of computer applications, self-organization, awareness of the role of illustration and graphics, personal interviewing skills, task and time management, appreciation of the potential dynamics of group co-ordination, awareness of sources and facilities outside university, and the confidence to construct their own hypotheses and ideas. All have reported a sense of achievement which has fostered self-confidence and personal assurance, and they have considered that the skills they have acquired will assist them to pursue a variety of career paths. As a result staff have also been able to construct fuller profiles of student abilities and personalities.

Although in some respects such work can be viewed as more demanding, and consequently less 'efficient', than traditional lecture-based teaching, it can yield positive benefits for staff. The projects have provided a rare opportunity to learn from and with students, combining what are all-too-often considered to be competing activities – teaching and research. Exercises which have employed computerized databases and spreadsheets have provided original material which can be incorporated into practical demonstrations and exercises or used as the basis for future research. The forging of contacts with local libraries, museums and archive services has led to the consideration of a variety of collaborative ventures which have already led to more substantial publications.

Conclusion

This chapter has been designed to foster debate about the relationship of academic history with popular perceptions of the discipline in the wider community, and to suggest ways in which students could be trained to evaluate those perceptions and to develop the skills necessary to communicate ideas and information to different audiences.

It has been argued that, by viewing the wider community both as a resource *and* as a potential audience, it is possible to pursue the subject matter of the discipline, promote the acquisition of transferable skills and produce benefits for staff, students and society alike. It has sought not to prescribe solutions but to offer examples and raise issues for consideration. Relatively minor amendments to existing course objectives, learning strategies and assessment procedures are capable of accommodating some of the objectives outlined above; considered as part of an integrated package of courses each of which concentrates on different elements of the agenda, it should be possible to attain most if not all of them.

Notes

1   *The Manufacture of Scottish history*, ed. I. Donnachie and C. Whatley (Polygon, Edinburgh, 1990), pp. 3–4.
2   G. Brown and M. Atkins, *Effective Teaching in Higher Education* (Methuen, London, 1988), p. 181.

Further Reading

In Britain, R. Hewison's polemical *The Heritage Industry: Britain in a Climate of Decline* (Methuen, London, 1987) occasioned much public debate and is still a provocative introduction to the subject. D. Lowenthal, *The Past is a Foreign Country* (Cambridge University Press, Cambridge, 1985), P. Wright, *On Living in an Old Country: The National Past in Contemporary Britain* (Verso, London, 1986) and P. Fowler, *The Past in Contemporary Society* (Routledge, London, 1992) are more measured, deeper explorations of the significance of the past in contemporary Britain. *The Museum Time Machine: Putting Cultures on Display*, ed. R. Lumley (Routledge, London, 1988) is more about practical issues, but it includes some examples from other countries. N. Merriman, *Beyond the Glass Case: The Past, the Heritage and the Public*

(Leicester University Press, Leicester, 1991) reviews the impact of theme parks and museums in the 1980s. J. G. Jenkins, *Getting Yesterday Right: Interpreting the Heritage of Wales* (University of Wales, Cardiff, 1992) is a critical survey of the impact of tourist-oriented museums in that country.

Debate has also developed along similar lines in other countries over the same period. In America, *Presenting the Past: Essays on History and the Public*, ed. S. P. Benson, S. Brier and R. Rosenzweig (Temple University Press, Philadelphia, 1985) explores how mass media, popular culture and 'public history' have influenced the way Americans have come to view themselves, while *Past Meets Present: Essays about Historic Interpretation and Public Audiences*, ed. J. Blatti (Smithsonian Institution Press, Washington DC, 1987) looks at the public responsibilities of historians and museum professionals. R. Johnson's *Making Histories: Studies in History Writing and Politics* (Hutchinson, London, 1982) points up the contested nature of popular historical consciousness, while *Museums, National Identity and National Ambitions*, ed. F. S. Kaplan (Leicester University Press, London, 1994) deals with how new nations of the nineteenth and twentieth centuries used or created a national cultural heritage for state purposes. This was certainly true of Ireland where the relative lack of academic revisionists' influence in determining popular conceptions of the past is the theme of R. Foster's 'History and the Irish Question', *Trans. Royal Hist. Soc.*, 5th series, 1983. Similar issues are also discussed in *The Manufacture of Scottish History*, ed. I. Donnachie and C. Whatley (Polygon, Edinburgh, 1990).

Ideas, contacts and sources for community-based research projects generally originate from individual teachers' historical expertise and knowledge and can clearly span an enormous range of subjects depending on location and the availability of sources. The Historical Association (59a Kennington Park Road, London, SE11 4JH) has an extensive catalogue of books and pamphlets on sources and approaches to research, including *Short Guides to Records*, ed. L. M. Munby, which is an invaluable collection of guides to twenty-four different classes of English sources; a further fourteen guides are available as pamphlets. The Association also publishes the 'Helps for Students of History' series which discusses sources, archives and approaches to specific subjects. The Conference of Regional and Local History publishes regular newsletters which include details of developments in regional history courses in British universities, and *The Local Historian* is an underrated journal which often contains pieces on unusual sources.

There are numerous guides to national and regional archives most of which are dealt with in books offering general advice to prospective local historians, although the sources they describe are, of course, also the raw material for academic history. These include K. Tiller, *English Local History: An Introduction* (Alan Sutton, Gloucester, 1992); S. Friar, *The Batsford Companion to Local History* (Batsford, London, 1991); P. Riden, *Local History: A Handbook for Beginners* (Batsford, London, 1983); W. B. Stephens, *Sources for English Local History* (Cambridge University Press, Cambridge, 1981); A. Rogers, *Approaches to Local History* (Longman, London, 1977). R. Perks, *Oral History: Talking About the Past* (Historical Association, London, 1992) and W. Baum, *Oral History for the Local Historical Society* (AASLH, Nashville, 1987) provide useful step-by-step practical guides for those contemplating undertaking oral history in their respective countries, but P. Thompson, *The Voice of the Past: Oral History* (Oxford University Press, Oxford, 1988) remains the best extended treatment of this particular approach which, if carefully and sensitively handled, is ideal for student project work within the local community. The journal of the British society, *Oral History*, also contains news of developments in this field.

13

Learning from Experience: Field Trips and Work Placements

Christine Hallas

In recent years higher education institutions have been attacked for their apparent deficiency in not providing an education that would adequately prepare students for the 'real' world of work. History as taught in higher education institutions has been particularly criticized, with some suggesting that it has no practical value and should not be a major subject in the curriculum. Academics have been accused of indulging themselves by giving students a narrow education that concentrated solely on history for its own sake and ignored the needs both of society and the individual student. The contention is that the student's experience has been purely cerebral and not practical. Historians have countered that history is a very practical subject, not least because historians have to go in search of their sources and be prepared to utilize any type of material which enhances the understanding of the issue under scrutiny. In addition, it is argued, the skills developed through the study of history can be utilized in non-history-specific environments such as employment.

Many historians have risen to the challenge posed by the criticism, and, as is amply demonstrated in this book, are now actively seeking, through a variety of means, to make their subject more clearly relevant to the needs both of society and of students. Practical experience for history students is clearly important and this chapter examines two types of activity – field trips and work placements – in which such experience can be successfully provided. The rationale for including these activities in a history course, the experiences of those taking part, some practical suggestions, and a case-study are presented in the following two sections.

Field Trips

Although the benefit of field trips for the study of history has been clearly demonstrated through the work of individual historians and some departments, notably at Leicester University, generally the use of fieldwork in higher education history courses has been sporadic.[1] As W. G. Hoskins noted 'most academically-trained historians are completely blind to the existence and value of visual evidence'.[2] More often than not, historians have regarded the field trip either as the central tool of the 'specialist' historian such as the archaeologist, or as the domain of the geographer, only to be borrowed on those few occasions when some light relief is required from sitting in the lecture hall. However, if planned properly and used as an integral part of a course, fieldwork can be a valuable aid both to the student's personal development and to his/her understanding of history. As Hoskins commented, there should be no opposition between fieldwork and documentary analysis: both should be part of a rigorous learning environment which should be analytical, scholarly and probing.[3]

In terms of advantages gained, field trips can serve a variety of purposes:

1 *Historical information.* Field trips can provide another dimension to the documentary evidence or they can be used as a starting point for identifying questions to be further explored in documents.[4]
2 *Context.* By visiting an area, issues under study can be placed in their social background and interrelationships between them can be identified.
3 *Additional issues.* Fieldwork frequently provides the opportunity for other topics or issues to be raised which could not have been easily incorporated into a lecture on the subject.[5]
4 *Empathy.* A sense of 'reality' is engendered and students can empathize more fully with their subject.[6]
5 *General development.* Fieldwork enlarges the historian's consciousness and encourages an open mind.[7]

Field trips also provide the opportunity to develop a variety of transferable skills:

1 *Observation skills.* Students can develop observation skills both with and without the aid of the lecturer.

2   *Analytical skills.* Students can assimilate information from a variety of sources and become familiar with different approaches to analysis.

3   *Independent learning.* The field visit is an ideal opportunity to encourage a greater independence of learning in students.

4   *Decision-making.* Visual or oral evidence can be used as a basis for decision-making.

5   *Teamwork skills.* If students are working in groups, the field trip can be of value in developing teamwork skills.[8]

Finally, all fieldtrip organizers note that the field visit provides an environment which encourages group cohesion and enhances the commitment and enthusiasm of students for their topic.[9]

There are, however, some difficulties, albeit of a largely practical nature, associated with incorporating field trips into courses:

1   In terms of resources, contrary to the situation for most geography courses, history departments do not usually have a separate fieldtrip budget. Given high transport and accommodation costs, it is, therefore, unlikely that most history departments could contemplate anything more ambitious than the short one- or half-day visit.[10]

2   Because the field trip requires careful planning and a detailed understanding of the topic and the environment, it is time-consuming. Even the 'one-off' visit takes a minimum of half a day and needs to be supported by extensive organization.

3   The field trip can cause logistical problems by disrupting one's own timetable and that of colleagues.

4   The field visit can be difficult to organize if large numbers are involved. Little useful work can be undertaken with groups larger than twenty, and a group size of twelve should be the optimum.[11]

5   The weather factor cannot be ignored for outside locations, and planning must incorporate alternative arrangements.

6   Unless students are carefully prepared they may regard the visit as a light-hearted day out and gain little from the experience.

Planning field trips

Given the difficulties listed in the previous section, the question arises when, if at all, should field trips be used? It is useful to note at this point that the type of course in terms of level has a bearing on the use and value of field trips. Fieldtrip organizers note that the maturity and natural enthusiasm of students following postgraduate or adult-education courses invariably results in maximum value being gained from fieldwork. As far as undergraduates are concerned, the field trip is likely to be of greatest value to those following history as a major subject and undertaking detailed studies. The field trip will not be of much value in short, non-intensive courses where it is likely to deteriorate into a passive exercise for students.[12] The criteria for incorporating fieldwork into any course must be the enhancement of the student's learning experience in relation to the achievement of course objectives. Fieldwork should not be confined to courses with a strong local or methodological emphasis. Many different types of courses, ranging from social, economic and political topics to national and international history, can benefit from the inclusion of a field visit.[13] Before embarking on a field trip the tutor must identify the purpose of the visit. Does the visit have the single objective of imparting some historical information or are there several objectives including, for example, understanding of concepts and developing skills?[14]

Once the purpose has been ascertained further questions need to be addressed such as: will the visit yield information that cannot be gained from another source?; will it enhance documentary information already acquired?; and will it enable students to empathize with their subject? How the field visit is handled depends upon its purpose. The 'one-off' illustrative visit may well have different requirements from the visit that is part of a larger scheme in developing students' skills in fieldwork. For example, one can go to 'observe' a battlefield, or to 'empathize' in a mill, or to 'understand' attitudes by examining architecture, or to be 'involved' in field walking and finding artefacts and collecting oral evidence.

The tutor has to be well prepared, both in knowledge of the site and in the significance of features. The field visit must include some preparatory work with the students even if this is only a discussion of the aims of the trip. The visit also requires some follow-up work. This may take the form of oral report and discussion and/or of written report but, at the very least, it must identify the extent to which the aims of the visit have been achieved. If possible the visit should be an integral part of the assessment process as this encourages students to approach the work seriously.[15] With respect to the actual field trip, although it is important that students take an active role and work independently, initially it is probably more valuable for the tutor to accompany the group around the site.[16] Students can then see how to approach fieldwork and can take part in a tutor-led discussion. This use of simple questionnaires on site is generally not advisable. However, if they are used, the quiz type of questionnaire, which tends to encourage students to be more interested in 'scoring points' than in thinking analytically, should be avoided. Guide sheets which include suggestions of types of questions to be asked of the site/artefacts can serve a useful purpose.

Case-study

At Trinity and All Saints' College, the field visit is an integral part of the history degree programme, which seeks both to impart information and to develop student skills and concepts.[17] The fieldvisit element of the course is designed to progress from introductory tutor-led visits to sites, record offices and museums to more sophisticated and independent use in the final year as part of special subject or dissertation units. Students undertake their first field trip within a few weeks of arrival at college, and the visit, to the model village of Saltaire near Bradford, forms the introduction to a method course, 'Sources and Their Use'. The aim of the visit is twofold: first, to encourage students, under tutor guidance and working in small groups, to ask questions of the environment as a starting point for examining documentary evidence, and, second, to develop group relationships among the new arrivals in a working and social (via a visit to a pub on the return journey) environment. Prior to the visit a brief background is provided and students discuss the type of questions which might be raised and answered on site. During the visit students refer to a guide list of questions and comments. The post-visit discussion centres upon information acquired from the visit; the value to the historian of using visual evidence; and problems of interpreting a site.

Later in the autumn term, first-year students, who have been examining copies of documents on campus, visit a record office to analyse selected original Parish Registers. As with their first visit, this places students in a different environment, gives them access to original sources and raises questions about the problems and advantages of examining such documents away from their original depository. Students write a report of their analysis and discuss their findings in class. In the spring term, students progress from examining individual sources to undertaking a six-week project based on a specific local area.[18] For this they are required to utilize local record offices and, as part of a group of about twelve students, undertake a tutor-led field visit to their chosen local area. Experience gained from the Saltaire visit is put to good use as students study the siting and the type of buildings. After at least one further visit to the record office, students compile written and oral reports and compare their results within their group. This exercise enables students to recognize the importance of identifying interrelationships between different features, such as the siting of a mill in respect of communications and the labour force. They also assess the value of additional information acquired from the site which might correct a misunderstanding of archive material or serve to demonstrate the significance of a particular written source.

The number of field visits students undertake after the compulsory first-year courses depends upon the options chosen. In their second year students following the Nineteenth-Century Studies option undertake two visits. One visit is to an industrial museum which is situated in an old mill. The aim of this visit is not only to examine interesting artefacts but to enable students to empathize. Demonstrations of steam engines which powered the mill and fast moving, noisy spinning machinery, bring home graphically the conditions in mills during the Industrial Revolution. This is a visit where students, with a guide sheet suggesting lines of enquiry, benefit from working in small groups without direct tutor support. Post-visit discussion centres on aspects of the industrial revolution and on the value of visiting museums. The second field visit, to Leeds city centre, is designed to provide more experience of analysing architecture and of using such a source to identify Victorian values. Prior to the visit students examine Victorian attitudes and discuss architectural styles. In the final year, students' use of the field visit will depend again on the options they have chosen. For example, the aim of visits in the Victorian Agriculture course is to provide a fuller understanding of agriculture by enabling students to visit farms, discuss farming practices with farmers, identify the processes which were in operation in the Victorian period, examine the remains of rural industries, and note the importance of transport links. Students also visit a rural museum which enables them to examine machinery and such Victorian innovations as drainage-laying systems. Students taking the Wars of the Roses course visit battlefields in order to empathize. They gain a fuller understanding of the course of the battle by listening to readings from documents while at the site.

Evaluations

Responses to questionnaires show that most students find field visits a valuable experience. They note that visits broaden their understanding of a subject, raise unexpected questions and help group dynamics which, in turn, has valuable repercussions both for class work and group tutorials. Student satisfaction is particularly high where they can see a direct link with the development of skills required for independent work. For example, 90 per cent of thirty second-year students find visits to record offices 'valuable', with 60 per cent placing such visits in the top category: 'very valuable'. Most final-year students, presumably with the hindsight of their dissertation research, also place these visits in the 'very valuable' category. The visit to examine the architecture of Leeds is very highly rated in terms of 'content', 'developing skills of observation', and 'demonstrating the value of the field visit as an important element of historical research'. Most students feel visits are valuable for improving group dynamics, with 75 per cent of final-year students believing they are 'very valuable'.

Students comment on the importance of field trips in terms of giving a sense of realism as well as extending their knowledge and understanding, and many note that field trips are 'really good fun'. Students also emphasize the need for careful preparation and integration in the course – Saltaire did not fully 'link with other work we were doing'; 'not bad as an introduction but no real relevance unless background provided'; 'one must remember that the place has changed'; 'always useful but not especially necessary'. They also emphasize practical considerations – 'better done in summer'; 'enjoyable although usually cold'; 'great fun if we don't have too far to walk'.

Staff also derive high levels of satisfaction from the field trip, particularly in respect of improving the students' learning experience. Although they comment that it is time-consuming in terms of preparation and actually accompanying the field trips, the consensus is that the returns in respect of gains for students (and, therefore, for tutors) make the effort worth while.

Conclusion

Tutors in history departments throughout the country note that there are problems in organizing and integrating fieldwork into history courses, particularly in respect of large student numbers and tight resources. However, they all comment on the value of fieldwork in respect of both the immediate acquisition of information and skills, and in the long-term development of the students.[19] The benefits are such that, as one method of history teaching and learning, the field trip is to be highly recommended.

Work Placements[20]

A government report published in 1985 noted 'higher education establishments need to go out to develop their links with industry and commerce . . . [and to establish] strong connections with their local communities'.[21] Largely in response to such pressures, there has been increasing interest in the value and use of periods of practical workplace experience as part of an undergraduate programme.

The debate in respect of work experience for history students centres on how far historians should be expected to become involved in such an exercise. Some historians still feel that placements have no relevance for the learning of history and that they should not take part in initiatives which, rather than aiding students' search of the past, address either the requirements of society or the students' career needs. However, many historians now maintain that history must not be isolated from the students' overall learning experience. Indeed, it is suggested that history has a very special part to play in the development of the whole student and that work placements can form one part of this activity.

Placements need not be approached as a narrow training for 'history' careers in museums or record offices. Professional placements can be part of a wider course objective which enables students to utilize in the workplace the concepts, skills and, in some cases, knowledge acquired in their history courses. This experience helps students to appreciate the value of the study of history as a preparation for virtually any career. Conversely, as a result of their placements, students are able to bring a greater understanding of the use of skills and concepts to their study of history.

Current practice and practical concerns

Essentially there are two types of work experience: the traditional placement where students are employed in a work environment for a block of time, and the project-oriented scheme where students are attached to an organization and undertake a specific task/project either on or off the workplace site. The former scheme may or may not be history-specific whereas the latter scheme is usually a history-based project and is often completed as a serial project rather than in a single block of time.

It is essential that historians who are considering introducing work-experience schemes identify precisely what they are seeking to achieve.

For example, those who want a project-oriented scheme which keeps work experience closely related to history and which has objectives such as skills in group work and/or computers, may wish to follow either the model of 'History in the Community' established at Lancaster University or Manchester Metropolitan University's 'Museum Placements' and 'Independent Study' models.[22] In the second-year unit at Manchester, students undertake project work for a local museum over a ten-week period. In the final year 'Independent Study' option students attend the place of employment for half a day per week over two terms and undertake a specific project for the employer. For those departments wishing to provide students with an experience closer to normal employment, the traditional block work-placement is the most appropriate model to follow. This is the approach adopted both for the Historical and Political Studies degree at Huddersfield University, where the scheme is organized at departmental level and the placement is directly related to History, and at Trinity and All Saints, Leeds, where the placement programme is arranged at institutional level and uses any organization that can offer experience commensurate with degree-level work.[23] These two types of block experience have different merits. The subject-specific placement has the obvious advantage of being related to history and students can see a direct connection between the content of their courses and their projects. The advantage of the non-history-specific approach is that, in recognition of the future careers of most students, it provides the opportunity to utilize the skills undertaken in the study of history in a general working environment. In addition, if there are high numbers of students to be placed, the non-history-specific approach can take advantage of a larger pool of organizations. Whichever model is chosen, the main objective should be to enhance student learning. This can be achieved during the placement by developing those transferable skills which have already been used in the history course, by introducing new skills, and by providing an experience of a work environment. Depending upon the individual student and the precise nature of the work experience, the skills which students should expect to gain experience of might include:

1   Researching and collating information.
2   Evaluating data.
3   Using initiative to develop novel approaches to handling a project.
4   Drawing conclusions on the basis of evidence.
5   Communication of findings orally and in writing.

6   Being a constructive team member and exercising team leadership.
7   Accepting, acting upon, and giving constructive criticism.
8   Developing computing skills.

The placement should also heighten the students' awareness of the need to be professional in their approach to work. While punctuality, taking responsibility and working independently are important for an undergraduate course, these issues are even more critical in an employment situation.

Problems and advantages of placements

As with most schemes, the placement system suffers from some disadvantages. The extent to which these are perceived as major obstacles will depend upon the priority given by department or institution to the scheme. If the scheme is accorded a high priority, this should result in a satisfactory level of planning and resources, and the negative elements should be minimized. Some of the difficulties and possible solutions are listed below:

1   To be undertaken successfully the placement system is not cheap. It is expensive in terms of tutor time and tutor and student expenses.
2   Placements can be disruptive to main-course teaching, though this disruption can be limited by careful course planning.
3   Some placements may not sufficiently challenge the student. However, if mechanisms are in place to brief fully and to vet properly organizations the likelihood of a poor placement is greatly reduced.
4   Students can be 'poached' away from their degree course. This rarely occurs if the employers are carefully chosen and properly briefed. Most employers are enlightened enough to recognize the importance of the students completing their degree course.
5   As the number of institutions providing placement schemes increases so does the difficulty of finding good placement organizations. This is a problem for which there is no easy solution.
6   The organization and supervision of placements is extremely complex and time-consuming.

Those institutions which have introduced placements into a history degree course note the importance of careful planning and adequate resourcing. Much of the success of a placement system lies in the commitment of all parts, or at least a large section, of the institution concerned in the scheme. If the programme is being introduced on a large scale, there should be an administrative placement officer and a tutor responsible for the whole scheme. In addition, there must be a placement tutor responsible for the individual student and for his/her placement organization.

In terms of establishing a pool of placement organizations, valuable contacts can be made by working closely with the local Chamber of Commerce or equivalent; advertising locally; writing to and visiting potential organizations; and pursuing contacts made by other members of staff and by students.[24] Where, as at Huddersfield and Manchester, specific history-related projects are required, the work in order to identify these is extremely time-consuming. However, although the possible number of organizations able to provide such projects is limited, the experience at Manchester indicates that with careful preparation in terms of developing and directing contacts there is no shortage of potential projects.[25]

Once the placement has been agreed it is crucial that there is adequate communication between the three parties: employer, student, and tutor. As far as possible, employers should be closely involved in placement planning and should be well briefed. It is important that each organization is visited by the tutor during the period of placement.

Case-study

Trinity and All Saints' College undertook an extensive review of its courses during the mid-1970s and, as a result, adopted a radical new course structure. Students enrol for a joint-degree course in a professional and an academic area. History students can follow a professional course in education, media, or management. History/education students gain practical experience through teaching practice and, following the education model, history/media or history/management students take part in a placement programme. Students undertake two six-week placements, the first in June/July of Year I, and the second in February/March of Year II.

Since its inception the placement system has grown rapidly and about sixty history students are now placed annually by the full-time placement officer.[26] A network of local and national placements has been established, through a variety of channels. Students request the type of placement they would like (for example, marketing, personnel, accountancy) and the placement officer attempts to match the students' preferences with available placement organizations. Some history students choose subject-related placements such as record offices, museums or heritage sites. Others prefer to use their skills in a non-history environment. If a suitable placement is not possible from existing contacts, the placement officer endeavours to arrange a new link. Alternatively, students can arrange their own placements. The student is not paid while on placement but does receive some travel expenses. If the student organizes a placement at some distance from college, he/she is responsible for the accommodation arrangements.

Prior to the placement the student is briefed and has to enter into a Learning Agreement with the employer. The Agreement is presented in general terms with the details of the particular placement being finalized between the employer and student at the pre-placement interview. Some organizations do not confirm their participation in the placement scheme until they have interviewed the student. This interview also enables the student to identify his/her role within the organization during the placement. Each student is assigned to a placement tutor with whom he/she has a pre-placement tutorial and is in phone/letter contact within the first week of the scheme. The student receives a visit from the tutor during the six-weeks' placement and is required to submit a report on completion of the placement.

Before embarking on the placement scheme the employer is briefed by the college placement officer as to the placement requirements. On completion of the placement the supervisor within the organization submits a report on the student's performance to the college. Although this scheme is not aimed primarily at the academic subject, for those students following history it provides invaluable experience which can be related both directly and indirectly to their history course. As a recent HEFC report on history at the college notes, 'students, staff and employers, all indicate that there is considerable reciprocal benefit between the attachment and the teaching and learning in history'.[27]

Student input

The rationale of the placement scheme is to enable students to be actively involved in the work environment, in a manner commensurate with their professional/academic attainment.[28] The student is required to examine the organization critically and to understand dynamics and the infrastructure from both a theoretical and a practical point of view. While on placement the student is expected to keep a diary of his/her work, to discover something about the industry as a whole and to provide an account of the specific organization with which he/she is involved. For example, a student working at a museum would be expected to examine the leisure/heritage/conservation industry as well as identifying the distinctive role of his/her specific museum. The student is also expected to undertake a project. This may be a piece of work which the employer requests or, if one cannot be suggested, a project may be devised by the student. For example, the student may work on the history of the organization, or may catalogue the archives, or analyse the effectiveness of the management structure or the nature of group dynamics. The diary, the organization analysis, and the project are included in the student's placement report which is submitted to the tutor. A student has to pass both placements in order to pass the course and hence gain a degree.

Evaluations

As far as history students are concerned the placement system provides a valuable experience. Even a 'bad' placement is of use in that it provides an insight into the type of career an individual might or might not like to follow. The student gains experience of a working/career environment, often with some degree of responsibility and usually with a high level of job satisfaction. Further, the placement sometimes results in the offer of a position with the organization at the end of the student's undergraduate course. Several history students have gained employment through this route.

Even though many students do not have a history-specific placement, they appreciate the value of the history course, particularly in terms of skills, for their placement work. For example, a student undertaking her second-year placement in the Tourist Department of Bradford Metropolitan Council commented that the skills learnt in her history courses were extremely useful. During the placement she was required to find and collate material, raise questions about the data, recognize bias, draw conclusions and present her findings in a manner appropriate for the tourist audience. A recent survey of the placement scheme demonstrates both the high value that students place on the experience and the importance of careful planning and good communication with all parties concerned.[29]

College staff agree that the programme is excellent when it succeeds but note that the maintenance of a high level of communication with employers, though desirable, is difficult. Most history tutors who take part in supervising placement students value the experience they gain

through such involvement. After visiting, for example, insurance companies, banks, museums, and heritage centres, tutors appreciate more
fully the skills required for different organizations and careers. As a
result, tutors are acutely aware of the importance of developing transferable skills within the history course. Apart from being concerned with
history-specific skills and concepts, the aims and objectives of the history
course explicitly seek to reinforce and expand upon skills students are
gaining elsewhere.

Most employers regard the scheme as being mutually beneficial for
themselves and students, and request that they be retained on the list for
future placements. A few organizations do not, or cannot, provide
students with a satisfactory level of stimulating work-experience. In
these cases the college seeks to ensure that the organization understands
more fully what is required. If the college is not successful, the organization is removed from the placement list. Due to the careful preparation
of students for placements, poor performance is kept to a minimum.
When there is an unsatisfactory report, the college undertakes a 'damage
limitation exercise'. It informs the organization supervisors that their
experience is atypical, ensures that they receive a 'good' student on
future placements, and monitors particularly closely the evaluation
reports from that organization.

Employers complete a confidential report as part of the placement
scheme. This gives them the opportunity to report on students and to
grade their performance as well as making general observations on the
scheme. Employers' reports frequently place history students in the top
category: 'The student quickly became a very valuable member of the
organization. The student was reliable, and conscientious showing
initiative and flair. If a suitable vacancy existed we would have been
happy to offer her/him a position.' For example, of eighteen reports for
second-year history students in 1992, 72 per cent were in the top two
categories on a six-point scale, with 44 per cent being in the highest
category. In 1993, of sixteen history students 94 per cent were placed in
the top two categories, with 63 per cent in the highest. Employers
generally see the report as important. They are prepared to spend time
completing the forms and frequently supply details, as the following
comments on history students demonstrate: 'Whilst on placement with
the museum, the staff found her a quick and bright learner'; 'a superb
placement! she showed enthusiasm, commitment to the company and
displayed excellent communication skills'; 'he has been an outstanding
placement . . . he has ironed out problems with the database we are using

with the archive material'; 'she proved to be flexible and capable of handling all aspects and all tasks seeking out news features, and stories and writing them up, suitable for insertion in the magazine'.

There are, of course, some less than complimentary comments but these are usually tempered with advice. For example, 'she needs to reflect on the importance of 'time' in a commercial organization'; 'the only area where there was a weakness was in the accuracy of her work. She may like to look at developing this in future, with the emphasis on checking all her work for accuracy, punctuation and spelling.'

Conclusion

The work placement schemes referred to in this chapter show the variety of approaches that can be used to provide history students with experience of employment. All who are involved note that, in order to achieve maximum benefit, the programme must be carefully organized and must be part of a coherent structure. Whichever model they have adopted, history tutors who take part in placement schemes feel that the learning experience of students is enriched.[30] Placements are excellent in terms of the general development and career aspirations of history students, and they are also an asset to a history course and enhance the work of history departments by providing students and staff with an interesting and enlightening experience. Insurance, banking, museums and the theatre certainly make a change from modern economic history or the politics of medieval England and yet, and perhaps not so surprisingly, there are many links between the university history course and the staff and student placement experience in the world 'out there'.

Notes

1   For the purpose of this chapter the 'field trip' is taken in its widest sense – of leaving the place of learning and going to a site to examine landscape, artefacts or documents. In this sense, field trips include visits to original sites and to depositories such as museums and record offices. Little has been written on the value of the field trip in history; geographers make greater use of this form of teaching and have published more extensively. However, in both subjects most of the literature has been directed at secondary rather than higher education. Much of what follows, therefore, has been distilled from such written material as is available from historians; many conversations with history colleagues in other higher education institutions; publications on geography fieldwork; and my own experience. My

thanks are particularly due to Peter Edwards of The Roehampton Institute of Higher Education, David Hey of Sheffield University, John H. Smith of Manchester University, and Keith Snell of Leicester University for their helpful comments.

2   W. G. Hoskins, *Fieldwork in Local History* (Faber, London, 1967), p. 183.

3   Ibid.

4   Hoskins notes that it was this inquisitiveness concerning the landscape that first led him to documents: ibid., pp. 21–3.

5   Comments from David Hey.

6   J. R. Gold et al., *Teaching Geography in Higher Education* (Blackwell, Oxford, 1991), p. 25.

7   C. M. Knowles, *Landscape History* (Historical Association, London, 1983), p. 5.

8   Many of the aims and objectives for the acquisition of skills are similar in different disciplines. For more detailed discussion, see Gold, *Teaching Geography*, pp. 25–7.

9   One organizer feels this element is so important that, where possible, fieldwork should be placed near the beginning of the course so as to gain maximum benefit.

10 Due to resource constraints, many departments have dropped or seriously curtailed their undergraduate field trips in recent years. However, for other courses, fieldtrip costs are usually included in the course fee. Organizers of these courses report a continued high level of use of field trips.

11 However, given resource constraints and increasing student numbers, larger groups are now frequently taken on visits. These can be subdivided to undertake exploration of the site with the tutor moving between the sub-groups.

12 Gold, *Teaching Geography*, pp. 33–4.

13 A multi-disciplinary approach can be taken to field trips. For example, Hey, in addition to collaborating with English and geography colleagues, undertakes fieldwork with geology tutors (examining types of stone, particularly in churches), and botany tutors (studying woodland and moors).

14 If the imparting of historical knowledge is purely in the form of an outside lecture with little-or-no student input, the value of the visit must be questioned. Perhaps the use of slides in the lecture hall would be more cost-effective and still achieve the objectives.

15 Gold, *Teaching Geography*, p. 34.

16 This is particularly true for undergraduates. Where the field trip is residential, it may be preferable to give an introductory lecture prior to fieldwork, provide students with brief details and a map, and let them work in small groups independently on the site. This can be followed immediately with a debriefing session and a second visit the following day.

17 From discussions with colleagues at other institutions it appears that the

inclusion of field trips is generally on an *ad hoc* basis depending upon the individual tutor and a specific module.

18 Students choose either a rural area (Addingham near Ilkley), or an urban area (Kirkstall, a suburb of Leeds).

19 Many students pursue interests generated by field trips either as a dissertation topic or after their course has finished. For example, as a result of taking part in a visit to examine types of building stone, a student undertook research on millstones which was subsequently published. Similarly, students involved in a field visit to working-class housing have undertaken research and published articles on housing in Manchester and Stockport. One of these students subsequently founded the Working-Class Housing Group in Manchester, to research and record housing threatened with demolition.

20 This section is based on an earlier article: C. Hallas, 'New Directions in Learning: History and Work Placements', *Push Newsletter*, 2 (1990), pp. 23–8.

21 *The Development of Higher Education into the 1990s* (HMSO, London, 1985), p. 4.

22 For details of the Lancaster initiative, see M. Winstanley, 'Group Work in the Humanities: History in the Community, a Case Study', *Studies in Higher Education*, 17 (1992), pp. 55–64, and 'History in the Community: Computer-Assisted Group Project Work', *PUSH Newsletter*, 3 (1992), pp. 38–45; D. Nicholls, 'Making History Students Enterprising: "Independent Study" at Manchester Polytechnic', *Studies in Higher Education*, 17 (1992), pp. 67–80, and 'Using Contracts in Project Placements', in *Using Learning Contracts in Higher Education*, ed. J. Stephenson and M. Laycock (Kogan Page, London, 1993), pp. 89–96.

23 For details of the Huddersfield initiative, see B. Roberts and M. Mycock, 'The Experience of Introducing Work-Based Learning on an Arts Degree Course', *Journal of Further and Higher Education*, 15 (1991), pp. 76–85, and B. Roberts, 'Work-based Learning: The BA (Hons) Historical and Political Studies Degree Course at Huddersfield Polytechnic', *PUSH Newsletter*, 3 (1992), pp. 28–34.

24 Nicholls, 'Making History Students Enterprising', p. 71.

25 Ibid., p. 75.

26 A college total of over 600 students is placed annually.

27 *Quality Assessment Report: Q58/94, Trinity and All Saints, History* (HEFCE, Bristol, 1994), p. 3.

28 This programme seeks to provide degree-level work experience, it is not a work-shadowing scheme.

29 P. Comley, 'Increasing the Vocational Element in Higher Education: The TASC Experience', Unpublished undergraduate dissertation, Trinity & All Saints College, 1992.

30   Winstanley, 'History in the Community', pp. 44–5; Nicholls, 'Making
     History Students Enterprising', p. 78; and Roberts, 'Work-based Learn-
     ing', p. 32.

Further Reading

Although there is a fairly extensive literature on the subject of field trips, little
of it is recent and much of it refers specifically to local history. Such advice as
is offered is either hidden in a few words of general introduction or conclu-
sion, or is found in texts belonging to disciplines other than history. However,
the following are useful: W. G. Hoskins, *Fieldwork in Local History* (Faber,
London, 1967), and *The Making of the English Landscape* (Hodder and
Stoughton, London, 1977 edn); W. B. Stephens, *Teaching Local History*
(Manchester University Press, Manchester, 1977); C. H. Knowles, *Landscape
History* (Historical Association, London, 1983); J. R. Gold et al., *Teaching
Geography in Higher Education* (Blackwell, Oxford, 1991), ch. 3; and G.
Gibbs, *Improving the Quality of Student Learning* (Technical and Education
Services, Bristol, 1992), ch. 10.

As work-experience schemes are a relatively new initiative within history de-
partments, there is little history-specific reading matter available on the subject. But see, C. Hallas, 'New Directions in Learning: History and Work
Placements', *PUSH Newsletter*, 2 (1990), pp. 23–8; D. Nicholls, 'Making
History Students Enterprising: "Independent Study" at Manchester Polytechnic', *Studies in Higher Education*, 17 (1992), pp. 67–80; B. Roberts and M.
Mycock, 'The Experience of Introducing Work-Based Learning on an Arts
Degree Course', *Journal of Further and Higher Education*, 15 (1991), pp. 76–
85; B. Roberts, 'Work-based Learning: The BA Hons Historical and Political
Studies Degree Course at Huddersfield Polytechnic', *PUSH Newsletter*, 3
(1992), pp. 28–34; M. Winstanley, 'Group Work in the Humanities: History
in the Community, a Case Study', *Studies in Higher Education*, 17 (1992), pp.
55–64, and 'History in the Community: Computer-Assisted Group Project
Work', *PUSH Newsletter*, 3 (1992), pp. 38–45.

For some general comments on student skills, see M. Guirdham and K. Tyler,
Enterprise Skills for Students (Butterworth-Heinemann, Oxford, 1992), pp.
126–31; M. Reeves, *The Crisis in Higher Education* (Open University, Buck-
ingham, 1988), chs 5 and 6; ed. J. Stephenson, *Using Learning Contracts in
Higher Education* (Kogan Page, London, 1993), J. Stephenson and M.
Laycock, pp. 80–121. D. Nicholls contributes a chapter 'Using Contracts in
Project Placements' (pp. 89–96), based on the 'Independent Study' course at
Manchester Metropolitan University.

14

History, the Curriculum and Graduate Employment

Peter J. Beck

Traditionally, history's role in providing an informed understanding of the past, including the roots of the modern world, has been reinforced by a capacity to illuminate and enrich a range of other disciplines within and beyond the humanities. But, during the late 1970s and 1980s changing views about the nature and purpose of higher education prompted concern about history's future. Business studies, computing, engineering, and science, which were *perceived* by policy-makers, funding bodies, and college administrators as subjects preparing students for specific careers, were favoured in a strategy rationalized in vocational terms. 'Non-vocational' subjects, like history, suffered more than their fair share of the fiscal, staffing, library and other constraints placed on higher education.

History seemed to be under threat. The History in the Universities Defence Group (HUDG) and the Campaign for Public Sector History (PUSH) were formed in 1982 and 1986 respectively, in response to fears about the contraction, even closure, of history-degree programmes.[1] Declining numbers of GCE A-level history candidates, alongside the tendency for secondary school history to be increasingly subsumed by integrated humanities courses, compounded the sense of crisis in the discipline, as articulated by the press in the mid-1980s.[2] Lord Blake, acting in collaboration with the Historical Association, highlighted history's problems in conferences held at the House of Lords, and lobbied the Department of Education and Science about the anxieties of the historical profession.

Debate centred around a number of questions:

- Was history in retreat?
- How did history fit, if at all, into the increasingly functional approach to higher education?
- Was a history degree irrelevant, even a disadvantage, for employment purposes?
- Could history be used for the promotion of transferable skills without compromising academic standards?

Parallel debates occurred elsewhere, most notably in the USA, where 'Public History' emerged as one response to decline and to charges of irrelevance.[3]

The attack occurred on a number of fronts, but the prime focus concerned allegations about history's lack of employment utility at a time when vocational relevance was adjudged a priority objective for higher education. The challenge came from several directions: from a government wanting higher education to be more relevant to 'perceived national needs'; from employers seeking more suitable recruits; and from students trying to avoid the growing ranks of the unemployed. The traditional 'ivory tower' stress upon the intrinsic academic merit of studying history was transformed from an educational virtue to a vice. History proved extremely vulnerable; thus, a *Daily Express* editorial, quoted on BBC Radio Four, complained that 'the end result has been that we produce far too many historians and not enough engineers, with considerable loss and harm to industry and economy'.[4]

Some historians, pressing the educational rather than training role of a history degree, criticized efforts to rationalize the subject according to the vague and ephemeral notion of 'relevance'. Others, acknowledging that employability and accountability had become the name of the game, accepted that the historian was not excluded from establishing, to quote Geoffrey Barraclough, 'a positive return' from society's investment in the history industry: 'In the long run, he will be judged – and history will be judged with him – by the contribution he makes in using his knowledge for the shaping of the future.'[5] At the very least, there arose a need to discuss and *present* history using the language of the marketplace; a trend encouraged during the late 1980s by the Department of Employment's 'Enterprise in Higher Education' initiative, the CNAA's 'Humanities and Employment' seminars, and Understanding Industry Trust's 'Pegasus' scheme.[6] The Higher Education Funding Council for England's (HEFCE) new Teaching Quality Assessment Exercise has kept up the pressure: thus, teaching assessors 'will wish to see student progress and achievement evaluated, including the development of intellectual and personal skills and questions of employability and employment'.[7]

Are contemporary pressures for relevance and enterprise really unprecedented? Despite denying that the past exactly repeats itself, historians often have a sense of *déjà vu*. Indeed, Peter Slee, writing as the Director of the Enterprise Programme at Durham University, identified continuities dating back to late nineteenth-century efforts to revive British industry. The resulting expansion of higher education benefited not only the more obvious 'vocational' subjects but also history and other disciplines.

> Within this general rationale presented by the new institutions, practitioners were keen to articulate the specific utility of their own particular discipline. . . . Academics – they included John Seeley (history), Thomas Tout (history) – were all unstinting in their efforts to explain in clear and simple terms the methods and means by which their own discipline could add to a student's marketable value.[8]

A history degree, though upholding academic values, was presented as useful in terms of training the mind for the broad range of management, marketing and other skills required to complement science: 'These "evangelical professors" . . . stressed process and method over content; thus, subject matter was merely a rigorous vehicle for developing transferable skills.'[9]

In the present day, things have moved on from the sense of crisis affecting history during the early and mid-1980s. History, characterized now by a rising number of GCE A-level candidates and buoyant demand for degree courses, has benefited from the recent expansion of higher education. But growth has failed to lessen the preoccupation with transferable skills. Indeed, recession, in conjunction with the HEFCE Teaching Quality Assessment Exercise and specific projects (e.g., the Royal Society of Arts' 'Capability in Higher Education' project), has concentrated minds upon this dimension.

Mature students, seeking to change career direction or to make up for past shortcomings in their education, are a growing presence in college life. But schools still provide the bulk of undergraduates, who largely view higher education as merely part of an automatic progression along a conveyor belt from cradle to the wider world via school and college.[10]

Their desire to continue an interest in history is often reinforced, occasionally even exceeded as a motive, by an anxiety to get away from home and sample the attractions of college life. Most students, albeit vaguely appreciating that higher education improves job prospects and fosters personal development, commence history courses with no clear idea of a specific career direction, particularly as compared to their counterparts following, say, business studies, or computing and engineering courses. At first sight, this appears an unwelcome feature, but there are advantages in delaying career choice until nearer the time of graduation. Despite ruling out certain careers (e.g., civil engineering, medicine), a history degree offers an element of flexibility that opens up other opportunities, especially as about 40 per cent of graduate vacancies are open to those from any discipline. There is also a wide range of postgraduate vocational training (e.g., accountancy, journalism, law, librarianship, personnel management, social work, teaching) and conversion courses (e.g., information technology).

What do History Graduates do?

History graduates are active, even prominent, in many spheres of public and commercial life. The list, headed by the Prince of Wales, covers several politicians (e.g., Kenneth Baker, Kenneth Clarke, Douglas Hurd, Neil Kinnock). Businessmen holding history degrees include Robert Gunn (Chairman of Boots PLC, 1985–90), Sir Robert Reid (formerly Chairman/Chief Executive of Shell, 1985–90, and Chairman of the British Railways Board since 1990), and Lord Sainsbury of Preston Candover (President of Sainsbury's since 1992). Other prominent history graduates include Sebastian Coe (now an MP), Rabbi Lionel Blue, Marmaduke Hussey (Chairman of the BBC Board of Governors), Salman Rushdie, Sir Roy Strong (Director of the Victoria and Albert Museum, 1974–87), John Tusa (Managing Director of the BBC World Service, 1986–92), and Brian Walden (broadcaster and former MP). In reality, most history graduates never achieve this kind of public visibility. Traditionally, the civil service and teaching – the latter category is now reviving after a period of decline – attracted a large proportion of history graduates, but today there exists a wide range of alternative career directions (figure 14.1): law; administration and management; buying, marketing and selling; banking, insurance and accountancy; librarianship,

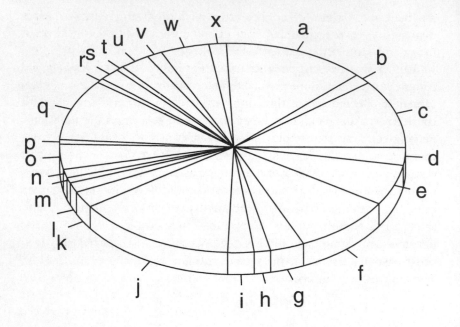

a)	Administration and management	13.4%	m)	Museum and Art Galleries	0.8%
b)	Personnel	1.6%	n)	Publishing	1.3%
c)	Buying, marketing and selling (including advertising, public relations)	10.7%	o)	Journalism	3.9%
			p)	Archive work	0.7%
d)	Management services (including computing, data processing)	2.7%	q)	Law	9.6%
			r)	Police	0.7%
e)	Secretarial and clerical	6.3%	s)	Armed Forces	1.9%
f)	Accountancy	9.4%	t)	Medical and nursing services	0.7%
g)	Banking	3.2%	u)	Social, welfare and religious work	2.8%
h)	Insurance	1.5%			
i)	Other financial work (e.g., investment, Stock Exchange)	2.5%	v)	Creative and entertainment (including broadcasting, film, theatre)	1.4%
j)	Teaching and lecturing	14.8%			
k)	Librarianship	2.5%	w)	Manual and non-professional occupations	4.5%
l)	Non-scientific research & information services	1.5%	x)	Other occupations	1.6%

Note
i) The figures of graduates entering work and training have been averaged over five years to avoid distortions caused by annual variations in categories recruiting relatively small numbers of graduates.
ii) Although it is possible to identify trends, several categories display considerable annual fluctuations. Care should be taken when comparing trends, which need to be interpreted in the wider economic context.
iii) The figures are based on first destination data kindly supplied by the Universities Statistical Record (i.e. graduates from former polytechnics and other colleges are excluded. The figures for 1991–92 graduates became available in July 1993.
iv) This table is based on returns covering over 15,000 history graduates, whose final year occurred from 1987–8 to 1991–2 inclusive.

Figure 14.1   History graduates: 1988–1992 career directions

archive and museum work; police and armed forces; and journalism. It is easy to forget that accountancy has attracted nearly 10 per cent of recent history graduates entering work and training.

Annual first-destination data prove the major source for informed comment on trends in the graduate job market as a whole, and individual careers in particular. But there are dangers in becoming obsessed with these figures for humanities subjects, whose graduates normally take longer to find suitable employment, but in due course do find it. A first-destination snapshot, taken six months after graduation, distorts the true picture, since most graduates categorized as 'unemployed' in first-destination data will find work sooner rather than later. This is recognised by the Association of Graduate Careers Advisory Services (AGCAS) and the Council for Industry and Higher Education: 'When you look at the figures, do remember that most of those who appear as unemployed or in short-term employment will in due course enter permanent employment; for most, this will be within the following few months.[11] Today's mobile labour-market means that a more representative picture would be secured some five or ten years after graduation, even if any person's career history depends on a range of imponderables – including personality, personal networks and luck – unrelated to the degree subject. Yet, the absence of long-term statistics means that, despite shortcomings, first-destination data provide the best available evidence regarding a history degree's role as an academic springboard for a diverse range of career directions.

What do Employers Require of Graduates?

At one time, employers, having specified the need for 'relevant' recruits, often proved unable or unwilling to articulate their precise requirements. More recently, greater thought has been devoted to expectations – for example, Prudential Corporation PLC specifies 'Key Criteria for Effective Performance of Graduate Recruits' – which tend to be organized around common categories, like academic achievement, motivation, analytical and decision-making abilities, written and oral communication, personal and interpersonal skills (e.g., teamwork, leadership), and managerial capabilities.[12]

The relatively large proportion of vacancies open to graduates from any discipline reflects not only employers' use of higher education for screening purposes but also their search for a broad range of personal and intellectual skills rather than specific subject expertise.[13] Touche Ross, a chartered accountancy firm recruiting some 400 graduates each year, informs applicants:

> Your personal qualities are far more important to us than your degree discipline. What matters is your ability to harness your talent so you can progress rapidly in the firm and take on responsibility at an early stage. . . . We look for people with drive and maturity, who are strong intellectually and have good skills with people.[14]

BMP DDB Needham, a large advertising agency, points out:

> We recruit from a variety of backgrounds, because we want different skills, different approaches to problem solving. This explains a range of degree subjects amongst our recent graduates that include Classics, History, Chemistry, Physics, Law, English, Geography and Aeronautical Engineering. The subject itself doesn't matter, but we are looking for excellence within it.[15]

In general, the prime focus is upon the possession of the 'right personal qualities' rather than a 'relevant' subject. Additional requirements comprise information technology, linguistic, numeracy, and teamwork skills, as suggested by extracts from recruitment literature:

- 'Intellectual ability is taken for granted (your degree tells us that), but you will need to operate effectively in teams, supporting and motivating others' (Unilever).
- 'Today we rely on teamwork as never before. . . . Working with others to get the best result is important' (BP).
- 'We require good mathematics and English O Level . . . foreign languages and IT skills are a bonus' (Touche Ross).

Employers and History

Historians are expected to sell their subject, but the views of employers and others outside the historical profession are more convincing. Lord Sainsbury, President of one of Britain's most successful companies, has recorded the benefits of studying history alongside his firm's willingness to recruit history graduates:

> I feel certain that my studies of history must have assisted me in many ways, hopefully including my ability to weigh different factors that are

required before making business decisions, and keeping relevant issues in due proportion. . . . There is no doubt that studying history stood me in good stead.[16]

Sirmilarly, John Tusa, a journalist and former Managing Director of the BBC World Service, has acknowledged his professional debt to history:

We, as journalists, rely directly on the skills and disciplines that spring from history. . . . We are only doing what historians do, namely, checking our sources, evaluating them, putting them in context, and seeking an explanation of events, often by setting them in a chronological sequence. . . . We might say that all journalism aspires to a condition of history.[17]

In 1990 the Council for Industry and Higher Education (CIHE), acting in collaboration with several 'captains of industry' (e.g., Robert Reid and Lord Prior, chairman of Shell UK and GEC, respectively), reported that graduates 'well trained and usefully educated in the humanities disciplines' made, and would continue to make, a 'useful', contribution to training the mind for the world of work:

The humanities have a central role in redefining and transmitting a common culture of objectivity, tolerance, judgement by relevant evidence, and fairness. . . . Employers of humanities graduates agree that interpreting demanding texts, distinguishing fact from assertion, and appraising doubtful arguments offer training in critical power and lucid expression; that well-taught history can familiarise students with the need to make balanced judgements on the basis of hazy and conflicting evidence . . . that close reading of literature sharpens people's critical faculties. . . . The critical techniques and traditions of the humanities can play an important role in giving graduates a measure of balance, making them aware of the limitations and implications of arguments and encouraging objectivity and disinterested enquiry. These too are business as well as academic virtues.[18]

The CIHE, viewing higher education as 'a bridge for humanities students into the world of affairs and employment', clarified the career value of specific academic skills: 'Business particularly values among its managers those who can stand back from the pressures of immediate opinions and alluring trends. Persuasive skills have their place, but so does the ability to see through them.'[19] This recalls Geoffrey Elton's emphasis on history's role in imposing a sceptical mind and offering an apprenticeship in criticism.[20]

History Courses, Skills and Work Experience

A recent Department of Employment paper criticized higher education for failing to adopt assessment methods that prepared graduates for employment. The report, noting that 'the essay and unseen examination are unchallenged', recommended that assessment methods were 'badly in need of review'.[21] This critique highlights the fact that education for capability has significant implications for modes of assessment, as well as for course development and teaching strategies.[22] In practice, well-taught history degrees have always promoted a range of useful historical skills – these included research, information processing, critical analysis of a diverse range of source materials, and written communication – but this 'training of the mind' element, as achieved through the acquisition and application of subject-specific knowledge, was generally overlooked as compared to content. More recently, several course teams, acknowledging that most graduates will not use their historical knowledge directly in their careers, have introduced changes expressly designed to foster abilities sought by employers. In general, the stress has been placed on work-related capabilities such as assimilating large amounts of material, making informed judgements, training the questioning mind, and discussing complicated issues logically and clearly with regard to the evidence, developed through an historical education rather than on the content of historical study. Nevertheless, syllabuses have been reconsidered as the prelude to being either amended or replaced by more innovatory proposals. Thus, syllabus descriptions, drafted as part of course development and validation processes, commonly include the acquisition of transferable skills among course objectives and learning outcomes. This is particularly true of colleges formerly subject to CNAA validation and review procedures.

Several questions have faced course teams:

- Which skills should be desirable attributes of their degree programme? Can history make a distinctive skills contribution?
- What is the appropriate balance between skills and content?
- Should skills be fostered in an integral or 'bolt-on' manner?
- Is it correct to argue that modularization reinforces efforts to enhance the utility of history courses (e.g., through enabling careers, IT and independent-study modules)?[23]
- Do assessment practices reflect adequately the espoused purpose of a course or programme of study? Do existing modes of teaching

and assessment discriminate in favour of certain abilities (e.g., to write lengthy essays, to measure factual recall) at the expense of others (e.g., oral communication)? Should it be possible for a student to secure a good degree grade without ever having spoken a single word?

• What experience should undergraduates be given in the writing of one-page reports or the making of oral presentations?[24]

• What type of relationship should exist between history tutors and the college careers office?

Recent changes in teaching and learning methods, though responding to pressures for relevance, have been prompted also by resource constraints, the advent of larger numbers of students, and the normal process of educational innovation. Christopher Clark, reporting on a seminar held at the University of York, noted that 'many colleagues believe in the possibility of implementing new methods capable of satisfying our own criteria, as historians, of sound educational practice'.[25] For instance, computing, as well as fostering logical precision, word-processing and IT skills, provides an additional dimension to the historian's study of quantitative and other projects, as highlighted by the HiDES software packages.[26]

Numerous examples of innovation highlighting the complementary nature of the historical and skills dimensions can be quoted. They include alternative forms of written work to the traditional essay and unseen examination, bibliographical exercises, computing and numeracy projects, oral presentations, distance-learning techniques, group work, and independent student learning.[27] There is also role-play, as employed at one college for teaching the Wars of the Roses: 'Role-play fosters students' ability to understand and argue complex issues of explanation and motivation. It enhances their historical understanding of the people they are studying. Role-play activities add an extra dimension by requiring them to think and make decisions swiftly when under pressure in dynamic situations.'[28]

Inevitably, the situation is patchy both within and between colleges. Work-shadowing was developed for the humanities course at Crewe and Alsager College, while at the University of Brighton the BA Humanities degree, which includes history, was designed with an explicit emphasis upon skills: 'The prime focus is placed upon students' ability to *do* things rather than on the mere acquisition of areas of knowledge. The degree's structure reflects the emphasis upon a developmental progression re-

garding the acquisition and practice of skills.'[29] Teaching and assessment
methods are designed specifically to fit within this framework, such as
the testing of oral as well as written skills.

At the University of Huddersfield the BA Historical and Political
Studies degree aims to equip students for the world of employment
through an emphasis upon a compulsory eight-week period of work
experience in their second year: 'Work experience was defined as providing the student with an opportunity to relate his/her studies to a work
situation of the type of employment commonly sought by arts graduates,
such as in the civil service, museum work, retail management, or attachment to a Member of Parliament.'[30] Initial feedback both from employers
and students was generally positive, even if it is premature to say whether
work experience proves a positive advantage in securing employment.
Some students received job offers (e.g., journalism, marketing) arising
out of their placements, while others realized which career areas to avoid
in the future. If nothing else, such schemes improve links between higher
education and employers, while extending the experience of history staff.
At Trinity All Saints' College, Leeds, the BA course includes two six-
week placements. 'The rationale of the attachment scheme is to enable
students to have experience of the work environment, hopefully, commensurate with their professional/academic attainment. . . . The attachment system is viewed primarily as a method of broadening the students'
educational experience rather than as a form of training scheme.'[31] 'Vocational applications of the historian's craft', a recently introduced second-year option offered at St Martin's College, Lancaster, interprets
work placement as 'the central aspect of the course' intended to promote
'an awareness of career opportunities'. The University of Northumbria
at Newcastle is among other colleges providing placement opportunities
to history students.

Against this background, how far have students themselves appreciated the nature and value of history-related skills? Can students convince
employers that they possess the requisite personal qualities? In practice,
history graduates have difficulty realizing that an employer is almost
totally uninterested in their knowledge of, say, the Thirty Years War or
Gladstone and British politics. Employers are more impressed by a
curriculum vitae (CV) containing a skills profile and evidence of participation in college extra-mural activities, than by a list of history courses
studied. As one employer asserted: 'Who you are is vital, not what you've
learnt in the past.'[32] Clearly, students require help in drafting CVs and
skills profiles, 'researching' the wide range of possible career directions

and training opportunities, discovering recent trends in the graduate labour market, and noting the specific skills sought by employers. Tutors could also help students, not only by writing references more attuned to the perceptions of employers but also by continuing to develop courses and modes of teaching and learning in a manner appropriate for the development of skills.

Conclusion

'Will a degree improve my job prospects?' is a question asked by an increasing number of students, and one given added significance at a time of recession characterized by higher-than-normal levels of graduate unemployment. Present-mindedness is best avoided when discussing careers, given the time-lags between study and work. Today's entrants to higher education will not be scanning job lists or attending 'milk round' presentations until the late 1990s when, hopefully, the demand for graduates should have improved. For AGCAS, 'the overall outlook for graduates continues to be encouraging'.[33] Despite current difficulties, graduates have better employment and financial prospects than any other group entering the job market. A degree qualification enables – it does not guarantee – a better type of job, higher starting salary, accelerated advancement, earlier positions of responsibility, greater job satisfaction, and improved long-term prospects. Many employers express a strong preference for graduates – for instance, Unilever regards them as the 'major source of senior management' – while certain occupations (e.g., law, teaching) specify 'graduate only' entry. At the same time, recession means that students must not only work harder to find a job but also consider a wider range of possibilities, including the need to accept, at least in the short term, what might be regarded as a post for which they seem over-qualified. Today, 'a graduate job' is being defined increasingly to mean 'any job a graduate is prepared to do'.[34]

There is always a risk that, if a degree is justified largely in terms of employment training, higher education will lose its integrity and fail in its fundamental objective of advancing scholarship and fostering the intellectual development of students. However, there is no reason why higher education should not also provide, to quote Robert Malpas, the chairman of Powergen, a 'relevant learning experience' preparing students for the rest of their lives.[35] In this vein, Robert Reid, writing as Chairman of Shell UK, has asserted:

The enhancement and enrichment of the mind confer a perspective on the individual which will be called on in their future direction of human affairs. It is the presence of this perspective which can produce the strategic thinking on which successful development and growth can be built. . . . We are not looking for knowledge in our recruits. We are looking for mastery of the processes by which knowledge can be acquired and a maturity and sympathy gained from exposure to the mainstream of intellectual thought.[36]

Within this context, a history degree should be seen as neither more nor less vocational than one in most other disciplines. History degree courses are not job-specific, but are work-related in the sense of providing a useful and cost-effective education fostering transferable skills, including the element of flexibility valued by employers. But history's specific career utility should not be exaggerated, particularly given the few openings existing for professional historians. A history degree, even one incorporating a significant skills component, is not in itself a qualification for business or industry; thus, graduates will often require further training specifically related to their chosen career.

This chapter's utilitarian focus should be complemented by an appreciation of history's wider value in the modern world, particularly at a time of fiscal constraint and renewed government efforts to steer students away from the humanities and social sciences. We continue to make substantial demands on history, which becomes functional in the sense that it helps any society to know itself and to understand its relationship with both the past and other societies. On becoming a *Sunday Times* columnist, Norman Stone, professor of history at Oxford University, explained: 'this is precisely what a professor of modern history ought to do: to set contemporary matters in a historical perspective'.[37] Historians, when challenged about the utility of history, could do worse than ask 'What kind of a population are you are going to have by the year 2000 if that population be historically illiterate?'[38] There is nothing new or unhistorical about having to justify the value of history.

Notes

1   D. Stevenson, 'The End of History?: The British University Experience, 1981–1992', *Contemporary Record*, 7 (1993), pp. 66–7. Advice provided by David Stevenson, Lecturer in International History at the London School of Economics and Secretary of History in the Universities Defence Group, is gratefully acknowledged.

2   *The Guardian*, 18 January 1986; I. Bradley, 'Don't Close the Book on History', *The Times*, 11 January 1986.

3   P. Beck, 'History Goes Public', *The Times Higher Education Supplement*, 21 January 1983, p. 13; *Public History: An Introduction*, ed. B. J. Howe and E. L. Kemp (Krieger, Malabar, 1986).

4   *The Daily Express*, 5 July 1980.

5   G. Barraclough, *Main Trends in History* (Houghton, New York, 1979), pp. 214–15.

6   P. Findlay, C. Martin and S. Smith, 'The Pegasus Project at Portsmouth Polytechnic', *Industry and Higher Education*, 1 (1987), pp. 67–9.

7   Annex to letter sent by HEFCE to higher education institutions, 2 July 1993.

8   P. Slee, 'Enterprise in Higher Education: The Unchanging Nature of the Contract between the State and Higher Education', *PUSH Newsletter*, 2 (1990), pp. 8–9.

9   Ibid., pp. 8–9.

10 M. Kogan, 'History', in *Higher Education and the Preparation for Work*, ed. C. Boys (Kingsley, London, 1988), p. 29.

11 Association of Graduate Careers Advisory Services, *What Do Graduates Do? 1993* (Hobsons, Cambridge, 1992), p. 20; Council for Industry and Higher Education, *Towards a Partnership: The Humanities for the Working World* (CIHE, London, 1990), p. 9.

12 B. Corby, 'Prudential Corporation', and D. Bradshaw, 'Classifications and Models of Transferable Skills', in *Art Graduates, their Skills and their Employment: Perspectives for Change*, ed. H. Eggins (Falmer Press, London, 1992), pp. 9–12, 39–112.

13 *Assessment Issues in Higher Education* (Department of Employment, London, 1993), pp. 32–3.

14 Association of Graduate Careers Advisory Services, *What do Graduates Do? 1993*, (Hobsons, Cambridge), p. 14.

15 Association of Graduate Careers Advisory Services, *What do Graduates Do? 1992* (Hobsons, Cambridge, 1991), p. 12.

16 Lord Sainsbury to the author, 29 June 1983 and 31 October 1985.

17 J. Tusa, 'History and the Wider World', *The Historian*, 3 (1984), pp. 11–12.

18 *Towards a Partnership*, pp. 1–5.

19 Ibid., p. 5.

20 'Thinking Aloud', *TV Channel 4*, January 1986.

21 *Assessment Issues in Higher Education*, p. 27.

22 K. Wilson, 'Curriculum Development and the Role of the Tutor', in *Arts Graduates*, ed. Eggins, pp. 186–90.

23 D. Watson, 'Humanities and Employment – the Institutional Perspective', in *Arts Graduates*, ed. Eggins, pp. 181–2.

24 Corby, 'Prudential Corporation', p. 9.

25   C. Clark, 'Innovation in History: A Report', *PUSH Newsletter*, 3 (1991), p. 46.

26   F. Colson, 'Information Technology and the Teaching of History: The Perspective from the HiDES Project', *PUSH Newsletter*, 3 (1992), pp. 6–17.

27   H. Woolf, 'Group Work in the Humanities at Wolverhampton Polytechnic', and P. Beck, 'Group Work in History at Kingston Polytechnic', *PUSH Newsletter*, 1 (1989), pp. 18–20, 20–3; RSA, *Higher Education for Capability*, 8 October 1991.

28   I. Dawson, 'The Use of Role-play in History Teaching at Degree Level', *PUSH Newsletter*, 2 (1990), pp. 34–8.

29   B. Brecher and T. Hickey, 'Teaching Skills through History: The new Humanities Degree at Brighton Polytechnic', *PUSH Newsletter*, 1 (1990), p. 15.

30   B. Roberts and M. Mycock, 'The Experience of Introducing Work-based Learning on an Arts Degree Course', *Journal of Further and Higher Education*, 15 (1991), pp. 76–85; B. Roberts, 'Work-based Learning: The BA (Hons) Historical and Political Studies Degree at Huddersfield Polytechnic', *PUSH Newsletter*, 3 (1992), pp. 28–34.

31   C. Hallas, 'New Directions in Learning: History and Work Attachments', *PUSH Newsletter*, 2 (1990), p. 25.

32   Needham, quoted in *GET 1992* (Hobsons, Cambridge, 1991), p. 233.

33   AGCAS, *What Do Graduates Do? 1993*, p. 10.

34   G. Wade, 'From Learners to Earners', *The Guardian*, 22 September 1992; T. Tysome, 'Currency of Degrees Devalued at Work', *The Times Higher Education Supplement*, 18 September 1992; A. Bevan, 'Falling Degrees of Expectation', *The Guardian*, 20 July 1993.

35   *Towards a Partnership*, p. 8.

36   R. Reid, quoted in *Towards a Partnership*, preface.

37   *The Sunday Times*, 15 April 1990.

38   M. Bentley, 'Analysis' programme, *BBC Radio Four*, 7 February 1991.

Further Reading

The broader context of developments affecting history in higher education is covered by D. Stevenson, 'The End of History?: The British University Experience, 1981–1992', *Contemporary Record*, 7 (1993), pp. 66–85, and G. Marsden, 'History in the New Universities', *History Today*, 43 (1993), pp. 60–1.

College careers offices offer a wide range of publications providing guidance on career directions and related matters. AGCAS's annual publication, *What Do Graduates Do?* (Hobsons, Cambridge), offers statistical guidance about the types of training and employment undertaken by history graduates in the past. The views of employers and others on the career possibilities and needs of humanities graduates are articulated by the Council for National Academic Awards, *Humanities and Employment: The CNAA Initiative. Humanities and Employment Briefing 1* (CNAA, London, 1990), and the Council for Industry and Higher Education, *Towards a Partnership: The Humanities for the Working World* (CIHE, London, 1990). Curriculum and teaching implications are mentioned, but these aspects are discussed more fully in individual chapters by D. Bradshaw, B. Corby and K. Wilson in *Arts Graduates, their Skills and their Employment: Perspectives for Change*, ed. H. Eggins (Falmer Press, London, 1992). Also relevant is M. Kogan's 'History', in *Higher Education and the Preparation for Work*, ed. C. Boys (Kingsley, London, 1989), pp. 21–38.

The value of a history degree in the wider world, particularly for employment purposes, is considered by A. L. Brown, M. B. Gauld and D. Murphy, *History. An Education for Life: History's Role and Value in Scottish Education* (Historical Association, Edinburgh, 1989); R. Harrison, 'History and Employability: History IS in Business', *Welsh Historian*, 6 (1986), pp. 6–8; and A. M. Kantrow, 'Why History Matters to Managers', *Harvard Business Review*, 64 (1986), pp. 81–8. The fullest discussion, plus a detailed and up-to-date bibliography, can be found in the third edition of the Historical Association's career guide and wall–chart written by Peter Beck and David Stevenson, *Careers Guide for History Graduates: A History Degree as a Bridge to the World of Work* (Historical Association, London, 1994). Several journals, most notably *The Historian, History Today, PUSH Newsletter* (1989–92) and *The Public Historian*, also include useful articles.

PART V

Assessment and Quality

15

Changing Assessment to Improve Learning

Alan Booth

Assessment procedures in history are still in most cases overwhelmingly traditional. If total reliance upon 'finals' examinations has virtually disappeared, students are typically assessed by an unadventurous combination of often heavily weighted end-of-course examinations and coursework essays, lightly leavened by an element of dissertation work. What these tasks test, what criteria are utilized to decide grades, and what is achieved in terms of student learning, are rarely made explicit. It is a system based on precedent rather than systematic reflection about the learning needs of history students in the 1990s.

There are many reasons for this. Assessment is a complex area, and experience suggests that most history tutors find it the least rewarding aspect of their teaching. As student numbers rise, and pressure to publish intensifies, 'marking' becomes even more disagreeable; an onerous and soul-destroying task to be despatched as quickly as possible, certainly not a field for reflection and innovation. The resulting ignorance about assessment methodology reinforces conservatism. In addition, current modes of assessment augment tutors' authority as the high priests of the most important ritual of a student's academic life, and both internal and external examiners naturally feel more comfortable with a system which conforms to their own professional background. Institutional factors reinforce the status quo. History courses are frequently locked into faculty or institutional regulations that standardize assessment procedures, and individual tutors often feel that they have little scope for manoeuvre, though there are indications that modularization can make this less so. Traditional assessment is administratively convenient. It can deliver an apparent consistency and comparability between modules within a department, between courses within an institution, and between history students and courses in different institutions.

Assessment, then, is rarely an important issue *per se*, and innovation in assessment generally lags far behind that in teaching methods and curriculum reform. For students, however, assessment is of overwhelming importance. Much recent research has demonstrated that students' perception of assessment is probably the most significant single influence upon their learning. As Sally Brown and Peter Knight point out: 'Assessment is at the heart of the student experience. Assessment defines what students regard as important, how they spend their time, and how they come to see themselves as students and then as graduates.'[1] Much time and effort is therefore expended in attempting to decipher what is important in the assessment process, for that is what will be given priority. 'Cue seeking', finding out what tutors' views are and what they see as important, becomes as important as learning itself.[2] In the process, students soon discover that tutors have very different ideas about what constitutes a good essay or presentation; that declarations about the importance of developing historical understanding are frequently found wanting against an examination system which often seems to demand little but memorization and surface learning.

To most students, assessment procedures appear remote and inaccessible; in the words of one researcher into student learning, 'hedged around with a thick bureaucratic mystique designed to form an effective barrier against the inquisitive'.[3] Common complaints are of essay marks mysteriously conjured-up with little explanation, by tutors who seem to be operating on widely differing views of what constitutes a good history essay. Writing an essay thus often seems like a game in which students try to tailor their work to the particular prejudices of the individual tutor. The lack of opportunity to see tutors' comments on examination scripts, to challenge marks, and the absence of satisfactory feedback on essays are also common criticisms. The following comment of a student who graduated with an upper-second degree in history in 1991, is a typical response:

> I would like to take this opportunity to stress a few points about the History course that I feel should be changed. Tutors' methods and approaches are extremely diverse. I found that to obtain good marks from various tutors I had to 'play the system', i.e. learn what they wanted; this greatly disrupted my development. Some tutors will always be better at

communicating, teaching etc., than others, but do the history staff have a set of guidelines?

Secondly, I feel that the history department seems largely unaware of the demands of employers. . . . As the graduate market place becomes more competitive the history department must come out of its ivory tower and include group projects, field trips and more active seminars as part of the course.

Finally, what is the function of exams? I study a topic for hours, involve myself in research and then have to answer a question on it in 45 minutes or an hour (if you're lucky). I feel that I am not allowed to show what I have learnt; exams place a student under great pressure that for historical study I do not think is appropriate.

This common sense of confusion, anxiety and powerlessness consti- tutes a real barrier to effective learning. It runs against the grain of all the considerable research literature on effective teaching and learning which now emphasizes the importance of active learning in student development.[4]

Assessment, then, is at the centre of student learning; not merely in measuring and grading what has been achieved but, importantly, in its potential to make it more active, and thus effective. If historians truly value the deepening of understanding, the ability to read sources sensi- tively and critically, to communicate clearly on complex issues and use historical skills to analyse, interpret and summarize issues and perspec- tives, improving assessment procedures should be a priority. In a recent review of the subject, George Brown has written: 'Put rather starkly, if you want to change student learning then change the methods of assess- ment.'[5] In order to consider how this might be achieved for history, it is helpful to examine some recent patterns in assessment procedure.

Trends in Assessment

What follows is a brief outline of some recent trends in assessment. Whilst for the sake of convenience they are considered separately, and as dualities, in practice they are often closely interconnected and can be used harmoniously together to produce a balanced assessment procedure.

Examinations versus coursework

In the 1960s and early 1970s a principal concern in assessment was the adverse effect of examinations on student learning. The disadvantages

were clearly exposed: examinations offer only one opportunity to demonstrate ability; allow some students to ignore much of a course and
concentrate their efforts into a final burst of revision; test only a narrow
range of skills; generate intense stress and provide little or no feedback
except at the end of a course.[6] Coursework is a more developmental mode
of assessment, reduces examination nerves, measures progress and increases the reliability of classification.

The trend towards greater coursework assessment in history has been
clear, and in the 1980s a greater variety of assessment tasks was introduced, particularly in the public sector institutions of the UK. However,
it has become clear that the benefits of coursework assessment in terms of
student learning are not automatic. Heavy coursework requirements can
result in similar problems to traditional examinations. Greater variety of
coursework assessment can lead to bunching of assessment, work overload and a retreat to surface learning. This too can increase stress and
destroy enthusiasm and motivation. This has particularly been a feature
of less well-thought-out modular-based systems, where assessment can
be relentless given the one semester duration of modules.

Formative versus summative

These terms relate to the purposes of assessment. Summative assessment
is basically judgemental, measuring, usually in terms of grades, how
much a student has learned on a course. It is essentially about producing
reliable and consistent grading procedures; this is clearly necessary, but
if too dominant can result in the passive, cue-seeking approach to learning characteristic of many history students. Formative assessment is
essentially developmental; about helping students to learn. Formative
roles include diagnosing strengths and weaknesses; providing guidance
on how to improve; consolidating work so far; helping students to reflect
on their own behaviour and on how they learn best. Feedback from
students, peers and external examiners might also be used by tutors
formatively to help them to develop their own teaching.

In practice, of course, a balance between formative and summative
assessment is necessary; indeed the two are inextricably interrelated. The
mark and comments on an essay, for example, could be said to have both
summative and formative purposes: both estimating the achievement of
the student and offering advice about how to improve. However, recent
research has strongly emphasized the need to pay closer attention to
more formative aspects of assessment if improving student learning is to

be a principal objective, and this has been a notable feature of recent innovations in the teaching of history, whether in the use of explicit criteria on marking sheets so as to encourage more detailed, structured and focused tutor comment, or in the introduction of self-assessment and peer assessment.

Student-led versus tutor-led

Increasing student participation in assessment has been a feature over the past twenty years. In history there has been greater student choice over essay questions, and more project work where students choose a topic to study in depth. In more innovative recent work, student self-assessment of coursework, seminar activities and project work has become more common.

Self-assessment can include a wide range of possibilities, from assessing one's performance against model answers or a tutor's comments on an essay to giving a mark to one's own work against a set of explicit criteria. Peer assessment involves assessing and receiving assessment from others, and is most often used in relation to oral presentations and group work led by students. It can involve discussion and negotiation between students, as well as assessment without discussion. The essential purpose, however, is students using their own judgements in order to develop greater responsibility for their own learning. Advocacy of peer assessment and self-assessment has been particularly strong in relation to courses where active learning is a key objective. Both can encourage a sense of ownership of assessment, increase motivation, and provide students with the opportunity to reflect more carefully on the processes of learning. There is also evidence that they may promote greater depth of critical analysis.[7] In developing their own skills of assessment, students become more vocal and less willing to accept uncritically what tutors say. If this might be considered a deterrent to tutors, it is also worth remembering that they also show more initiative, commitment and enthusiasm.

Collaborative versus competitive

The school system fosters an ingrained competitive ethos which continues strongly into higher education. Current assessment practice in history tends to emphasise individual, competitive skills at the expense of collaborative activity. Where students are placed in their group is a frequent question when results are fed back. Whilst this has some advantages in terms of motivation, collaborative assessment in history can deepen understanding of the subject and historical interpretations. Demand for teamwork skills from employers in the 1990s and the increase in student numbers have also combined to raise the profile of this type of assessment in history.

Assessing collaboratively can involve all students receiving the same mark for a piece of work, or students negotiating an individual mark with the members of their team. In this latter form it is a more adventurous use of self-assessment and peer assessment. Whilst there are difficulties in introducing group assessment (and these are explored in the following chapter), the reported advantages in terms of student learning are an increase in motivation, the incentive to work as a team and the negotiation, reflection and attention to the processes required for effective group work. Setting it up also requires greater collaboration and negotiation between tutor and students, and this itself can help students to feel more involved in their own learning.

Explicit versus implicit criteria

Since the 1980s most history programmes, prompted by the mounting scrutiny of internal and external quality audits, have developed clearer course objectives. Some teachers have also made explicit the criteria for assessing student work, particularly in essays but also in group activities. In the most innovative work, students have been encouraged to formulate their own criteria, often in negotiation with the tutor.[8]

The use of explicit criteria sheets for marking assessed work has been a prominent feature of recent changes in assessment, and examples can be seen in the following chapter. They have many advantages: they encourage clear thinking about objectives on the part of tutor and student; enable students to know what is considered important and help to avoid the cue-seeking that often dominates student learning. They also facilitate more consistent marking: a criteria sheet is a useful reminder of what is most important.

Product versus process

Formal assessment in history typically involves judgement of a final product, such as an essay or project. Some teachers, however, have begun to look at the processes involved. This has been particularly evident in group work in history, where evaluating the ways a group operated and the contribution of individuals to the process is increasingly regarded as an important part of improving team skills. Process assessment is easiest to operate when it is formative, but it can be used summatively as a means of achieving a more holistic assessment of student performance. Again, this type of assessment is often self- or peer-based and allows students to develop their own assessment skills, and to recognize and reflect on the value of the means of producing something rather than narrowly focusing upon the end product. It enables students to explore what has happened in addition to what has been produced, and this attention to process can often improve the quality of the final product.

Content versus competencies

Since the late 1980s the UK Enterprise in Higher Education initiative has particularly promoted a skills-based approach to student assessment. It has encouraged the development of a wider range of skills; for example, critical thinking, working together, communicating, decision-making, time-management, leadership. Students can be expected to adapt these essentially transferable skills to a variety of situations, most notably in employment. If students can demonstrate 'competence' in these skills, this is one way of assessing them and the quality of education they receive. This forms the basis of current attempts to measure the 'outcomes' of student learning.

The dangers are that a reliance on transferable skills can ignore the often subject-based ways in which students learn best, and that identifying skills can become very prescriptive. Measurement is also a difficulty. Even first-year history undergraduates show some 'competence' at everything, and it is very difficult to define, never mind finely grade, skills such as critical thinking or communication. How to decide what constitutes a suitable level of achievement is also not easy. The result can be a set of generalized outcomes unrelated to the specifics of historical understanding which are difficult to measure in a meaningful way. Alternatively a long list is produced of detailed outcomes so specific as to be trivial, though some progress on distinguishing levels has been made in the General National Vocational Qualification.

None the less, the competencies/outcomes approach does challenge historians to state explicitly what is important in their discipline, what students should be expected to learn, and to communicate this clearly to students so that they can more easily choose between modules or courses. In this way it can be an important motivator to students, as well as a useful focus for a departmental review of assessment procedures. It has also encouraged experimentation in the formal assessment of skills such as oral communication and teamwork hitherto generally ignored in the formal assessment process.

Introducing New Modes of Assessment

Changing assessment to promote more effective learning is inevitably about making difficult practical choices about what you think is important. This might include not only educational priorities but also your own time and effort. To review teaching in this way is not an easy task, nor is it always comfortable. It is important to remember that there are no perfect solutions, but in thinking about change it is essential to keep firmly in mind the key objective of improving student learning, and choose a blend of assessment tasks and methods which works for you and your students in your particular context. The following are offered as general pointers to introducing change:

Think carefully about what you want to do   This might sound obvious but it is important to base change on strong reflective practice, and this carries its own reassurance to students. If you want to encourage deep learning in essay writing, for example, set questions which require students to think critically about the topic and test their reading and understanding, not ones which encourage them to be descriptive as in narrative.[9] Particularly, try to ensure that assessment tasks and methods are congruent with module and programme objectives, and that the balance and combination of the elements of assessment are educationally sound and time-efficient. Always keep in mind that assessment is an integral part of teaching not a bolt-on addition. A powerful yet simple review mechanism of existing procedures is provided by Brown, who suggests focusing initially upon learning outcomes and then considering appropriate teaching and assessment strategies.[10] He poses four key questions: What kinds of things do I want my students to learn on this module? What opportunities will be provided? What assessment tasks will be set? What methods of assessment will be used? Doing this kind of audit of your teaching can also tell you what sort of change you might be comfortable with, and thus how likely you are to succeed in taking your students through it.

A review of what students think about existing assessment and how it could be improved can also be productive, both in providing information and convincing them of your intentions. If you have a large class, you might want to concentrate on one new area, such as oral communication skills or report writing. Finally, it is often useful to do some reading from the recent literature on teaching. As with historical research, others' work can generate ideas, save you re-inventing the wheel and often reassure you that what you want to do makes sense.

Start small Most innovations evolve gradually, and even relatively small changes in assessment can make a big difference. Initially, you might also feel more confident with incremental change, and so might your students. For example, if you want to introduce self-assessment or peer assessment do so on a formative basis at first to see how it works. The more you change at once the more potential there is for something to go wrong and the harder it will be to identify the source of the problem. Often the simpler your innovation, the more effective it will be and the firmer the foundation for more complex strategies such as assessing group projects.

Give clear guidance Explain to students the reasons for the introduction of new assessment methods and how they relate to what you are trying to do. It is particularly important to let students know what is expected of them, which assessment tasks count towards grading and how much each element contributes to the final course-mark. Explain how it will benefit them: self-interest is a powerful force for the acceptance of change. Handouts can be helpful to focus thought and discussion on what is required.

Make criteria explicit Openness and honesty are appreciated by students; in this area they are vital. In summative assessment it is particularly important to address the criteria being used. This helps to reassure students and also facilitates consistency of marking, which itself generates confidence. Criteria can be student-generated, or there are now many criteria checklists available for most assessment tasks and methods. Getting students to generate criteria is not easy; they will initially try to pass the responsibility to you. It can be useful to ask them to work in smaller 'buzz' groups, first deciding criteria then prioritizing them. These lists can be put on a blackboard or flip-chart and after a general discussion a composite list produced. This can then be used to produce a checklist for assessment.[11]

Involve students   Student resistance to change can be a major obstacle. The general lack of prior experience of more student-centred assessment methods leads to understandable anxieties: assessed oral presentations invoke fears of public humliation; self-assessment and peer assessment generate concern about competence to perform this difficult task, and about possible bias and loss of trust between members of a group. Experience of working to hidden agendas makes for cynicism. Convincing students otherwise means encouraging ownership of what they are to do. Negotiation is important. Offering choice of methods is always popular; setting criteria and self-assessment and peer assessment will involve them even more fundamentally in the assessment process. There are obviously different levels of involvement, but at the very least it is important to listen to and respect student views. Assessment works best on learning when it is something done in partnership with students, as well as something done to them.

Provide support   Greater responsibility can be terrifying. Final-year undergraduates will be more confident than second or first years; students will be more confident later in a module than at the beginning. Think about how you feel when you are asked to do something new, especially in public. Self-assessment is particularly difficult for those with low self-esteem, and may pose particular problems for some mature and overseas students. Listen to what students say and encourage them to express fears and difficulties. Providing training can help. This is time-consuming but if done well at the start of a course can save time later by reducing anxiety and aiding clarity. If possible, use this time to allow students to practise what is required before assessment counts. Allow students to practise use of the OHP if you think that is important (and you have access to one!). For written exercises, examples of previous years' work can be very helpful.

Employ a variety of tasks and methods   This will provide more, and more interesting, opportunities for students to demonstrate their knowledge and skills, and produce a more rounded and reliable picture of what a student has learnt. History is not just about writing essays: if you think oral presentation is important, assess it. Peer assessment is useful if you want to focus on teamwork; self-assessment can make students reflect on the ways they learn best. Encourage students to try different ways of running seminars: using debates, mock trials and role-play are all useful ways of developing discussion skills. Writing a report or book review provides an alternative to essays and raises awareness of the requirements of addressing different audiences. Flexibility is an important element of active learning. However, in extending the range of assessment be careful not to overload the assessed coursework, as this will result in anxiety and shallow forms of learning. Also pay careful attention to the weighting of the different elements, so that the final consolidated mark does represent the balance and priority of skills you want to assess.

Pay attention to timing It is better to begin innovative work with first-year undergraduates. This accustoms students to varied methods in what is often a progress year, and formative assessment is particularly appropriate in the early stages of a course. It is also important not to assess students formally immediately after a public presentation or group activity, when they might be feeling vulnerable, or only at the end of a course when there is little they can do about it. Always give plenty of warnig about when assignments are to be delivered.

Make time for feedback Too often this is paid only lip service, but effective feedback will give momentum to the process of change as you go through the module and is a critical part of improving student learning. History students correctly regard feedback as a principal hallmark of good teaching: especially in helping them to study more effectively and in increasing their sense of confidence and general well-being. It needs to be prompt, clear and helpful; that is, indicating how they might improve in an encouraging fashion.

A short timetabled de-briefing session after an oral presentation or student-led seminar can offer a useful means of obtaining peer evaluation as well as providing tutor feedback. Group feedback sessions can often be used to discuss essay problems. Student self-help groups can be even more effective when large numbers are involved, as can model answers or feedback sheets on essays which enable boxes to be ticked so that students can immediately see their strengths and weaknesses. Talk to students about what sort of feedback they want and what is possible; time used for feedback needs to be productive.

Be pragmatic   All assessment is an uncertain process, and introducing new methods will always pose problems. No matter how much you have thought it out, some issues will only become apparent once you have begun, and others will prove more difficult than you originally thought. If you have a lot of students, concentrate on what you think is really important; you may not be able to do it all. If things are going wrong, talk to your students and renegotiate if you can. If not, review procedures at the end of the first year, though avoid too much change on a single run-through. Remember to be positive: experience can only be gained by making mistakes. In this kind of teaching you are not trying to appear infallible.

Get connected   Finally, it is important to recognize that new assessment methods can be seen as threatening by colleagues. If you can get others to do the same you will feel less isolated. Departmental seminars, course review meetings and appraisal are some of the methods that can be used to persuade others of the advantages of your innovations at a wider level. Mentoring and peer-observation schemes can also provide you with support at departmental level. Even if colleagues remain unconvinced, such activities can help you to explain and legitimize what you are doing and help defuse ill-informed destructive comment. Handouts for students, examples of work, student feedback, results, and external examiners' comments can all be useful evidence in support of change.

However, it is also important to recognize that change may be necessary at the departmental level. A departmental review may be a useful means of examining the coherence of assessment practices across the degree programme as a whole.[12] Assessment may be locked into faculty or institutional regulations and this will need addressing, perhaps through the institution's Quality Assurance structure. Staff development officers or educational development advisers can also be useful allies in promoting change. They may be able to run institution-wide training events on changing assessment, and often have good contacts throughout the institution who can provide support and advice.

Conclusion

Changing assessment to encourage active learning has the potential to change the ways that students approach the whole history curriculum. It follows that putting student learning at the forefront of assessment procedures should be a primary objective for history tutors. However, improving student learning is not merely a matter of introducing new assessment techniques, important though this is; the ways in which they are introduced and implemented are critical. A strong reflective practice is required, in which appreciation of student perceptions of effective learning and respect for students as learners are allied to the use of a variety of assessment tasks and methods providing students with greater responsibility for their own learning. The chapter which follows examines more fully the possibilities opened up by recent developments in assessment for active learning in one key context for historians, that of group activities.

Notes

1   S. Brown and P. Knight, *Assessing Learners in Higher Education* (Kogan Page, London, 1994).
2   On how students approach learning, see J. Biggs, *Student Approaches to Learning and Studying* (Australian Council for Educational Research, Victoria, 1987); N. Entwistle and P. Ramsden, *Understanding Student Learning* (Croom Helm, London, 1983); *The Experience of Learning*, ed. F. Marton, D. Hounsell and N. Entwistle (Scottish Academic Press, Edinburgh, 1984); *How to Get a First Class Degree*, ed. H. Arksey (Lancaster University Unit for Innovation in Higher Education, Lancaster, 1992).
3   P. Ramsden, *Learning to Teach in Higher Education* (Routledge, London, 1992), p. 181.
4   See the introduction to this volume for a discussion of active learning, and further reading on the subject.
5   G. Brown and M. Pendlebury, *Assessing Active Learning*, (CVCP, Sheffield, 1992).
6   On the problems of assessment by examinations, see C. Buckle and R. Riding, 'Current Problems in Assessment: Some Reflections, *Educational Psychology*, 8 (1988), pp. 299–306.
7   See S. Brown and P. Dove, *Self and Peer Assessment* (SCED Paper no. 63, Birmingham, 1991); D. Boud, *Implementing Student Self-Assessment*, (HERDSA Green Guide no. 5, 1986); Brown and Pendlebury, *Assessing Active Learning*, module 1, ch. 9. On the reliability of student self-assessment, see also D.Boud and N. Falchikov, 'Quantitative Studies of Student Self-Assessment in Higher Education: A Critical Analysis of Findings', *Higher Education*, 18 (1989), pp. 529–49. On student attitudes, see E. Williams, 'Student Attitudes to Learning and Assessment', *Assessment and Evaluation in Higher Education*, 17 (1992), pp. 45–58.
8   For an example in project work, see D. Nicholls, 'Making History Students Enterprising', *Studies in Higher Education*, 17 (1992), pp. 67–80.

9 Setting essay and examination questions is difficult no matter how experienced the tutor. Some practical advice is given in D. Hounsell and R. Murray, *Essay Writing for Active Learning* (CVCP, Sheffield, 1992).
10 Brown and Pendlebury, *Assessing Active Learning*, module 1, p. 103.
11 Marking with overt criteria is critical to the success of assessment as a facilitator of learning. For further advice, see Brown and Knight, *Assessing Learners in Higher Education*.
12 This important issue of facilitating change at the level of the system is dealt with in Brown and Knight, *Assessing Learners in Higher Education*, chs 11–12. See also M. Atkins, J. Beattie and W. Dockrell, *Assessment Issues in Higher Education* (Department of Employment, Sheffield, 1993), pp. 68–70.

Further Reading

Whilst there is little specifically on history, there are some good recent works which offer practical advice on assessment which is relevant to teachers of history in higher education. G. Brown and M. Pendlebury's, *Assessing Active Learning* (CVCP, Sheffield, 1992) provides a review of the recent literature, self-study questions, practical tips and exercises and useful case studies. M. Atkins, J. Beattie and W. Dockrell, *Assessment Issues in Higher Education* (Department of Employment, Sheffield, 1993) is a thought-provoking analysis in relation to the purposes of higher education. S. Brown and P. Knight, *Assessing Learners in Higher Education* (Kogan Page, London, 1994) provides a thorough general survey of assessment issues and practices, with some good advice.

Short practical exercises are the forte of G. Gibbs: see especially his *53 Interesting Ways to Assess your Students* (Technical & Educational Services, Bristol, 1986), and *Assessing More Students* (PCFC, Oxford, 1992) for ideas on assessing larger classes. On self-assessment and peer assessment, *Self and Peer Assessment*, ed. S. Brown and P. Dove (Standing Conference on Educational Development, no. 63, Birmingham, 1991) contains case studies, reflections on use and practical advice. D. Boud, *Implementing Student Self-Assessment* (Higher Education Research & Development Society, Green Guide no. 5, University of New South Wales, 1986) also offers some useful guidance on feedback, as does T. Crooks, *Assessing Student Performance* (HERDSA, Green Guide no. 8, University of New South Wales, 1986).

For those who want a systematic study in depth, J. Heywood, *Assessment in Higher Education* (John Wiley, London, 1989) provides a comprehensive review of the research literature. D. Rowntree, *Assessing Students: How Shall We Know Them?* (Kogan Page, London, 1987) provides a stimulating and thought-provoking account of the underlying rationale of assessment. It is important to see assessment as part of teaching, and amongst the most successful general works to integrate assessment into a wide-ranging review of teaching and learning are N. Entwistle, S. Thompson and H. Tait, *Guidelines for Promoting Effective Learning in Higher Education* (University of Edinburgh, Centre for Research on Learning and Instruction, Edinburgh, 1992), and P. Ramsden, *Learning to Teach in Higher Education* (Routledge, London, 1992).

16

Assessing Group Work

Alan Booth

Group work is an umbrella term for a wide variety of activities in history teaching. It includes seminar discussion and the less-familiar group projects, as well as work in tutorials and self-help groups which tends to focus more upon students' reactions, problems and study skills. This chapter examines some recent developments in the assessment of group work, including both activities in groups and activities by groups of students.

Group work has many benefits for student learning. In groups, students have the opportunity to test and refine a wide range of skills through discussion with their peers. The potential gains in terms of motivation, understanding of the subject and personal development are well-documented in the research literature. None the less, as history tutors' comments on seminars (the most common form of group work in history) frequently reveal, the reality is not always so positive, even in student-led seminars. Their complaints about low levels of student preparation and participation are often matched only by students' resentment of the dominance of one or two individuals, or the tutor. As class sizes in history have risen, so dissatisfaction has intensified. Large classes certainly do not make learning easier but, equally, learning in groups has never been merely a function of assembling a number of people together. The group needs to work as a group, and recent work has explored how this might be achieved, emphasizing the importance of increased student autonomy, reflection on the process of learning and explicit attention to communication and teamwork.[1]

The most direct means of encouraging the development of these qualities is through assessment. Assessment is the single most important influence on student learning. This does not mean that marks themselves are always of overwhelming importance; in self-assessment and peer assessment schemes, for example, the value may lie more in the written or verbal comments than in the mark as a record of assessment. None the less, students are eminently practical and give priority to what is assessed over what is not; what is overtly valued in the assessment system not what is said to be important by the tutor. Giving group work a realistic value in final assessment procedures legitimizes it in the eyes of students, and gives real power to a teaching activity that students themselves say they find particularly rewarding. In these ways assessment both motivates and underlines the importance of a range of skills traditionally under-represented in historical training. It can make students think more carefully about the nature of their subject, as well as developing a range of skills of use not only to future historians but in employment generally. Few graduates today escape the ubiquitous oral presentation at employment interviews; most are asked to work in teams. Finally, assessing group work in combination with other modes of assessment adds variety to assessment tasks, relieving the monotony of repeated essay writing for student and tutor alike, and generating a more representative picture of student attainment. As Brown and Knight forcefully point out:

> Some universities have got into a rut, believing, for example, that history is about writing essays. The best that can be said about this is that it is a nonsense view of history and purblind as a response to the pressures on universities to demonstrate the breadth of their students' achievements. Multiple methods are necessary to assess multiple talents for multiple audiences.[2]

For convenience, what follows focuses upon the areas of oral communication, teamwork and student reflection which recent work has suggested can lead to more effective learning in groups. It should be emphasized that assessment is seen here not merely as a means of measuring progress and attainment but, crucially, of facilitating them.

Assessing for Communication: Oral Presentations and Poster Sessions

Oral communication involves a variety of skills, including presenting and explaining, listening and responding. In history it is usually formally experienced in the presentation of a paper as a lead-in to seminar discussion and, less frequently, in the form of the viva voce between a student and examiner(s) in the assessment of project work or a borderline examination case. Vivas can also be used in group work as a final quality check, to explore individual contributions to a group report if one student seems to have contributed insufficiently, or perhaps to seek further information on a group performing particularly well, badly, or on a borderline. Both seminar papers and vivas can test communication skills and allow the individuality of the student to come out, but both also have disadvantages. The routine boredom of the traditional history seminar paper is a common complaint of students and tutors alike, while even in the most skilled hands vivas can be intimidating as well as time-consuming.

The most frequently employed recent alternatives have been oral presentations and poster sessions. These are closely related. Oral presentations usually include both a presenting and questioning session. They can be organized in class and can be assessed on the spot, with peer assessment being a common element. Posters are normally used as part of the assessment of group projects to display the fruits of a group's research in an attractive fashion. More sophisticated poster exhibitions use photographs and facsimiles of historical documents. Like oral presentations, they can be used as a focus for subsequent questioning and discussion, and as a supplementary task to a written report in both group projects and student-led seminars. In larger classes they can provide a more time-efficient alternative to oral presentations, though there is an obvious need for greater production materials such as flip-chart sheets, marker pens, Blu-tac, etc. Video recording is an asset for training, feedback and monitoring purposes, though it can inhibit performance and is often unavailable as well as time-consuming to set up. Most history tutors will probably find access to aids such as an OHP and flip-chart more realistic, though students will need guidelines on how to use them to effect. At the very least students will need access to photocopying facilities so that handouts can be prepared for all the group.

Both oral presentations and poster sessions can be organized on an individual or group basis. Experience suggests that they are most effective when careful groundwork has been done. Students need to be very clear about the purpose of the exercise, as public presentation of work can generate considerable anxiety. Allowing students to choose their topic from a list of possibilities is a good way of gaining co-operation. Providing training or a practice run, and producing clear guidelines about what is to be expected from a good presentation or poster are also fundamentally important. An example of a poster created by previous students is always helpful, and can be used to allow students working in small groups to generate their own assessment criteria. Discussing these criteria in an introductory session is an important source of reassurance. If students are unwilling to generate criteria themselves, using one of the many available format sheets such as those in figures 16.1 and 16.2 can help. These can focus discussion, and provide an excellent means of

Presenter: _____ **Group No:** _____

	1	2	3	4	5

SKILLS

Preparation: Knowledge of subject. Script familiarity.

Content: Appropriateness to audience. Interest, clarity depth, scope. Achievement of aim.

Structure: Suitable introduction. Logical development. Balance. Summing up.

Delivery: Audibility. Tone. Pace. Fluency.

Timing: Within allocated time. Balance between sections.

Visual Aids: Clarity. Appropriateness. Impact.

Response to Questions: Relevance. Succinctness. Well-managed.

QUALITIES

Confidence: Self-assurance. Awareness of abilities.

Impact: Presence. Enthusiasm. Authority.

Manner: Attitude to audience and subject. Relaxed. Humour.

Non-verbal: Audience Scan. Posture. Mannerisms. Gesture.

Total

Grand Total

OVERALL EFFECTIVENESS (please circle) A B C D

A   A lucid and fluent communicator with a flair for oral expression, very well structured work and high impact.

B   A good communicator with a logical, methodical approach. S/he imparts messages clearly and effectively.

C   A sound communicator who has to work hard. Reasonably effective in expression but without much flair or imagination.

D   An inadequate communicator who struggles to master the basic skills. Message is either confusing or lacks depth and substance.

Figure 16.1   Presentation review sheet

1. Purpose
   Clear, self-explanatory ☐ ☐ ☐ ☐ ☐ Confused, unclear
   Comments: 5 4 3 2 1

2. Design
   Visually attractive,   Unattractive,
   striking impact   ☐ ☐ ☐ ☐ ☐ wrong level of
   Comments: 5 4 3 2 1 detail

3. Creativity
   Novel, surprising,   ☐ ☐ ☐ ☐ ☐ Dull, obvious
   different   5 4 3 2 1
   Comments:

4. Structure
   Clear, logical structure ☐ ☐ ☐ ☐ ☐ Confusing,
   Comments: 5 4 3 2 1 meandering

5. Analysis
   good use of evidence,
   clear and concise   ☐ ☐ ☐ ☐ ☐ Poor grasp of
   analysis   5 4 3 2 1 evidence and
   Comments: argument

Total Score (out of 25):

Figure 16.2 Poster assessment sheet

introducing peer- and self-assessment methods which are well suited to this type of activity. If students prove resistant to peer assessment, using it only formatively is a way forward, perhaps as supportive evidence in a written report.[3]

Oral presentations and poster sessions can be very effective in increasing students' confidence and developing oral communication in a structured fashion. They also encourage students to summarize complex material clearly and concisely. Posters also focus particular attention on layout issues and the need for clear structuring. Openness, negotiation and, especially, clear guidelines and criteria are critical, and this is even more pertinent if peer assessment is to be involved.

Assessing for Teamwork: Group Projects and Student-led Seminars

Teamwork skills are becoming more in demand in academic, professional and managerial careers. The most significant attempts to develop these skills in history have been in group projects and student-led seminars.

Group projects are a relatively recent development in history teaching, though individual project work is very common and its benefits well-established. Students particularly appreciate the opportunity to study a topic of their own choice in depth, and produce a longer piece of, sometimes original, historical writing. The gains in terms of independence and initiative, research and organizational skills, and general confidence and maturing of historical understanding are often considerable. Self-motivation can be a problem for students, however, and supervizing, monitoring, marking and providing feedback can be onerous. In a context of rising numbers, group projects are a means of preserving the benefits of project work whilst also encouraging commitment and the development of collaborative skills such as chairing, negotiation, leadership and facilitating.

Group projects seem to work best with teams of about four to six: large enough to allow a good mix of individuals but small enough to encourage a strong group identity to emerge and to discourage idlers. Reports suggest that students at all levels enjoy working together, and that the negotiation encourages a deeper-than-usual thinking through of the approach to and execution of the project. Even the occasional personality conflicts that arise or the problems of someone not contributing fully can be an opportunity to explore and develop negotiation skills.

Student-led seminars run by a group of students and on which they are assessed, are easier than group projects to accommodate within a traditional lecture and seminar format. They also encourage teamwork, independence of learning and a more direct element of peer tutoring. There are many variations possible on this method. On one American history course at Loughborough University, at the beginning of each seminar the students brainstormed possible issues on the topic for discussion in order to generate a structured agenda for their seminar. Similarly, in an Intellectual History class at the University of Vermont, the group as a whole divided into smaller buzz-groups to work out the key questions that needed to be discussed on a particular issue, and set up an agenda for the seminar. On a Seventeenth Century course at Durham University, seminar groups of ten students decided which areas they wished to cover from a thematic list, devised their working methods and appointed group leaders to chair each session and lead debates on papers given.[4]

In group projects and student-led seminars students take considerable responsibility for their own learning. Clear guidelines and criteria for assessment are therefore essential, and format sheets are useful in this respect. At Griffith University, project work in history is marked on a format sheet divided into categories relating to research and use of sources; comprehension of content; analysis and synthesis; evaluation; presentation. Each of these is subdivided into specific components. A similar sheet classifies projects into five key categories: information gathering; structure and organization; use of evidence; historical analysis and argument; presentation.[5] In the humanities degree at Brighton University four broad areas of competence are identified in seminar work: preparation, presentation, chairing and leading discussion and participation. Each is further divided into its constituent elements and student performance is assessed by the tutor on a five-point scale from 1 (First) to 5 (Fail).[6] A similar schedule is reproduced in figure 16.3.

There are problems, however, in formally assessing collaborative

Twenty per cent of marks are awarded for your presentation at the seminar. The criteria are as follows:

Criteria	Marks	Comments
Content Opening, clarity of argument or explanation, overview, conclusion	0 1 2 3 4 5	
Evidence Literature review, use of sources interpretation and analysis	0 1 2 3 4 5	
Presentation Fluency, use of audiovisual aids, handouts, body language	0 1 2 3 4 5	
Discussion skills Listening, responding to questions, engaging others in the discussion, managing the group and individuals	0 1 2 3 4 5	

Total mark

Your best skills

What needs improving

Tutor/student

Date

Figure 16.3   Seminar presentation and discussion

Source: From *Assessing Active Learning*, ed. G. Brown and M. Pendlebury (CVCP, Sheffield, 1992).

work. The following issues are frequently mentioned by history tutors who have tried this type of assessment: Should every student receive the same mark? What about lazy students who capitalize on others' efforts? Who should mark? How reliable are students as markers? There are no easy answers, but it is very important to explain the issues clearly to students, and allow them to discuss them. You might, for instance, encourage them to decide for themselves whether they should receive individual marks or a collective mark. On the other hand a team mark will emphasize the need to work together, and will encourage co-operation and negotiation. A team mark can easily be generated on a submitted project, but it is also possible to set a co-operative examination with the project teams working together in different parts of the classroom. If you wish to try using a team mark in, for example, seminar work led by a group of students, perhaps the best advice is to be cautious and weight this part of the overall assessment lightly at first. Experience suggests that between 15–20 per cent of total assessment on a module is given over to group seminars. This is large enough to motivate well, but small enough to allow individual effort in the module to be rewarded. Not weighting this type of assessment too heavily can also help to assuage some of the doubts of less adventurous or sceptical colleagues concerning this type of assessment.

If you wish to derive individual marks from a group effort, one simple means is to use a combination of self-assessment and peer assessment for the process of working together, and tutor assessment for the final product.[7] The tutor assessment can be weighted more heavily and will thus be more influential, and if you are concerned that students will be too generous in marking each other this might be a solution. A meeting between seminar leaders and tutor immediately after a seminar for the purposes of evaluation is simple and effective. This might be followed by a short report from each student, including a personal commentary on the way the group worked together, their contribution, strengths and weaknesses, and possibly on the conclusions drawn. If you require greater student involvement in final assessment, give the group a total mark which is divided up by the group members. They have to give marks above and below the norm to individuals according to contribution. This can also provide a sanction against uncommitted students.[8] Getting all students to keep a learning journal can also provide some means of keeping track of individual effort and contribution, especially if this is used as part of a final 'viva' interview. On a programme of student-led seminars, a self-assessment sheet for students to evaluate their contribution across the whole seminar programme (such as that in figure 16.4

Ten per cent of the total course mark is an assessment of your contribution to the seminar's effectiveness. Consider how you have contributed to the seminars during the whole of the term. For each of the criteria listed below comment upon how you think you have performed. Note that what your tutor is looking for is self-critical awareness, so do not exaggerate your strengths or your limitations. Finally, for your overall performance suggest a mark out of 100.

NAME . . . .

A   ATTENDANCE AT AND PREPARATION FOR THE SEMINARS

B   QUALITY OF YOUR INFORMATION TO THE GROUP. TO WHAT EXTENT DID YOU SUPPLY INFORMATION AND IDEAS THAT WERE USEFUL TO THE GROUP?

C   RECEPTIVENESS TO THE IDEAS OF OTHERS. TO WHAT EXTENT DID YOU ALLOW OTHERS TO CONTRIBUTE AND LISTEN TO WHAT THEY HAD TO SAY?

D   FACILITATING THE GROUP'S COHESION AND ENCOURAGING OTHERS TO CONTRIBUTE.

YOUR SUGGESTED MARK   . . . . %

TUTOR'S MARK   . . . .

TUTOR'S COMMENTS

Figure 16.4   Contribution to seminar's effectiveness: self-assessment form

Source: From A. Jenkins and D. Pepper, *Enhancing Employability and Educational Experience* (SCED Paper No. 27, Birmingham, 1987).

developed at Oxford Brookes University) can be combined with tutor assessment of individual sessions in order to provide a stronger element of self-assessment, and a means of rewarding effort across the semester or year.

Assessing collaborative activities does have its difficulties, but in my own experience and that of several colleagues these are far outweighed by the advantages in terms of student learning, especially the development of co-operative spirit, group solidarity, enthusiasm and motivation and greater reflection on the process of learning. Nor does the available evidence suggest that when students are involved in assessing themselves and each other they are generally more generous than the tutor. In this type of work some element of self-assessment and peer assessment is generally essential to generate student commitment and to maximize the benefits.

Assessing for Reflection on the Process of Learning

Focusing on the final product or performance can obscure the important developmental aspects of production. Reflection on the process of learning is itself essential for the development of communication and teamwork skills, and the success of group work in general.[9] It is important for students to be able to recognize problems, develop ways of addressing them, and check the effectiveness of their solutions. In order to encourage reflection, activities need to be explicitly focused on the process of learning.

Tutorials between a teacher and a small number of students are a common means of encouraging reflection and providing feedback. They can be academic or pastoral in emphasis, but are especially useful for enabling students to discuss progress, strengths and weaknesses and how to improve learning skills, as well as general course review. Tutorials are time-consuming but important in improving learning. The critical thing is that the time is used effectively. It is therefore useful for students to do some preparation. Writing an agenda to be handed in before the meeting or completing a self-assessment sheet on their performance over a module can be a useful means of ensuring a structured and pointed discussion.

Student self-help groups are an alternative where large student numbers make it difficult for tutors to see students regularly. They are set up by students and run by them for mutual support, allowing them to meet more frequently to address questions and issues arising from lectures and seminars. Self-help groups are often run by students at a similar stage of their course, but to give them greater structure and direction more experienced students can profitably be involved. One example of this at Leeds University involved a proctorial system where each third-year 'proctor' was responsible for a group of ten first-years. Proctors prompted discussion, took notes and gave advice. Problems they encountered were common ones in group work: the student who dominates discussion; students who say nothing; the deadly silence. Both proctors and first-year students gained from sharing experience. First-years were able to address topics which they found difficult to confide to teachers, as well as general learning issues, and if necessary these could be passed back to teaching staff to help in course development. Third-year students gained experience of the process of teaching, and both sets of students felt an increase in active engagement with the subject and a real sense of community.[10] Obviously such a system needs to be carefully set up and monitored to ensure that it is taken seriously, but it can be an effective way of enabling students to reflect on issues of teaching and learning in a non-threatening environment.

Checklists can be directly targeted at the process of learning. This is particularly useful in collaborative activity, and also provides a mechanism for monitoring this difficult aspect of group work. One example is provided in figure 16.5, and can be used to provide information for discussion in a tutorial as well as focusing students' attention on the meaning of teamwork skills and underlining their importance.[11]

Learning contracts are a variation on the same idea, and help to clarify what is expected at the start of a course or project. A learning contract is

Most of our meetings were confused	1 2 3 4 5	Most of our meetings were well organized
We often got sidetracked	1 2 3 4 5	We stuck to the task most of the time
We didn't listen to each other	1 2 3 4 5	We did listen to each other
Some talked too much and some did not talk enough	1 2 3 4 5	We all contributed to the discussion
We did not think through our ideas sufficiently	1 2 3 4 5	We thought through our ideas well
Some got aggressive and and some got upset	1 2 3 4 5	We were able to argue and discuss without getting upset
Most of us seemed to be bored by the discussion	1 2 3 4 5	Most of us seemed to enjoy the discussion
Most of us did not improve our discussion skills	1 2 3 4 5	Most of us did improve our discussion skills
Most of us did not learn much	1 2 3 4 5	Most of us did learn through our group work

How could the group have worked better?

Any other comments on the group or the course?

NAME:

GROUP:

Thank you for your views. There will be an opportunity to discuss the overall reactions of the group at our next meeting.

Figure 16.5 How our group worked

Source: From *Assessing Active Learning*, ed. G. Brown and M. Pendlebury (CVCP, Sheffield, 1992).

negotiated with students and involves setting ground-rules for the behaviour of a group or objectives for group work. This can be more or less formal. For student-led seminar work a simple but workable set of rules can be established by the group as a whole, as in the case-study later in this chapter. For group project-work a formal learning contract might be more appropriate. At Manchester Metropolitan University each student negotiates a simple formal contract to establish a framework within which his or her project proceeds. The document lays out name, course, project outline, method of assessment, deadlines, time of meetings, etc., and is signed by student and tutor. This contract can be altered as priorities change, and provides an agreed reference point to begin discussion if a session fails or a group or individual is not working effectively.[12]

Learning contracts encourage students to review their needs, skills, knowledge and understanding at key points of a project or course, and allow renegotiation if circumstances change. Whilst much work still needs to be done in this area, learning contracts can be a flexible assessment tool strongly encouraging reflection and ownership which are central to active learning.

The *learning journal* or *teamwork log* also enables students to write notes about their experience of the way their seminar or project group is working. Students can be asked to record observations, problems or ideas for action on an individual or group basis. In the case of collaborative work, minutes of meetings, problems encountered, how they were addressed and how effectiveness was monitored in the group might be the focus of the journal. The journal can be submitted with a final report as part of formal assessment, or used to write a separate report on the process of working together. It can also be discussed with the tutor as part of a self-assessment at a feedback tutorial. It is important to emphasize that students will have to produce evidence of their journal, or experience suggests that it will not be taken seriously.[13]

Finally, a learning contract and project journal can be used to build a wider *Record of Achievement*, a developmental profile of progress through the whole degree course. Although as yet the construction of these for higher education is in its infancy, they can help students to reflect on their progress within and between years, and in relation to key objectives and skills. A Record of Achievement can demonstrate much more clearly than a simple degree classification what a student has achieved over their degree course as a whole in terms of knowledge, skills and understanding. Clearly, they have to be explicitly laid out, and the purpose of the exercise, how it fits into the degree structure, how it is to be monitored and what are key issues to address need to be carefully explained.[14] The development of a Record of Achievement which could be widely used in history degree programmes would be a timely innovation, given that they are likely to become more widespread in the future.

Limitations of space have inevitably restricted discussion to a handful of the many assessment tasks suitable for group activities. Others can be found in the works under the Further Reading sections of this and the preceding chapter. What follows is intended as a practical demonstration of some of the things described above, in the hope that it will provide a stronger flavour of group work assessment in action. It is not intended as a model of good practice to be adopted wholesale, but as an example of one person's choice from the many possibilities.[15]

Case-study: Assessing Student-led Seminars in History

Organization

The module described runs over a half-year semester with a group of, on average, fifteen finalists taught in one fortnightly two-hour seminar. Its theme is popular culture in the Industrial Revolution period, and the topics covered include the changing process of work and artisanal values, the factory system, working women, leisure and recreation, urban and rural riots and protest, industrial discontent, popular religion, Methodism, schooling and education, the new police, and the issue of class consciousness. Each student will work with two or three colleagues to lead one seminar. The group as a whole is responsible for the efficient running of the seminars.

The first session is an introductory one, where the group as a whole discusses objectives and skills to be developed via a handout 'Guide to the Module'. They choose, from a list, the topics the module will cover and which topic they will lead. Sessions 2–5 are led by the students. Prior to the seminar, the leaders decide what their individual roles will be; attend a consultation meeting with the tutor; prepare and circulate a structured agenda within the first week comprising objectives, critical questions, factual issues, debates, etc.; prescribe specific individual reading for each member of the group; provide instructions on the intended methods for facilitating discussion; prepare handouts and overheads as necessary. At the seminar, the leaders each give a short introductory presentation for five minutes outlining their objectives, methodological issues, etc.; direct the group through the agenda; ensure everyone contributes and take responsibility for tutoring the group, with guidance from the tutor. Session 6 provides an opportunity to draw together the themes of the module and discuss general issues and revision.

Formulating criteria

Clear criteria are critical for confidence on a module which is dependent upon the active co-operation of the students themselves and which gives them a great deal of responsibility.

An effective way of establishing general ground-rules for measuring the success of the whole programme of seminars, as well as generating a sense of ownership, is to divide the group into buzz groups, each of four or five students. They are asked to think about the best seminar they have ever had and what made it so; or the worst and what made it so bad, if they fail to think of a good one. This latter suggestion usually focuses the mind quickly, as well as giving them a chance of getting to know one another. Each group has about ten minutes to produce five or six main principles of a 'good' seminar, which they put up on the blackboard. The lists produced are compared and a composite list of 'rules' for conducting the seminar drawn up. A list of the 'tutor's view' of what constitutes a good seminar is used for comparison, and is always very similar; a fact surprising to the students but not to anyone familiar with the findings of research into student learning. In the 1994–5 session the student list was as follows:

1 Everyone takes responsibility for preparation.
2 A clear structure is in place in each seminar.
3 Everyone participates.
4 Discussion is to the point.
5 Different viewpoints are aired and respected.
6 A variety of approaches are adopted.
7 Nobody dominates.
8 A relaxed atmosphere prevails.

Students are also provided with a Seminar Evaluation Sheet (figure 16.6) which can be refined by the group in the introductory session. It contains material generated from the module documents and previous years' experience, and provides clear criteria against which performance will be

Running the seminar counts as part of your final assessment. The assessment criteria are as follows. For more detailed guidance please refer to the module handouts.

Criteria	Mark	Comments

Preparation

1 Extent of reading
2 Clarifying roles
3 Deciding objectives
4 Structuring the agenda
5 Producing the agenda on time
6 Distributing reading tasks

Presentation

1 Introducing the topic
2 Explaining aims and objectives
3 Speaking clearly and confidently
4 Use of handouts/other material
5 Maintaining interest in the topic

Managing the group

1 Moving the agenda along
2 Maintaining relevance
3 Summing up where necessary
4 Involving everyone
5 Not allowing anyone to dominate
6 Encouraging a relaxed atmosphere
7 Timing the discussion

Discussion/Analysis

1 Awareness of historical issues
2 Stimulating informed discussion
3 Taking account of others' viewpoints
4 Responding to questions
5 Providing information
6 Deciding what is relevant
7 Clarifying discussion
8 Drawing a positive conclusion from the group

STUDENT: _____ **TOTAL MARK:**_____

Your best skills:

Things to work on:

Figure 16.6   Seminar evaluation sheet

measured, as well as acting as a shorthand guide to group leaders to assist their preparation.

In discussing the evaluation form two issues usually arise: How much weight should be given to each section? Should each group leader receive the same mark? The issue of who should mark is dealt with in the following section. It is possible, and probably better, to allow the group to decide this for itself in the introductory session; it is certainly essential for them to discuss these issues so that all is clear and agreed at the outset. On the question of weighting, the most straightforward solution is to give each section equal weighting and this is what the group invariably decides, if asked. More difficult is the allocation of marks. As two or three people are usually running the seminar, should they be given the same or individual marks? I have found that the best way to tackle this issue is to put it to the group, possibly using buzz groups, and reach a collective decision. There is invariably some debate about the respective merits of individual versus collective marking, and airing the concern is important in itself.

Some solutions to this problem have been suggested earlier in this chapter. Personally, I have found it useful for all group leaders to receive at least the same mark for preparation unless there is very good reason for them not to. Co-operative preparation is essential, and a joint mark seems only fair on this section and encourages teamwork. Some colleagues prefer to give the group leaders the same mark throughout, and there is a real logic to this in terms of encouraging co-operation. However, I have tended to prefer giving individual marks overall, feeling that this does acknowledge differing contributions and abilities, and have not found that it causes problems if it is made clear at the outset. However, it can be useful to allow the group to devise a ceiling on the amount of difference between group leaders, if they wish. Most groups choose not to do so, though some have settled on about 10 per cent, and this gives ample marking flexibility as the degree of divergence is only exceptionally more than this.

Assessment procedures

The overall assessment of the module comprises the following elements: one essay (35 per cent); seminar work (25 per cent); written examination (45 per cent).

For each seminar there is a combination of formative and summative assessment. After each session there is a de-briefing session for the group leaders who are usually keen to talk about how it went and think through the issues before they write their final report. This also supplements and reinforces the initial thinking about the process in the weekly consultations with group leaders before the agenda is produced. Both act as an ongoing means of reflection and evaluation, and as a means of support. The group leaders tend to construct their own agenda in the light of the perceived success or otherwise of previous seminars, and this provides a good opportunity to discuss objectives, structuring an agenda and techniques for facilitating discussion.

For the purposes of formal assessment, the group evaluates each seminar during the final ten minutes. A good way to do this is simply by asking those running it to send round a sheet asking each member to comment on the seminar, including both supportive points and ways it might have been improved. This has the advantage of being supportive whilst allowing some scope for critical reflection, and avoids the tedium of filling out a larger evaluation sheet which might also threaten the goodwill upon which the seminar depends. It also provides the group leaders with additional information upon which to base their final report. The group leaders then submit individual reports within three days of the seminar drawing upon the peer comment, and with sections on conclusions of the group on the topic, the process of preparation and their view of the meeting, including strengths and weaknesses. They are frequently exceptionally astute in their awareness of what transpired and invariably honest, sometimes too self-deprecating – a point which can be raised in the feedback by the tutor.

All the available information is then assessed formally by the tutor on the Seminar Evaluation Sheet, where a final overall mark is generated and advice offered as to how they might improve in particular aspects. My own experience has been that the students prefer the final assessment to be done by the tutor, on the grounds that summative peer assessment will destroy the co-operative spirit which builds up quickly in the group. I have no strong feelings either way on this and, ideally, the students might play a stronger role. However, if they are not used to doing this or feel unhappy with it, it seems better to go for an 'impure' system which works rather than a pure one which is theoretically more correct but fails to work. Much will depend on the context and the students, and I have found that the more-confident group leaders will readily self-assess on the evaluation sheet provided, with the tutor acting as final arbiter. I do not make it compulsory, though the more familiar the students are with the system the more willing they are to self-assess. A greater level of self-assessment or peer assessment is to be encouraged, particularly in semester 2 of the final year, and in my experience when this happens the self-assessed marks are rarely very different from those which I would have given myself.

Finally, self-assessment is also used as part of a short final-feedback session with each student discussing their performance over the seminars as a whole, and is organized using a format sheet as in figure 16.4 above.

Student evaluation

The response from students to assessment of the seminars has been overwhelmingly positive. In feedback they have made the following points. First, that seminars are such an important method of teaching and learning that they ought to be assessed, and this is particularly true where much effort is expected in them. Secondly, that it is good to have variety in the assessment process. Why, some asked in reply to a questionnaire, do history students have to do quite so many essays? Thirdly, and most important, it increases motivation and participation. All admit that this module has made them read more for seminars than they normally do. Everyone feels a duty to prepare and contribute, from a sense of solidarity with those running the seminar and in the knowledge that they too will have to do the same and will need everyone's co-operation. Enlightened self-interest can be a powerful motivator. Fourthly, and relatedly, the assessment criteria force them to focus and reflect upon what skills they need to work on to run the group effectively, and this lends an extra interest to the traditional discussion of a historical topic. Finally, the by-product of the seriousness with which the seminars are treated is that the atmosphere is more relaxed than usual. Although some mentioned feeling apprehensive at the beginning, this feeling quickly passed and the seminars were both enjoyable and rewarding.

The tutor's view

Several colleagues have tried this method. All report benefits in terms of motivation, group spirit and reflection. The shared responsibility and accountability seem to bind the group together and make everyone work for the seminars in a way that is not always common, particularly in a group of fifteen or more. In addition, the students share their knowledge better because everyone is contributing. Hitherto, a few students might dominate and this led to resentment that they were contributing their points to others who made no return, and among the rest that they were being dominated and forced to listen to what this minority wished to talk about. The rules drawn up by the students themselves make this much less of an issue. The students also become far more aware of the mechanics of group work, and the subtleties and complexities of group and personal interaction and communication. In this way their confidence grows and they become more adventurous, open and flexible. They are no longer so defensive when contradicted by others in the group, and are more willing to push their own ideas out further. Although they become more critical and active as learners, they also seem to develop a greater awareness of the difficulties of teaching through seminars. This tolerance of tutors' fallibilities is a useful by-product.

Perhaps the two key problems are generating individual marks and the reliability of marking. When peer assessment is used in association with clear assessment criteria, experience suggests that marks generated by students rarely differ greatly from those that the tutor would award. It is true, however, that group work can lead to higher marks than essay work, partly because there are more people to work on a piece of work, and individual weaknesses are concealed behind the strengths of the more able. This can advantage weaker students at the expense of the academically outstanding, though attention to the weighting of seminar assessment can help. The real problem over reliability is not this, however, but the process of monitoring which generally establishes reliability through second markers and external examiners. Whilst these have experience of moderating essay work, and can see the final product, they can have difficulty appreciating the exact circumstances of a seminar or oral presentation without expensive, and potentially disruptive, resort on the part of the tutor to videorecording. In some instances of this type of work, both second marker and external examiner have to witness at least one seminar presentation. This is undoubtedly good practice, and can be worked into a departmental scheme of peer observation of teaching. Where time constraints do not allow this, the best way forward is a variety of inputs of peer assessment, self-assessment and tutor comment which relate not only to presentation but also to content and analysis. Together these can provide a more complete picture, and enable effective monitoring to occur.

Conclusion

The research literature on assessment for learning suggests that if your purpose is to equip your students with a range of skills appropriate to historians in the 1990s, then multiple methods of assessment are a necessity. This chapter has focused upon assessment to encourage effective learning in groups, and has argued that assessment of group work offers a productive and practical addition, or alternative, to more traditional modes of assessment. If you value group work and want your students to value it, then assess it. Whilst not without its difficulties, the benefits in terms of student motivation and learning are considerable. There is no single correct way to assess this type of activity but, as with assessment generally, choosing a varied and balanced range of assessment tasks and methods will probably work best. Most likely to be successful are those which increase students' responsibility for their own learning. To support this, clarity of assessment criteria and negotiation are particularly important. In these ways the oral communication, teamwork and reflective skills necessary to effective learning in groups can be facilitated, and group work realize its potential as a powerful method for encouraging effective learning in history.

Notes

1 D. Jaques, *Learning in Groups* (Kogan Page, London, 1991); S. Griffiths and P. Partington, *Enabling Active Learning in Small Groups* (CVCP, Sheffield, 1992); N. Entwistle, S. Thompson and H. Tait, *Guidelines for Promoting Effective Learning in Higher Education* (Edinburgh University, Centre for Research on Learning and Instruction, Edinburgh, 1992).

2 S. Brown and P. Knight, *Assessing Learners in Higher Education* (Kogan Page, London, 1994), p. 23.

3 For advice on running poster sessions and oral presentations, and for alternative assessment formats, see G. Brown and M, Pendlebury, *Assessing Active Learning* (CVCP, Sheffield, 1992), and S. Mandel, *Effective Presentation Skills* (Kogan Page, London, 1988).

4 A. Wilson, 'Structuring Seminars: A Technique to Allow Students to Participate in the Structuring of Small Group Discussions', *Studies in Higher Education*, 5 (1980), pp. 81–4; H. Steffens, 'Collaborative Learning in a History Seminar', *History Teacher*, 22 (1989), pp. 125–38; Report on a course, 'British History 1558–1689' by A. Fletcher for the workshop on 'Innovative History Teaching', University of York, 1990.

5   J. Heywood, *Assessment in Higher Education* (John Wiley, London, 1989), pp. 272–3; Brown and Pendlebury, *Assessing Active Learning*, module I, p. 62.

6   B. Brecher and T. Hickey, 'Teaching Skills through History', *PUSH Newsletter*, 1 (1990), pp. 17–19. A similar seminar classification system is used at Stafford College with HND students where staff assessed in relation to Preparation and evidence of research; Quality of content; Quality of presentation; Promotion of discussion and reasoned arguments; and Ability to summarize. See also, H. Watson, 'Developing an Evaluative Technique for Assessing Seminar Work', *Collected Original Resources in Education*, 13 (1989), pp. 1–5.

7   For the working out of this method in detail, see N. Falchikov, 'Self and Peer Assessment of Working Together in a Group', in *Self and Peer Assessment*, ed. S. Brown and P. Dove (SCED Paper no. 63, Birmingham, 1989).

8   For advice on how to do this, and format sheets to help, see G. Gibbs, S. Habeshaw and T. Habeshaw, *53 Interesting Ways to Assess your Students* (Technical and Educational Services, Bristol, 1988), pp. 103–8. Other useful suggestions are to be found in Brown and Knight, *Assessing Learners in Higher Education*, pp. 62–3.

9   See especially, G. Gibbs, 'Assessing Teamwork Skills', *Bulletin of Teaching and Learning*, 5 (1990), pp. 6–9. For a 'red card' system for dealing with problem members of a group project, see M. Lejk, 'Team Assessment: Win or Lose', *New Academic*, 3 (1994), pp. 10–11.

10 P. Ericson and N. Cohen, 'Proctorials: A Student View', *New Academic*, 2 (1993), p. 13. On the whole area of peer tutoring, see *Explorations in Peer Tutoring*, ed. S. Goodlad and B. Hurst (Kogan Page, London, 1990).

11 For another example relating to the process of chairing a seminar, see Gibbs, 'Assessing Teamwork Skills', p. 8.

12 D. Nicholls, 'Making History Students Enterprising: "Independent Study" at Manchester Polytechnic', *Studies in Higher Education*, 17 (1992), pp. 67–80. *Learning Contracts*, vol. 2, ed. S. Brown (SCED Paper no. 72, Birmingham, 1993) also contains an article by Nicholls on learning contracts in history project-work as well as much general practical advice. See also S. Griffiths and P. Partington, *Active Learning in Small Groups* (CVCP, Sheffield, 1992), and G. Anderson, D. Bond and J. Sampson, 'Expectations of Learning Contracts', *Capability*, 1 (1994), pp. 22–31.

13 Advice on constructing learning diaries is contained in D. Jaques, *Supervising Projects* (Oxford Polytechnic Press, Oxford, 1988). For their use in history courses, see Steffens, 'Collaborative Learning', pp. 130–4; V. Reber, 'Teaching Undergraduates to Think Like Historians', in *History Anew: Innovations in the Teaching of History Today*, ed. R. Blackey (California State University Press, Long Beach, 1993).

14 For more information on Records of Achievement, and some case studies in their use, see *Using Records of Achievement in Higher Education*, ed. A. Assiter and E. Shaw (Kogan Page, London, 1993); J. Bull and S. Otter, *Recording Achievement: Potential for Higher Education* (CVCP, Sheffield, 1994). Also interesting is P. Trowler and K. Hinett, 'Implementing the Recording of Achievement in Higher Education', *Capability*, 1 (1994), pp. 53–61.

15 For a similar experiment in another context, see P. Daniel, 'Assessing Student-led Seminars through a Process of Negotiation', *Journal of Geography in Higher Education*, 15 (1991), pp. 57–62.

Further Reading

The general works noted for the previous chapter all contain useful material, but especially good are G. Gibbs, *Improving the Quality of Student Learning* (Technical and Educational Services, Bristol, 1992) and G. Brown and M. Pendlebury, *Assessing Active Learning* (CVCP, Sheffield, 1992) which provide examples of criteria sheets and other material which can be customized for a wide variety of group activities. Although clumsily titled and relating to geography, A. Jenkins and D. Pepper's *Enhancing Employability and Educational Experience: A Manual on Teaching Communication and Groupwork Skills in Higher Education* (SCED Paper, no. 27, Birmingham, 1987), has some excellent group-work exercises and assessment formats which can be used in history teaching. *Self and Peer Assessment*, ed. S. Brown and P. Dove (SCED Paper, no. 63, Birmingham, 1991) provides thoughtful case-studies on attempts to introduce self-assessment and peer assessment into group work. Useful guides to group work in general, with good advice on encouraging active learning are D. Jaques, *Learning in Groups* (Kogan Page, London, 1991) and S. Griffiths and P. Partington, *Enabling Active Learning in Small Groups* (CVCP, Sheffield, 1992).

17

Assessing the Quality of Education in History Departments

George Brown

This chapter provides a perspective on the assessment of teaching in history. It explores the issues underlying current approaches to assessing quality that are being developed in Britain and, particularly, in England. The exploration is set in the context of the nature of assessment, of quality and of teaching and learning in history. The chapter is not concerned with the mechanics of obtaining labels of 'excellence' or 'quality approved' nor with providing a chronological sequence of events that led to the present system. Rather it seeks to clarify the tensions, limitations and values that are implicit in current approaches to assessment of the quality of education in history departments.

Assessment

The term 'assessment' for appraising the quality of teaching and learning is a cultural import from the United States. Like many imports from the United States in education and health, it sits uncomfortably with many of our values, assumptions and language usage. Inevitably there are confusions arising from the indigenous use of the term for assessing student learning and the use of the term for reviewing the education provided by a department. Both types of assessment share common characteristics. Both are based upon the procedure of taking a sample, drawing inferences and estimating worth. Common weaknesses are:

- the sample does not match the stated outcomes;
- the sample is drawn from too narrow a domain;
- the sample is too large or too small;
- absence of well-defined criteria;
- unduly specific criteria;
- variations in the inferences drawn by different assessors of the sample;
- variations in estimates of worth.

Both types of assessment influence the nature of learning and performance. It is well known that changing the mode of assessment changes the mode of student learning. Measuring performance on given criteria changes performance towards those criteria. If the criteria are not appropriate for the purposes of the task then one may end up fulfilling the criteria but not performing the task well. Operationalism and its attenuated form, accountism, have conceptual and structural weaknesses. These rather abstract descriptions are manifest in the assessment of students' work, in course design, in course management and in the assessment of the quality of teaching and learning. A more detailed discussion of assessment, particularly in relation to student learning, may be found in Brown and Pendlebury.[1]

The purposes of assessment, whether of student learning or of the quality of education provided by a department, contain inherent conflicts. Assessment may be criterion-referenced or normative. The former relies on predetermined standards that a student or a department is expected to achieve; the latter upon rank ordering according to some hidden or explicit criteria. Strictly speaking, if a department or student meets the criteria they should receive the appropriate grade. In practice, considerations of better and best affect decisions–particularly funding decisions. Assessment may be primarily formative: it may provide feedback that assists students or departments to reflect upon their goals and on ways of improving. It may be primarily summative: a series of judgements or recommendations. The distinction between formative and summative assessment is not clear cut. Summative assessment can, if expressed appropriately, provide meaningful and useful feedback and thereby aid development. Formative feedback may involve multiple points of summative feedback. Both summative and formative assessments involve judgements and judgements are based on values – which may or may not be explicit to the assessors themselves or to the assessed. Finally, there are conflicts between the judgemental and developmental purposes of assessment. These conflicts are shot through student learning, staff appraisal, academic audit, the research selectivity exercise and the quality assurance exercise. Achieving a satisfactory balance that satisfies all those concerned is not easy.

There is, inevitably, debate about what counts as good assessment. Issues of fairness, reliability and validity predominate. Fairness implies equality of opportunity and treatment; reliability implies consistency of approach; and validity implies appropriateness of methods of truth-seeking. Purposes and context are central to estimates of what is good assessment. All of these are deep problems. None the less, most people agree that:

- the purposes, dimensions and criteria should be clear to the assessors and the assessed;
- they should be used consistently by the assessors;
- the sample of activities observed should be representative of all the major dimensions being assessed;
- the dimensions should be related to the purposes of the assessment;
- the inferences drawn should be consistent;
- the estimates of worth should be consistent with the inferences and the criteria.

Many of the criticisms of the quality assessment procedures may be fitted in to the model of assessment described above. Conflicts of purpose, variability across and within subject assessments, the sample of activities assessed, the methods of assessment and the grading system of worth in the English system of quality assessment have all been criticized.[2] The Barnett report advocated the use of profiles and the abolition of global categories of excellence, satisfactory and unsatisfactory. The report from the History in the Universities Defence Group, claims there is 'a substantial lack of confidence in the Assessment Exercise'.[3] Its criticisms seem mainly directed at the inadequacies of the assessors, who themselves are historians.

Similar criticisms have been directed at the assessment of student learning for many years.[4] Yet many history departments persist in using methods of student assessment that are seriously flawed. Many of the same departments complain when a not dissimilar method to their own for assessing student learning is applied to the quality of their provision of student learning. The same weaknesses are also endemic in staff appraisal schemes in universities.[5] Yet many universities who seem unwilling to develop their appraisal schemes are willing to criticize the efforts of the national Funding Councils. It is sometimes forgotten that the Funding Councils' methods of assessment, at the time of writing this chapter, have been in operation for less than two years. The Funding Councils seem more responsive to comments and criticisms than many departments and universities are responsive to the comments and criticisms of their students and staff.

Quality: Rhetoric and Reality

In discussions of higher education, the term 'quality' is in danger of becoming a confusing predicate. Its popularity may be attributed to its connotations and therefore its usefulness as a rhetorical device and as a cloak for hegemonic intention. Quality has been identified variously as 'Exceptional, Perfection, Consistency, Fitness for purpose, Goal achievement, Effectiveness in achieving institutional goals, Value for money, Transformation of students'.[6] Beneath these overlapping definitions there are two conflicting concepts. The first may be traced to Plato and the second to Aristotle. The Platonic concept is based on absolute or ideal standards to which teaching and learning should aspire. National standards of history degrees and rank ordering of history departments emanate from this concept. The Aristotelian notion is teleological: quality is assessed by the fitness for purpose of methods and strategies of learning and teaching. Absolute standards are not relevant. Arguments within the Aristotelian paradigm centre on appropriateness of methods for purposes and, arguably, on appropriateness of purposes for different student populations. Platonic approaches begin with principles that are predetermined by the 'guardians' of society. In managerial language, these are expressed as performance indicators. They are potent: modes of measurement do change phenomena. Aristotelian approaches begin with reflections upon experience. These may lead to differing notions of 'good' according to purposes, context and the shifting boundaries of experience.

There are of course similarities are well as differences between these approaches, but they are a convenient way of highlighting conflicts. The conflict between the absolute and the relative is redolent in theories of history and the purposes of history. In a less obvious way it shapes debates about the assessment of quality, and the assessment of student learning. Circular 3/93 stated that 'The quality of teaching and learning in a diverse sector can only be understood in the context of an institution's own aims and objectives.'[7] The approach is apparently intended to be Aristotelian with a touch of Platonism. The outcomes of the exercise were, according to 3/93, to be explicitly related to funding. The interpretation of those outcomes has been Platonic with a touch of Aristotelianism. A grade of excellence is not seen as 'goodness of fit' so much as the 'best in the country' by intending students, their parents, employers and by some historians.

Related to this issue are comparisons across subjects. Table 17.1 provides the overall results of the first round of Quality Assessments conducted by the HEFCE. Ninety self-assessments were received for History, with fifty-seven of these claiming excellence. Forty-one Quality Assessment visits were made to older (26) and newer (15) universities (formerly polytechnics and colleges in the public sector). Sixteen of the seventeen grades of excellence were awarded to departments of history in older universities. One College of Higher Education, received a grade of excellence. No department of history in ex-polytechnics received a grade of excellence. Of the fifty-seven awards of excellence across the range of subjects assessed, fifty were from older universities. Thirty-seven of those departments that were rated excellent also received a 5 (the highest score) in the Research Assessment Exercise (RAE) of 1992. Of those which were given the lowest score, only six were rated excellent in teaching.

These results are open to various interpretations. As indicated above, the notion of excellence is supposedly based upon closeness of fit between purposes and methods. But the grades of excellence are often read as high standards in teaching. The variation across subjects is not read as closeness of fit of purpose and method so much as that teaching in history is better than in chemistry and mechanical engineering. This view is,

Table 17.1 Distribution of HEFCE grades

	Excellent	Satisfactory	Unsatisfactory
Chemistry	12	56	0
History	17	73	0
Law	19	48	0
Mechanical Engineering	9	63	2
Totals	57	240	2

incidentally, in line with a study of students' perceptions of the quality of courses in universities and colleges in Australian universities.[8] The data may be interpreted as confirming the time-honoured view that the quality of teaching and research is intimately related. It may be used to demonstrate that the teaching of history is better in older universities than in newer ones. It indicates that those departments with more well-qualified students on entry, better staff–student ratios and more library resources' provide a better education.

Such interpretations are not without controversy. They highlight how the results of an assessment, intended (ostensibly) to be sensitive to diversity of mission and intake, can be converted into a league table of national standards. They suggest that variations in the results may, in part, be attributed to variations between and within assessors of different subjects. In short, the purpose, content and methods of a system of assessment always require regular scrutiny.

Teaching and Learning for what Purposes?

Before assessing any phenomenon, it is useful to know the nature of that phenomenon and its purposes. Teaching is predicated upon learning. That is to say, learning, not teaching, takes primacy, particularly in higher education. Wright expressed it thus: 'At the very heart of the activity of higher education must be placed the processes by which students learn and a concern for the processes that facilitate them.'[9] Conceptions of learning and teaching underpin not only approaches to teaching and learning but also course design, course management and the assessment of student learning. At this point it may be useful to distinguish between *expressed* values and *implicit* values. An individual or a department may write eloquently about the nature of learning yet the same individual's or department's course design and modes of assessment may reveal a primitive conception of student learning and, therefore, of teaching. The most common of the primitive conceptions of teaching is the transmission model: transmission, reception and recitation of what has been learnt. Few historians espouse such a primitive model, yet some courses are dangerously close to it. An examination of the underlying conceptions of teaching and learning implicit in the course documents of a department provide a sound basis for a review of the quality of teaching and learning. This approach is used by quality assessors and many other course evaluators.

A broad, if somewhat rough and ready, conception of learning encompasses changes in skills, knowledge and understanding brought about by experience and reflection upon that experience. This description does not deny the importance of knowledge-acquisition so much as place it in context. A knowledge of the Treaty of Versailles is necessary before one can adequately analyse the problems of Germany in the 1920s. A transmission model *per se* is unlikely to generate such analytical skills in students. Reflective learning has been shown in many fields to be a *sine qua non* of moving a learner from the status of novice towards the status of expert.[10] Entwistle, in a thorough review of how undergraduates learn, concludes that:

> Where they have been carefully planned and properly implemented, attempts at encouraging active learning have been uniformly rated favourably by teachers and students. There is also evidence that freedom in learning or student autonomy together with good teaching which encourages students to form their own conceptions, will lead to deep approaches to learning which enhance personal conceptual understanding. Such understanding is a necessary first step in being able to apply knowledge in novel contexts and solve related problems. Adding to conceptual understanding, skills which have been developed through experiential learning (from Simulations, Projects and work placements) will further strengthen the ability to make these applications. A further step is to use collaborative learning, with it's opportunities for developing communication skills and the explicit discussion of the group dynamics involved. These methods seem to foster the social and personal skills so necessary both in working and in everyday life.[11]

Entwistle's conclusions almost provide a programme of action for lecturers and departments of history.

From this discussion, it follows that teaching might best be considered as the provision of a wide range of opportunities to learn. It includes transmission but it also includes other forms of face-to-face teaching, other learning opportunities, assessment of student learning, course design and course management. It is in this generic sense that the Funding Councils use the term 'teaching'. Their programmes of assessing teaching quality reflect these components of teaching. At the heart of their approach is concern for the quality of the students' learning experiences: 'Teaching and learning are inseparable: teaching involves the whole management and promotion of student learning by a variety of methods, including access to a wide range of learning resources.'[12]

The broad conception of learning provided above is rather more subtle than it might appear. In particular, the term 'skill' is problematic. It encompasses psychomotor skills such as using a PC; social skills such as working in groups; cognitive skills such as reading critically; analytical and interpretative skills and the skills of synthesizing evidence and creating new perspectives. Few historians would dispute the importance of these skills in the study of history. What they might object to is the notion that these skills can be learnt *in vacuo*. Skills are grounded in content and the content shapes the skills. Despite the claims of the advocates of National Vocational Qualifications and General National Vocational Qualifications,[13] skills are not identical across subjects nor do they readily transfer across contexts. The overwhelming weight of evidence indicates that knowledge and understanding of different contexts are necessary for transfer.[14] The skills of analysis and synthesis in history and histopathology do have distinctive differences. Subjects do differ in the nature of the core concepts, in the structures of the discipline, in the truth-criteria used and in the methods of arriving at truths. Only a blind zealot would think otherwise. However, these differences do not excuse historians from considering what skills are learnt, and might be learnt, by students in their history courses.

Given there are differences in emphases and skills between subjects and departments, how can one assess the national quality of teaching and learning in higher education? The answer proffered by the Funding Councils was, ostensibly, to use the notion of fitness of purpose. As indicated earlier in this chapter, that notion has its roots in Aristotelian ethics and it sits uneasily in a context of accountability and national standards.

The relationship between skills, knowledge and understanding is a complex epistemological problem that has recently re-emerged in discussions of higher education.[15] Put crudely, the overlapping domains are concerned with *know how* (skills), *know that* (knowledge), *know why* (understanding). Skills are seen, *inter alia*, as ways of acquiring and managing knowledge and of developing understanding. Understanding is sometimes subsumed under knowledge, and sometimes understanding is seen as a higher order than knowledge. These differing conceptions may be found in the competency movement and in different approaches to academic disciplines. They have deep implications for teaching, learning and assessment within history, or indeed any academic subject, but there are no abrupt transitions across categories and there are dangers in attempting too precise a set of delineations when considering what one wants students to learn in history or from their higher education.

The Purposes of Higher Education

Argument about whether skills, knowledge or understanding takes primacy is part of the debate of the purposes of higher education and therefore of the purposes of teaching history in universities. Those concerned with vocationalism are likely to stress the importance of skills and their transferability, and those concerned with truth-seeking are likely to stress the importance of understanding. Vocationalist perspectives neglect that knowledge and understanding of different concepts and contexts are the prerequisites of transfer. Those concerned with knowledge-seeking and understanding neglect that the development of skills is necessary for improving the acquisition and management of knowledge and for deepening understanding. Concern with the development of higher order skills is not only useful to students but also for the development of history as an academic subject.

The wider debate concerning the purposes of higher education is at least as old as Hippocrates. The question then posed was: Is the learning of medicine an education or a training? The debate has see-sawed between vocationalism and liberalism ever since. The debate is a false antithesis. There is a continuum of views from specific vocationalism through what might be called liberal vocationalism, to vocational liberalism to liberalism and beyond. As a rule of thumb, prestigious departments and universities are more likely to be liberal than vocational, and less prestigious universities to be vocational rather than liberal. Although it is likely that there is a whole spectrum of views from extreme vocationalism to postmodernism within history departments, it is likely that most departments are towards the liberal end of the continuum.

These parts of the continuum provide different purposes for higher education. In their cogent and scholarly analysis of the assessment of student learning in higher education, Atkins, Beattie and Dockrell distinguish and discuss the evidence and assumptions underlying four broad overlapping purposes:[16]

- specific vocational preparation;
- preparation for general employment;

- preparation for knowledge creation;
- general educational experience.

They point to significant gaps in our knowledge of whether higher education is achieving its present purposes, to the shift towards specific or general employment-related outcomes in many courses and universities, and to the changes in the student population.

The purposes of higher education cannot easily be separated from the people involved or from their other intentions and motives. As well as purposes, one needs to consider *whose* purposes. In times of unemployment, it is hardly surprising that history students are likely to be more concerned with the relevance of their education to job-seeking. Only about half of the present graduates entered permanent employment within six months of completing their degree. Forty per cent of jobs advertised do not specify a subject. Major employers receive, on average, ninety applications per vacancy.[17] Employers concerned for the future of their companies may look towards higher education for some solutions to their problems. But their claims to be concerned to recruit undergraduates with the requisite skills seem to be mingled with a concern to recruit from the most prestigious universities. A government eager to appear to be solving unemployment problems may prefer to keep a substantial group of young people out of its unemployment statistics. On the one hand it claims that it wishes to expand the system from an elitist to a mass higher education system; yet, on the other hand, it reduces student grants and thereby excludes potentially able students of the less prosperous sectors of society. A mass higher education system of 40 per cent of young people has been advocated recently by the Confederation of British Industries to increase brain power, creativity and motivation.[18] Given that organization's commitment to no minimum wage for employees, to no maximum salary for directors, and to dismantling the existing support structures for the unemployed then one wonders whether expressed purposes belie some hidden intentions. It would seem that the conflict of vocationalism and liberalism together with expressed and implicit values applies as much to employers and government as to academics.

Although instrumental purposes of higher education are in the ascendancy, it is worth repeating some cautionary notes. Narrow vocationalism is a naïve goal for history courses when so many of their graduates enter a diversity of occupations and may change careers. Even if they do not change jobs then their jobs may change. A sound basis of the skills involved in knowledge acquisition and understanding may serve them better than attempts to make history more vocational. Newman, in the language of his day, expressed this view most eloquently:

> It is the education which gives a man a clear conscious view of his own opinions and judgements, a truth in developing them, an eloquence in expressing them, and a force in urging them. It teaches him to see things as they are, to go right to the point, to disentangle a skein of thought, to detect what is sophistical, and to discard what is irrelevant. It prepares him to fill any post with credit, and to master any subject with facility. It shows him how to accommodate himself to others, how to throw himself in to their frame of mind, how to bring before them his own, how to influence them, how to come to an understanding with them, how to bear with them.[19]

This is not to deny the value of some vocational influences. Work-based learning can provide opportunities to develop and apply skills in different contexts that can enrich students' understanding of history as well as of workplaces. Employers and past students can provide useful suggestions on course development. Government initiatives, such as the Enterprise in Higher Education project, have been shown to have had an impact upon course development and methods of teaching.[20]

The Purposes of Teaching in History

The above debate impinges upon the purposes of history teaching in universities. Whilst it would be rash to lay down a programme of purposes and methods for all history departments to follow, the following broad questions should be considered by any history department interested in the quality of its students' learning:

- What kinds of things do we want students to learn in our history courses?
- What opportunities are provided?
- How do we assess their learning?
- What criteria do we use?

The answers to these questions are interlinked. They provide a sound basis for self-assessment and reflection. And just as reflection upon learning aids a student to deepen his or her approach to learning history, so too can reflection by history departments lead to deeper approaches to teaching and assessing history students. Finally, it is worth noting that the reports of Quality Assessors and, earlier, of HMIs and other course reviewers, indicate that weaknesses are often found between the expressed aims of a department and the methods of teaching and assessment that it uses.

The State of Quality

The assessment of education in history departments of older universities, in so far that it existed, was based upon occasional visits by the subject committees of the University Grants Committee and by the external examiners. The task of the latter was to be a guardian of standards and to protect students from gross iniquities. This normative approach may have been satisfactory when the system of higher education was relatively small and stable. Now that departments have different missions and intakes the role of the external examiner is gradually changing towards that of evaluator of courses and assessment procedures. The conflict of maintaining national standards whilst being sensitive to the purposes and intakes of a department is inherent in this new role.[21]

Polytechnics and colleges were subject, initially, to the procedures of the Council for National Academic Awards, and to regular inspections by HMIs.[22] Both bodies provided independent assessments of the quality of education and the impact of government policies on education. On the recommendations of the Policy Studies Institute of the Conservative Party, these bodies were disbanded in 1992–3. Subsequently, two strands of quality assessment emerged. The first was initiated by the CVCP and it is, at present, the Division of Quality Audit of the non-statutory Higher Education Quality Council. It is primarily concerned with the effectiveness of the quality assurance procedures in universities: it has no legal or financial authority. The second is the Quality Assessment Divisions of the Higher Education Funding Councils for England, Northern Ireland, Scotland and Wales. The Funding Councils have a statutory obligation, under the Further and Higher Education Act of 1992, to ensure that provision is made for assessing the quality of education in institutions for whose activities they provide funding. Their concern is primarily the quality of education provided by subjects.

Division of Quality Audit

The remit of the Division of Quality Audit is to explore the mechanisms of quality assurance within universities. In the words of its director:

> It describes, analyses and makes judgements on the effectiveness of quality assurance mechanisms and structures in respect of six main areas: design and review of courses; teaching, learning and the student experience; academic staff; student assessment and degree classification; promotions material and feedback and verification systems. . . . Reports have both formative and judgemental elements but do not offer categorical judgements of the 'satisfactory/unsatisfactory' type.[23]

The report, *Learning from Audit*, provides an analysis of the term 'quality assurance system' and an analysis based on the audit reports to sixty-nine universities. It suggests that a system of quality assurance could be defined as something which:

- is clear in its specifications of roles, responsibilities and procedures;
- enables institutional aims and objectives to be achieved;
- informs decision-making;
- is free from individual personal bias;
- is repeatable over time;
- involves all staff;
- includes the specification of standards and acceptable evidence;
- prompts continuous improvement.

These echoes of Weber are, of course, part of a wider revolution in public services. The notional departments of individuals who pursue their research and teaching relatively independent of their colleagues are being replaced by departments that have financial and bureaucratic responsibilities. Together with student charters, mutual surveillance and the managerial language of customers, providers, transparency, drivers, front-loading and milestones, they pave the way for increasing hegemony whilst appearing to increase democracy, ownership and openness.

The analysis of the reports on many institutions provides a summary of areas for further consideration. Amongst its observations are those shown in figure 17.1. The full report should be of interest to anyone concerned with the quality of education provided in history departments and universities.

'The extent to which teaching and learning is evaluated, both across and within institutions remains variable and is sometimes absent.' [p. xvii]

'There are serious concerns about the adequacy of provision of library services, due in the main, to the great increase in student numbers.' [p. xix]

'In some cases the library is not involved in programme approval and review. This is one aspect of a wider problem; a lack of co-ordination of academic and resource issues was noted in some universities.' [p. xix]

'The training of lecturers to be effective teachers tends to be short, voluntary and concentrated at the start of a career, and is generally focused on full time staff.' [p. xxi]

'Staff development activities are often not adequately monitored or reviewed to assess their effectiveness.' [p. xxi]

'Most universities have introduced staff appraisal schemes, yet these often require greater monitoring and oversight to assess their use and value and to determine staff development needs.' [p. xxi]

'There is concern that students (within and across universities) may not be receiving fair and equal treatment in terms of the marking scores used to assess performance, the criteria used, or the methods used to record achievement (e.g., degree classification).' [p. xxii]

'The methods used to monitor the effectiveness of assessment practices are, mostly, rudimentary.' [p. xxii]

'The duties of external examiners and their impact upon the operation of programmes within universities often vary considerably.' [p. xxii]

'There is variation in the distribution of external examiner reports, and in the mechanism for ensuring that appropriate and timely action is taken on the results.' [p. xxiii]

Figure 17.1 Observations of quality assurance systems in universities

Source: Higher Education Quality Council, *Learning from Audit* (HEQC, London, 1994).

Quality assessment: purpose and methodology

Whereas the Division of Quality Audit focuses upon mechanisms, the Quality Assessment Divisions focus upon the quality of education provided to students. There are differences in approaches, particularly between the Scottish and English system. The Scottish system is based on published, specific criteria. The English system is rather more coy: 'The council does not wish to be prescriptive. However, the Council believes that institutions will find it helpful to have guidance on the areas to be covered . . .'[24] The discussion of methods that follows is based upon the HEFC for England, the largest of the Funding Councils.

The purposes of the quality assessment as set out in 3/93 were:

- to ensure that all education for which the HEFCE provides funding is of satisfactory quality or better, and to ensure speedy rectification of unsatisfactory quality;
- to encourage improvements in the quality of education through the publication of assessment reports and an annual report;
- to inform funding and reward excellence.

The Barnett report pointed to the tensions between these purposes.[25] A consultative circular (2/94) was published in June 1994, and this paved the way for the purposes given in Circular 39/94:[26]

- to secure value from public investment;
- to encourage improvement . . . through publication of reports . . . ;
- to provide effective and accessible public information on the quality of the education for which the HEFCE provides funding.

Funding of a university or college may be partially blocked if one of its departments receives an unsatisfactory grading on one or more of the core aspects of provision. These aspects are:

- curriculum design, content and organization;
- teaching, learning and assessment;
- student progression and achievement;
- student support and guidance;
- learning resources;
- quality assurance and enhancement.

The broad criteria underpinning these aspects of provision are given in the annex to the circular.

The existing system of grading departments as excellent, satisfactory or unsatisfactory is therefore being dropped in favour of profiles based on the aspects of provision and linked to a four-point grading system similar to that used in the Research Assessment Exercises.[27] This system will remove the label of 'satisfactory', with all its connotations, and the grade of excellence, which some departments were pleased to receive if only for their marketing of courses. Instead, those that receive a grade of 2 or more will be rated as 'quality approved' on that aspect. No mention has been made so far of the links between grades of excellence and funding. In the earlier scheme it was proposed that grades of excellence would provide opportunities to obtain more government-funded places for students; whereas grades of 4 or 5 in RAEs may accrue increases of income estimated to be between £14,000 and £24,000 per member of staff. One does not need to be an economic historian to recognise that such discrepancies in financial incentives would do little to increase interest in the quality of educational provision.

The self-assessment report is the core document in the process of quality assessment. Some have objected to the work involved in preparing the document, but it is a useful exercise. Self-assessment and reflection are, as mentioned in relation to student learning, key processes in developing professional expertise. It is therefore not unreasonable for a department to be asked to reflect upon its approaches to educating students. Indeed some historians have always been concerned to improve their teaching. Now the responsibility for the quality of teaching rests firmly with all departments, not merely with individuals who have a strong interest in teaching.

A cause of concern in the pre-1995 system was the use of the self-assessment report as the sole method of estimating whether a department is satisfactory. (Those claiming to be excellent were visited if their claim was upheld by independent readers of the document.) The approach was confined to the HEFCE which has to monitor the quality of over 5,000 departments in over a hundred universities and colleges. It was mindful of costs and so adopted a sampling approach analogous to that used by external examiners of undergraduate courses. The external examiner looks at the weakest and best, and the border lines and at a sample from the middle range. He or she assumes that the methods of marking are reliable, consistent and valid within a department unless there is evidence to suggest otherwise. On this basis, students are awarded firsts (excellent?), upper seconds, lower seconds, thirds, passes (satisfactory?) and, occasionally, fails (unsatisfactory?). The system is accepted for assessing undergraduate learning but it was not, apparently, acceptable for assessing the provision for undergraduate learning.

The self-assessment document is used by quality assessors in two ways. First, the intrinsic validity of the document is explored. Inconsistencies, weak links between claimed objectives and evidence of teaching and assessment, underlying tensions and issues, and the strategies that are being developed to cope with emerging problems are all considered. In the early stages of Quality Assessment, there was a gap between those experienced at writing course documents for external assessment and those less used to an external system. Informal reports from HEFCE suggest this gap has closed; description has given way to analysis. Certainly the results of the first round of assessments do not indicate that the less experienced were disadvantaged. The second approach tests the extrinsic validity of the claim. Documentary analyses, analyses of students' course-work and examination scripts, interviews, meetings, informal discussions, direct observation of teaching are used to test hypotheses arising from the reading of the self-assessment document and to assemble evidence on which to draw inferences and make estimates of worth in relation to the broad dimensions of the assessment exercise.

Despite the views of some Vice-Chancellors and others, the *system* of assessment is valid. This is not to say it cannot be improved. Estimates of the impact of resources and the direct observation of teaching are particular difficulties. But the main difficulties are not of validity so much as reliability. The core of the difficulties is the instruments of assessment: the assessors. These are recommended to the HEFCE by Vice-Chancellors and Principals, so Vice-Chancellors and Principals have some responsibility for the selection of the assessors. Those of professorial rank are preferred. Often that rank is not attained through expertise in teaching but through research and scholarship. They receive a short training course of about fourteen hours and a briefing session. (The training is to be extended to three days.) They then conduct the assessments of their subjects in other universities and departments who may have other traditions and assumptions about learning and teaching. In the early stages they are learning the procedures of observing, discussing and writing sections of the report. Soon after learning these procedures they stop. The benefits that they gained are fed back to their own departments. But they may not be called upon again until the next round of assessment, which may be in five years' time. Given these circumstances, it is hardly surprising that there is variability across assessment teams or across subjects. This variability is likely to be greatest in areas where the assessors have least expertise. It is manifest in the reports on individual departments. Indeed the reports on the quality of education in history departments, together with the summary report,[28] would provide an interesting project for a history student or tutor with an interest in contemporary documentary analysis.

The usual length of visit is three days. Some say this is too long; others that it is too short. Those in favour of longer visits point to the complexity of course provision and the need for greater samples of teaching and discussion. Those who prefer shorter visits argue that the course documentation is sufficient for a judgement to be made and that it is not necessary to sample face-to-face teaching.

We would argue that as face-to-face teaching remains the experience of the majority of students in history it should remain part of the assessment and criteria of quality of the education provided in history departments. This is not to deny that the observation of teaching is more open to an individual's value judgements and to primitive notions of teaching and learning than is the scrutiny of course documents. Rather it is to suggest that a more thorough training in observation of teaching and learning in history is required, together with the development of understanding of perspectives and research on learning and teaching in history. This is the single most important route to improving the quality of education in history and for ensuring that historians make informed, consistent, professional judgements of what counts as good teaching and learning in a particular history course. The difficulty of assessing a task should not deter us lest we fall into one of the traps of accountism: of only measuring those things that can be measured easily. Finally, in considering assessment systems, it is worth remembering that it is easy to dissect and criticize a system: it is less to develop a system that will satisfy all of its users.

Part of the problem of assessing quality of provision in a subject is the link between funding and ascribed status – but here again there are analogies between the importance of accurate degree classification for the future careers of students and the labels of 'excellent' or 'quality approved' for the development of departments and universities. It is at least arguable than funding for teaching should be linked to funding for individual universities based on their *agreed* mission. Assessment and Audit could be united and visits take place no more than every five years. The system of sampling would be sufficient, on technical grounds, for summative judgements of the quality of the system. But it might not provide motivation for departments to develop their teaching and it would not satisfy the whims of our present political masters.

Quo Vadimus?

This chapter has outlined the nature of assessment, quality, teaching and learning. The chapter has pointed to the inherent conflicts between assessment for judgemental purposes and for developmental purposes and it has shown how the Platonic and Aristotelian notions of the 'good' permeate the debate on quality assessment. It has indicated that the underlying conceptions of teaching may be inferred from course documents and this conception may be related to the avowed claims in the document. Direct observation of teaching provides one of the checks on the validity of the claims of a department for its provision of education. Whilst face-to-face teaching remains the major vehicle of teaching then it should remain a feature of the assessment process. The present system of quality assessment was examined in the light of the discussions earlier in the chapter. The weaknesses of the present Quality Assessment system are more related to issues of reliability than of validity. The Funding Councils have demonstrated their willingness to respond to criticisms and, one suspects, they may have had vigorous debates behind closed doors with ministers and senior civil servants who were more concerned with the system's capacity for summary judgements and control than with the quality of the assessment process or of the educational provision itself.

So what does the future hold? Historians and, latterly, chaos theorists, warn of the dangers of predictions in complex systems. The task is approached cautiously. The shift from an elitist to a mass higher education together with a marketing philosophy has brought in its wake a diminution of the collegial model of governance and an increase in managerialism. Quality assurance will probably be a feature of higher education in all industrialized nations well into the next century.

In the immediate future in Britain, Quality Assessment and Quality Audit will continue to be fine-tuned. Within the next few years they are likely to be conjoined, ostensibly for efficiency gains. Whether the emphasis will be weighted more towards development and fitness for purpose or more towards summary judgement, national standards and payment by results, is dependent upon wider political movements. Whether assessors remain temporary, part-time staff or become a cadre of trained, full-time specialists who are able to offer professional expertise and judgement is again dependent upon wider issues. A commitment to the quality of the assessment process itself implies a commitment to fairness, and to improving the validity and the reliability of the system. These commitments raise issues of values in a democratic society and each has implications for cost and for professional approaches to the provision of undergraduate education. Whether Britain remains as democratic as it has been since 1945 is open to question. Changes in the core values of the powerful will, as ever, be reflected in the myriad of systems of control that permeate a society, its culture, and its educational provision.

Notes

I should like to thank Ian Bull and Alan Booth for their comments on the draft of this chapter.

1   G. Brown and M. Pendlebury, *Assessing Active Learning* (CVCP, Sheffield, 1992).
2   R. Barnett, *Assessment of the Quality of Higher Education: A Review and an Evaluation* (University of London Institute of Education, London, 1994); History in the Universities Defence Group, *Teaching Quality Assessment of History by the Education Funding Councils of England and Wales, 1993–94* (HUDG, Hull, 1994).
3   HUDG, *Teaching Quality Assessment*, p. 3.
4   See for example, J. Heywood, *Assessment in Higher Education* (John Wiley, Chichester, 1989).
5   See, I. Bull, *Appraisal in Universities* (CVCP, Sheffield, 1990).
6   A. Burrows, D. Green and L. Harvey, *Criteria of Quality* (University of Central England, Birmingham, 1992).
7   HEFCE, *Assessment of the Quality of Education: Circular 3/93* (HEFCE, Bristol, 1993), para. 11.
8   P. Ramsden, 'A Performance Indicator of Teaching Quality in Higher Education: The Course Experience Questionnaire', *Studies in Higher Education*, 16 (1991), pp. 129–50.
9   P. Wright, 'Putting Learning at the Centre of Higher Education', in *Access and Institutional Change*, ed. O. Fulton (SRHE, Guildford, 1989), pp. 99–110.
10 H. P. A. Boshuizer, G. R. Norman and H. G. Schmidt, 'A Cognitive Perspective on Medical Expertise: Theory and Implications', *Academic Medicine*, 65 (1990), pp. 611–21.
11 N. J. Entwistle, *The Impact of Teaching on Learning Outcomes* (CVCP, Sheffield, 1992), p. 29.
12 HEFCE, *Assessment of the Quality of Education*, para. 1.
13 G. Jessup, *Outcomes: NVQs and the Emerging Model of Education and Training* (Falmer Press, London, 1991).
14 J. Annett and J. Sparrow, 'Transfer of Training: A Review of Research and Practical Implications', *APLET Journal*, 22 (1989), pp. 116–24; J. Bruner, 'Another Look at New Look 1', *American Psychologist*, 47 (1992), pp. 780–3; J. G. Donald, 'Knowledge and the University Curriculum', *Higher Education*, 15 (1986), pp. 267–82.
15 R. Barnett, *The Limitations of Competence* (Open University Press, Buckingham, 1994).

16 M. J. Atkins, J. Beattie and W. B. Dockrell, *Assessment Issues in Higher Education* (Department of Employment, Sheffield, 1993).

17 Association of Graduate Recruiters, *Graduate Salaries and Vacancies, 1994* (AGR, Cambridge, 1994).

18 Confederation of British Industries, *Thinking Ahead: Ensuring the Expansion of Higher Education in the 21st Century* (CBI, London, 1994).

19 J. H. Newman, *The Idea of a University* (Longman Green, London, 1947 [1853]), Discourse VII.

20 HMI, *A Survey of the Enterprise in Higher Education Initiative: A Report by HMI* (Department of Education and Science, London, 1992).

21 G. Brown, G. Gordon, J. Partington, *Handbook for External Examiners in Higher Education* (CVCP, Sheffield, 1993).

22 HMI, *The English Polytechnics: An HMI Commentary* (HMSO, London, 1989).

23 Higher Education Quality Council, *Learning from Audit* (HEQC, London, 1994), p. vi.

24 HEFCE, *Assessment of the Quality of Education*, para. 19.

25 Barnett, *Assessment of the Quality of Higher Education*.

26 HEFCE, *Further Development of the Method for the Assessment of the Quality of Education: Circular 2/94* (HEFCE, Bristol, 1994).

27 HEFCE, *The Quality Assessment Method from April 1995: Circular 39/94* (HEFCE, Bristol, 1994), para. 23.

28 HEFCE, *Quality Assessment of History 1993–94: Subject Overview Report* (HEFCE, Bristol, 1994).

Further Reading

Essential reading for those concerned with Quality Assessment in England is the HEFCE's *The Quality Assessment Method from April 1995* (HEFCE, Bristol, 1994) and the HEQC's *Learning from Audit* (HEQC, London, 1994). The latter is also useful for all readers with an interest in the quality of educational provision. The summary report on history, *Quality Assessment of History 1993–94: Subject Overview Report* (HEFCE, Bristol, 1994) is somewhat self-congratulatory but it does provide a survey of educational provision in history departments.

For a broader view of quality and quality issues one should read *Quality Assurance in Teaching*, ed. R. Ellis (Open University Press, Buckingham, 1993). The chapter by Brown provides a review of research on effective teaching, and the chapter by Elton discusses quality and standards in teaching. The policy document, P. Partington and L. Elton, *Teaching Standards and Excellence in Higher Education: Developing a Culture for Quality* (CVCP, Sheffield, 1993) provides a discussion of ways of estimating excellence in teaching, and the policy document by G. Brown, *Staff Development for Teaching: Towards a Coherent and Comprehensive Framework* (CVCP, Sheffield, 1994) provides suggestions for staff development for individuals, department and universities.

CVCP has also published a series of twelve modules on effective teaching and learning. Of these the most useful to historians and history departments are: G. Brown and M. Pendlebury, *Assessing Active Learning* (CVCP, Sheffield, 1992), which provides research on assessment, as well as practical guides on all aspects of assessment together with activities for workshops. S. Griffiths and P. Partington, *Enabling Active Learning in Small Groups* (CVCP, Sheffield, 1992) provides guidelines and suggestions for approaches to tutorials and seminars. The accompanying video is most useful for analysing and discussing small-group teaching. The module by M. O'Neill and G. Pennington, *Evaluating Teaching and Courses from an Active Learning Perspective* (CVCP, Sheffield, 1992) contains examples of various approaches to evaluating teaching and courses, and a series of short articles by lecturers who have evaluated their teaching. The text contains some suggestions for workshops on evaluating teaching and courses.

A brief guide on promoting effective learning is provided by N. Entwistle, S. Thompson and H. Tait, *Guidelines for Promoting Effective Learning in Higher Education* (Centre for Research on Learning and Instruction, Edinburgh, 1992). A longer guide that also reviews the literature and offers practical suggestions is G. Brown and M. Atkins, *Effective Teaching in Higher Education* (Methuen, London, 1988). The text by P. Ramsden, *Learning to Teach in Higher Education* (Routledge, London, 1992) is a thoughtful account of research and practice that takes as its starting point the importance of developing the capacity for deep learning. For those interested in conducting research on teaching, the annotated bibliography in part two of *Teaching and Learning in an Expanding Higher Education System* (Committee of Scottish University Principals, 1992) provides a useful starting point.

Index

Abercrombie, M. J. L. 112
academic audit 2, 195, 300, 309,
    310, 311, 316
academic leadership of
    departments 147–8
action research 13, 145 *see also*
    questionnaires; teaching, peer
    review of
active learning 6, 51–2, 100–3,
    213, 235–6, 263, 265, 271, 304
    characteristics of 8–12
    in seminars 111–26, 142, 280–9
A-level 35, 242, 244
American Historical Association 5
Ankersmit, F. R. 76, 78, 80
approaches to learning 9–10,
    113–15, 132, 134–5, 220, 262,
    264, 304–5, 308–9 *see also*
    active learning; learning,
    student reflection on
Aristotle 301–2, 316
Asante, M. 45
assessment of history departments
    298–317 *see also* evaluation
assessment of students 9, 10, 11,
    115, 130–2, 134, 162, 166,
    168, 179, 188–9, 195, 200,
    214–15, 219–20, 227, 250,
    261–73, 276–95
    case study of 288–94
    group work 276–95
    in seminars 123, 142–3, 280–4,
    288–93
    introducing new modes of 141,
    214–16, 219–20, 251, 268–72
    oral presentations 142–3, 215,
    277–80
    poster sessions 277–80
    self and peer 9, 11, 185–8, 265,
    266, 270–1, 277, 280, 282–4,
    289–94
    trends in 263–8
Association of Graduate Careers
    Advisory Services (AGCAS)
    247, 253
Atkins, M. J. 306
audio visual *see* visual media

Baldwin, J. 50
Baldwin, S. 192
Barnett report 312
Barraclough, G. 243

Beattie, J. 306
Bennett, T. 76–8, 85, 88, 89, 90
  Formalism and Marxism 88
  Outside Literature 88
Bennett, W. 45
Blake, Lord 242
Bland, M. 60
Boud, D. 112
British Association for Local
  History 213
British Universities Film and
  Video Council (BUFVC) 198,
  200–1
Brown, G. 263, 268, 299
Brown, S. 262, 277
Buzan, T. 123

Campaign for Public Sector
  History (PUSH) 242
Capability in Higher Education
  244
careers *see* employment of
  graduates
Carr, E. H. 87, 88, 89, 90
Cary, L. 39–40, 43
  Black Ice 39–40
case-studies
  a gendered history course 68–70
  assessing student-led seminars
    288–94
  constructing a theory course
    87–91
  designing a history degree 33–6
  distance learning courses 180–9
  field trips 228–30
  history and the community
    215–21
  work placement 234–8
Clark, A. 60, 63
Clark, C. 251
collaboration
  of staff 6–7, 49, 144–9, 272 *see*
    also team teaching; teaching,
    peer review of

of students 11–12, 25, 51–2, 98,
  102, 116, 124–5, 207, 216,
  226, 265–6, 276–95
Colleges *see* Universities and
  Colleges
Collier, G. 124
Committee of Vice-Chancellors and
  Principals (CVCP) 309
computer-assisted teaching and
  learning 11, 31, 155–73, 216,
  219
  course design for 163–7
  current practice in 160–3
  goals and objectives of 159–60
  instructional software for
    168–72
computer
  as tool 156–67
  as instructor 167–72
Computers in Teaching
  Initiative 6, 160
Confederation of British Industries
  (CBI) 307
Conference of Regional and Local
  History (CORAL) 213
contemporary history 30–1
Council for Industry and Higher
  Education (CIHE) 27, 247,
  249
Council for National Academic
  Awards (CNAA) 21, 243, 250,
  309
Crow, J. 41, 44
curriculum development
  gender in 55–70
  history theory in 75–91
  planning for change 4, 21–37,
    141, 242–5
  race in 39–53
  see also case-studies; computer-
    assisted teaching and learning

Daily Express 243
Darwinist theory 67

de Pisan, C. 60
Derrida, J. 77, 84, 87, 89
distance learning 98, 129
distance teaching 178–90
  character of 179–81
  course aims and objectives for
    182–5
  logistics of 189
  self-assessment in 185–8
  tutor assessment of 188–9
Dockrell, W. B. 306

electronic seminars 169
Elton, G. R. 8, 29, 84, 87, 88–9,
  90, 249
  Return to Essentials 89
empiricism 83–4, 87
employers 36, 113, 233–8, 243,
  247–9, 252–3, 263, 266, 307–8
employment of graduates 2,
  242–54
Enterprise in Higher Education 6,
  216, 243, 267, 308
Entwistle, N. 12, 304
ERASMUS 35
ethnicity *see* race and history
Ethnic Notions 45
evaluation
  formative and summative 137–8
  of courses 103, 135–8, 138, 141,
    220–1, 229–30, 236–8
  of teaching 103, 105–6, 135,
    139, 141–7, 293–4
  see also assessment of
    departments; Teaching
    Quality Assessment
excellence in higher education 2–3,
  45, 298, 302, 312
experiential learning *see* learning
  from experience
external examiners 131–2, 261,
  264, 272, 294, 309, 313

facilitator 112, 126, 144–5

feedback
  for tutors 105–6, 137–8, 149,
    220, 264, 293
  for students 125, 189, 262, 264,
    271, 281
  see also evaluation
feminist theory and approaches 57,
  58, 61, 63–4, 77
field trips 225–30
  case study of 228–30
film *see* visual sources
Foucault, M. 87, 88, 89
Fox-Genovese, E. 85–6
Freire, P. 51

Gates, H. L. 44
gender and women's histories
  58–60, 65–8
gendered critiques of history 61–3
General National Vocational
  Qualifications (GNVQ) 267,
  305
George, D. 60
Gibbs, G. 107, 114, 115
Giroux, H. 51
Gladstone, W. 192
group work *see* collaboration

Habeshaw, S. 111, 123
'heritage' issues *see* history and the
  community
Her Majesty's Inspectorate (HMI)
  309
Herodotus 79
higher education, aims and
  purposes of 1, 45, 50–1,
  112–13, 306–8
Higher Education Funding Council
  (HEFC) 3, 6, 21, 32, 129,
  235, 243, 244, 301, 302, 304,
  305, 309, 312–14, 316
Hippocrates 306
Hirsh, E. D. 45
Historical Association 242

Historical Document Expert
    System (HiDES) 169, 171,
    251
*Historical Journal of Film, Radio
    and Television* 201
historicism 82
history as historiography 76–81,
    86–7
history and ideology 47, 81–2
history and the community 207–21
  case-study of 215–21
  objectives of 211–12
  rationale for 208–11
  strategies for 212–15
History in the Universities Defence
    Group (HUDG) 242, 300
history course outlines 68–70,
    89–91, 180–1
History Courseware Consortium
    UK 31, 156, 171
history education, aims and
    purposes of 26–7, 55–6, 58,
    62, 231, 308–9 *see also* higher
    education, aims and purposes
    of
history teaching, traditions of 3–6,
    22–5, 43–4, 55–8, 65, 75, 99,
    128–9, 132–4, 191–2, 199,
    208–11, 224, 242–5, 261–3,
    277
history theory 75–87
Hitler, A. 192–3
Hoskins, W. G. 225
hypermedia 156, 169–72

Imperial War Museum 198
independent learning 9, 112, 181,
    226 *see also* active learning;
    approaches to learning
information technology 31, 34,
    106, 187, 212, 218, 219 *see also*
    computers; computer-assisted
    teaching and learning

Institute of Communication
    Studies, Leeds 199
International Association of Media
    Historians (IAMHIST) 201
InterUniversity History Film
    Consortium (IUHFC) 199,
    201

Jameson, F. 85
Jaques, D. 112, 125
Jones, T. 5
*Journal of Regional and Local
    Studies* 213

Knight, P. 262, 277
Kolb, D. 10

learning, contexts of 12, 115, 149
    see also active learning;
    approaches to learning
learning contracts 286–7
learning cycle 10
learning from experience 10–11,
    224–38, 304 *see also* field trips;
    history and the community;
    work placement and
    experience
learning journals 283, 287
learning, student reflection on
    10–11, 52, 146, 219, 284,
    285–8, 304, 308–9
lectures
  basic purposes of 107–9
  criticisms of 97–100
  organization and structure of
    103–6
  special effects in 106
  student participation in 100–3
  teaching and learning in 97–109
Lerner, G. 61
Lewis, J. 62
library resources 1, 25, 30, 32, 158,
    208, 213

local history *see* history and the
     community; fieldwork; work
     placement and experience
Lougée, C. 168
Lower Manhattan Project 163

Malpas, R. 253
Marton, F. 113
Marwick, A. 84, 87
Marxism 62, 79, 81, 85, 86, 88, 89,
     181, 183
Meyers, C. 5
Middleton, R. 160
modular programmes 2, 24, 28, 32,
     33, 34, 128–9, 250, 261–2, 264
Monaco, J. 194
motherhood 67–8
multiculturalism 34, 44–5, 49 *see*
     also race and history
Museum of the Moving Image 201

narrative turn *see* textualist
     arguments about history
National Curriculum for
     schools 21, 24, 25, 26, 56
National Film and Television
     Archive (NFTVA) 198
National Film Theatre 201
national histories 23, 27, 29, 33,
     43–8, 56, 196, 210–11
Newman, J. H. 308

objectivity in history 47, 55, 65, 87,
     129

Pankhurst, E. S. 61
Partnership Awards 6
past/history distinction 76–80
Pendlebury, M. 299
Perspectives 5–6
Phillips, U. B. 41
Pinchbeck, I. 60, 63
Plato 301–2, 316

poster sessions 277–80
post-structuralism 58–60, 64, 66,
     75, 87, 89
Power, E. 60
Prior, Lord 249
project work, student 10, 25,
     215–17, 218, 226–8, 281 *see*
     also collaboration, of students
Pronay, N. 194, 199
PUSH Newsletter 7
pyramiding 119

Quality Assessment *see* Teaching
     Quality Assessment
quality assurance 6, 131, 146–7,
     272, 300, 309–11, 316
questionnaires
     examples of 136, 139
     uses of 103, 115, 133, 135, 137,
     138–40, 142, 228, 229

race and history
     classroom exercises for 51–3
     curriculum issues of 39–53
     multiple meanings of 41–3
     teaching of 43–53
Ramsden, P. 8, 115
Ravitch, D. 44
Record of Achievement 287–8
Rees, L. 194
Reid, R. 245, 249, 253
research and teaching, relationship
     of 3–5, 6, 28, 32, 134, 148,
     209, 302–3
Research Assessment Exercise
     (RAE) 2, 3, 129, 209, 300,
     302, 312–13
Riley, D. 59
Roberts, J. M. 180–1
Rogers, C. 11
Rorty, R. 87, 88–9, 90

Sainsbury, Lord 245, 248

Säljö, R. 113
Samuel, R. 86–7
school curriculum *see* National
　Curriculum
Schreiner, O. 60
Scott, J. 59
Seeley, J. 244
seminars 111–26, 277–94
　absent friend in 125
　electronic 169
　evaluation of 139–40, 141, 143,
　　279–94
　ground rules for 118–19, 289
　hidden agendas in 116
　icebreakers for 117–18
　nature and importance of
　　111–13
　product or process? 115–16
　seating arrangements 120–1
　size of 119
　student-led 123–6, 142–3,
　　281–4
　student participation in 51–3,
　　121–5
　tutor authority in 117
　see also assessment of students
Semonche, J. 168
skills *see* transferable skills
Slee, P. 244
Spiegel, G. 84–5
staff appraisal 2, 137, 300
staff training and development 3,
　6, 132, 146, 272 *see also*
　teaching, peer review of
Stearns, P. 3, 27, 28
Stenhouse, L. 117
Stone, L. 84–5
Stone, N. 254
Strachey, R. 61
student-centred learning 2, 9, 46,
　52, 57, 212 *see also* active
　learning
students

backgrounds of 2, 23–4, 26, 35,
　39–40, 56–7, 104, 244–5
control over learning 8–9, 52 *see*
　also active learning
exit performance of 130–1
increased number of 1–2, 23, 24,
　25, 97, 128, 261
views of teaching 133–4, 262–3
study abroad 35–6

Taylor, P. 199
teaching and research *see* research
　and teaching
Teaching History 7
teaching, peer review of 144–7 *see*
　also Teaching Quality
　Assessment; assessment of
　history departments
Teaching Quality Assessment 6,
　21, 32, 129, 243–4, 298–317
　purpose and methodology
　311–17
team teaching 49, 162 *see also*
　collaboration, of staff
teamwork *see* collaboration
Terry, P. M. 112
textbooks, student 7, 44, 49, 108,
　121, 133, 169, 170, 185, 208
textualist arguments about
　history 84–7
theory *see* history theory
Thind case 41
Thom, D. 62
topic web 122–3
Tout, T. 244
transferable skills 11–12, 27–8, 31,
　34–6, 115–16, 159, 193, 200,
　211–12, 213–14, 220, 225–6,
　232–3, 243–4, 250–4, 267–8,
　304–5, 306
Tusa, J. 245, 249

Understanding Industry Trust 243

United States Supreme Court 41
Universities and Colleges
   Brighton 251, 282
   Cambridge 3, 22
   Coleraine 199
   Crewe and Alsager 251
   Durham 244, 281
   East Anglia 198, 199
   Edinburgh 162–3
   Glasgow 6, 161–2
   Griffith 282
   Harvard 45
   Huddersfield 232, 234, 252
   Joennsuu 35
   Lancaster 199, 215–21, 232
   Leeds 285
   Leicester 225
   Loughborough 281
   Manchester Metropolitan 232,
     234, 287
   Metropolitan State 5
   Northumbria 22, 33–6, 252
   Open 7, 13, 129, 178–90, 199
   Oxford 3, 22, 32, 254
   Oxford Brookes 284
   Princeton 45
   Queen Mary and Westfield 199
   Southampton 169
   St Martin's 252
   Sussex 199
   Trinity and All Saints 228–30,
     232, 234–8, 252
   Tulane 163

Vermont 281
Warwick 199
York 251
US Census 42

value added 130, 220
Viewfinder 201
visual media, teaching with 179,
   187–8, 191–202
visual sources,
   courses using 199–200
   help and advice with 200–1
   importance of 26, 191–3
   problems of 193–9

Ward, K. 199
Wardley, P. 160
White, H. 76, 78–9, 81–90
Wilson, A. 122–3
Wollstonecraft, M. 60
woman-centred history 64–5 *see*
   also women's history
women's history 58–61, 62–5 *see*
   also gender and women's
   histories
work placement and
   experience 217, 231–8,
   250–4, 308
   case-study of 234–8
Wright, P. 303

Zinn, H. 47–8